Feeling Asian American

NATIONAL WOMEN'S STUDIES ASSOCIATION /
UNIVERSITY OF ILLINOIS PRESS FIRST BOOK PRIZE

For a list of prize winners, please see our website at www.press.uillinois.edu.

Feeling Asian American

Racial Flexibility Between Assimilation and Oppression

WEN LIU

UNIVERSITY OF ILLINOIS PRESS
Urbana, Chicago, and Springfield

1 2 3 4 5 C P 5 4 3 2 1
♾ This book is printed on acid-free paper.

Library of Congress Cataloging-in-Publication Data
Names: Liu, Wen, 1987– author.
Title: Feeling Asian American : racial flexibility between assimilation and oppression / Wen Liu.
Description: Urbana : University of Illinois Press, [2024] | Series: National Women's Studies Association/ University of Illinois first book prize | Includes bibliographical references and index.
Identifiers: LCCN 2023042126 (print) | LCCN 2023042127 (ebook) | ISBN 9780252045790 (cloth) | ISBN 9780252087905 (paperback) | ISBN 9780252056673 (ebook)
Subjects: LCSH: Asian Americans—Social conditions. | United States—Race relations.
Classification: LCC E184.A75 L582 2024 (print) | LCC E184.A75 (ebook) | DDC 305.895/073—dc23/eng/20231101
LC record available at https://lccn.loc.gov/2023042126
LC ebook record available at https://lccn.loc.gov/2023042127

Contents

Acknowledgments

This book has been both challenging and pleasurable for me to write. This research project first began around 2012 when I moved to New York City and got involved with transnational Asian American activist work. As a Taiwanese American immigrant forming my own sense of belonging in academia and in the United States, this book has become an integral part of my intellectual, political, and personal journey.

For many years, I had the blessing of working among passionate and brilliant mentors and colleagues in the Critical Social Psychology program at the Graduate Center, City University of New York. I am deeply grateful to my adviser, Michelle Fine, for her ongoing encouragement and support for the type of scholarship I wanted to pursue, which could often be quite unorthodox and ambiguous in its disciplinary forms. My close colleagues from the Affect Studies collective at the Graduate Center—Akemi Nishida, Rachel Liebert, Ali Lara, Michelle Billies, and Colin Ashley—were instrumental in shaping the ways I think and write today, even though we are now located in different continents and time zones. I am deeply indebted to Celina Su, Susan Opotow, Sunil Bhatia, Tamara Buckley, and Kyoo Lee, who have seen many different drafts of this book project and continued to intellectually support me even in times of doubt. I am grateful for my former colleagues Vivien Ng, Barbara Sutton, Rajani Bhatia, and Janell Hobson at the Women's, Gender and Sexuality Studies Department at the University of Albany, State University of New York; these colleagues were generous and welcoming, and trusted in my capacity to complete this project. This book would not have materialized without the National Women's Studies Association's First Book Prize committee's recognition as well as the support of editors from the University of Illinois Press, especially Dominique Moore.

Networks and friendship across the United States and Taiwan were crucial for facilitating my thinking on the subject, especially my comrades from New York's API People's Solidarity and New Bloom: Ayumi, Meejin, Brian Hioe, Daniel Yo-Ling, and many others. Thank you for the countless conversations we have had about politics and belonging. Special thanks to Daniel Yo-Ling and Oliver Fulgler for their meticulous edits on multiple drafts of this manuscript. I am immeasurably grateful for my fellow queer and feminist Sinophone scholars who have always challenged me in how to approach the world with both critique and hope: Charlie Yi Zhang, Lin Li, Fan-ting Cheng, Eno Chen, Eva Li, Howard Chiang, Ying-Chao Kao, and Adam Chen-Dedman.

It would have been impossible to have the time and psychological endurance to write this book without the support of my family and partner who have always made sure that I am well taken care of and encouraged me to pursue what my instincts feel right. This book is for them.

Feeling Asian American

INTRODUCTION

Feeling Asian American

What does it feel like to be Asian American? The COVID-19 pandemic has not only drastically restructured global politics and social relations but also rearticulated Asian visibility and vulnerability worldwide. Video footage of Asian-bodied people being attacked in the streets, on public transit, and in businesses was widely circulated via social media, illustrating horrific scenes of one attack after another and marking a rise in anti-Asian violence in the United States and beyond. As the outbreak landed in the United States around March 2020, Donald Trump's naming of COVID-19 as the "China virus" undoubtedly brought the specter of the Cold War between the United States and China to center stage as well as reattaching the century-old stereotype of "yellow perilism" to Asian Americans. Throughout the first and second pandemic years, Asian Americans mobilized and took to the streets, holding protest signs that said, "Not Your Model Minority" and "We're Not Invisible" to defy the racist attacks—a collective identity could emerge from such a moment. However, there is an awkward and uncomfortable disconnect between the Asian American professional class and disproportionally visible Chinese and East Asian body that has galvanized these tragic events to gain more political leverages and those who were attacked, especially in the high-profile cases such as the elderly Thai man, Vicha Ratanapakdee, who died from physical assault in Oakland, California, and the six Asian female massage workers who were murdered during the Atlanta spa shootings in March 2021. These victims have mainly been Asian immigrants who are seldom included in the typical narrative about being "Asian American."

In the rare moments when Asian Americans have been in the national and international headlines, Asian American politicians like Andrew Yang, the former Democratic presidential candidate who was running for New York City mayor, have called for racial and national unity during this period of heightened racialization, emphasizing the need for Asian Americans to "embrace and show our Americanness."[1] However, these assaults on Asian people of diverse ethnicities, who do not share the same migration histories, cultural lineages, or feelings about *Asian* as a panethnic racial category, demand a more complicated narrative about Asian racialization and a different way of relating to the state beyond a racial minoritarian framework. Certainly, each of the cases and the victims in the video footage necessitates a story of its own, yet what threads them all together is an intensified feeling of a collective sense of racial injury. This *Asian American feeling* of injury—oftentimes invisible and unspoken—can be heightened during times of racial attacks. For instance, the killing of Vincent Chin, a Chinese American drafting technician in Detroit, in 1982 has been brought up repeatedly during COVID-19 to illustrate a continuous thread of anti-Asian violence, a common racial history of Asian Americans, and the formation of a pan-Asian identity. Only in times of brutal injuries do we see mass numbers of Asian Americans of different ethnic communities—for example, Japanese and Chinese—mobilize under the category of *Asian Americans* with common interests. Asian Americanness, otherwise, seldom exists beyond academic or political discourses. The *New York Times* writer Jay Caspian Kang points out the inconsistency and contradiction of Asian American as a racial category as it "assumes kinship between people who do not speak the same language, and, in many cases, dislike one another."[2] Although there are undeniable embodied cultural and affective similarities among Asian Americans, solidarity in non-crisis times, in fact, seems unlikely. The feeling of collective injury serves as an effect of what Karen Fields and Barbara Fields term "racecraft," which refers to a pervasive belief and psychological imagination that race exists objectively.[3] To view Asian Americanness as an effect of racecraft is in no way to call it irrational or unreal but to emphasize how an affect is turned into a "vivid truth" via our day-to-day actions and imagination.[4] It turns racial ideologies into seemingly biologically real matters that govern our activity and subjectivity.

In *Feeling Asian American,* I argue that Asian Americanness is as much an institutional construction of the racial category as it is a form of self-subjectification. To feel Asian American is to sense a collectivized history of racial injury, despite its categorical internal demographic and ideological heterogeneities.

Rather than understanding Asian Americanness as a biologically and culturally coherent racial group, the book traces the turns and shifts of how Asian Americanness is felt and seen through American psychology. To approach it as an assemblage does not make these feelings less authentic or real but instead calls attention to the material conditions, scientific discourses, and psychological techniques that have assembled the public's capacity to sense and name these feelings as specifically *Asian American.* To feel Asian American is to always sense and embody foreignness from the nation, to be treated like a national security threat, to be placed outside of the dominant paradigm of racial relations, and to experience a sense of resentment about the unfulfilled American dream. Asian American feelings help construct the paradigm of "beyond Black and white" in US racial discourses, a place of neither victim nor oppressor but something in between. Although "white supremacy" can serve as a temporal holder for the Asian American feelings of rage, silence, and vulnerability, it seems inadequate to explain the way that Asian Americanness continues to fail to account for the contradictory representations of both the disease-ridden, foreign body of the yellow peril and the post-racial, assimilating model minority. The professional class's alignment with the model-minority framework has also failed to resolve these contradictory Asian American feelings but enhanced the perpetual unfitness of being neither "American" nor "Asian" enough.

The invocation of affect in this book aims not only to disarticulate the overdetermined negative affect attached to a taken-for-granted presence of the Asian American subject but also to make explicit the autonomy of affect[5] that has driven the production and consolidation of Asian American as a biocultural and racial category with a distinct combination of culture, value, cognition, and politics. Following Brian Massumi's concept of affect as a synesthetic force that circulates between the *virtual* and the *actual* of things,[6] the two sides of my investigation in this project—one of the virtual (the Asian American subject) and another of the actual (the material fields and social forces that make the subject legible)—are inseparable units that together assemble a point of view and a specific sensation that can be understood as Asian Americanness. The turn to affect in the field of cultural studies has emerged out of this analytical exhaustion from both the representational model of identity and the poststructuralist critique of identity. In *Imagine Otherwise: On Asian Americanist Critique,* Kandice Chuh posits that Asian American is a subjectless position, which indicates "a term *in difference from itself*—at once making a claim of achieved subjectivity and referring to the impossibility of that achievement."[7] The deconstructive effort of Asian American studies critically reflecting on the discipline and knowledge production via the category of Asian American has thus been focused on articulating a position of the marginalized in relation to hegemonic power and the internal instability of racial term. However, the book questions whether the political and theoretical project of Asian American marginalization and representational difference is still productive in the time of the rise of China and right-wing authoritarianism in the West, when marginalization—embodied and expressed through the injured affect—can be mobilized toward reinforcing both white racial domination and geopolitical binarism. Therefore, rather than situating Asian American in a fixed position of the marginalized, the use of affect captures its capacity that has not yet been fully manifested and is always already changed when we start to describe its shape and form. As Patricia Clough articulates, affect is infra-empirical. The psychological tools of classification and categorization only provide us the empirical data of "behavior, discourse, reported-experience, and cognizant ideas" when affect is no longer here.[8] Ali Lara accurately describes the ephemeral quality of affect: "When affect has been captured and passed to be expressed in the phenomenological realm from which we collect our empirical data, it has already become something else."[9]

To conceptualize Asian American as an affective assemblage means that we will always fail to capture its full picture. This problem, however, should not be understood merely in representational terms, which we can mend by adding more subjects to the conversation. The queer critique of identity has already warned us that no matter how intersectional our analysis, the assumed presence of subjecthood continues to haunt and linger in it. Queerness, as a theoretical approach and a politics against identity, has since become an expansive field of inquiry beyond the sexual body and matter. Despite these transgressive turns against queer-as-a-subject, Jasbir Puar posits that queerness "nevertheless surfaces as an object in need of excavation, elaboration, or specularization."[10] Thus, the project at hand for this book is to resist the impulse of characterizing what Asian Americanness is and instead to illustrate *what it can do* through following the residues of the emotional excess persistently attached and stuck to the Asian American figure. Although the book does not claim to take on the task of ontologizing Asian American feeling, it is situated within the tension of illustrating a historically, politically, and geographically particular emergence of the Asian American affect and its inseparable relation and co-constitution with—and juxtaposed to—other racial affects. In the same vein as José Esteban Muñoz's conceptualization of brownness, the Asian American feeling cannot be legible without thinking it through the multisubjective relations of imperial expansion, settler coloniality, state violence, vulnerability, border formation, and the institutions of neoliberal multiculturalism.[11] In the words of Muñoz,

"Brownness is not white and not black either, yet it does not simply sit midway between them."[12] Like other racialized affects in North America, Asian American feeling is made visible through its articulation of difference from the public perceptions of Blackness and brownness as well as its impossibility of becoming whiteness, yet it is neither simply a lesser intensity of Blackness along a racial hierarchy nor on a comparable racialization scale with brownness. Indeed, arguments of its position being "beyond Black and white" have been criticized by Asian American scholars as not only inaccurate but potentially bolstering anti-Black political practice by exceptionalizing Asian American positionality to triangulate between Blacks and whites.[13] Christopher Patterson also points out that the space of Asian American politics has been dominated by "yellow" forms of East Asianness. In his articulation, the lens of *brown transpacific* de-essentializes the dominance of East Asian racial injury and explicates multiple forms of imperial racial capitalism.[14] The turn to a concept of Asian American feeling thus demands an alternative opening, not from "beyond Black and white" but "alongside" the plural racial, colonial, and geopolitical forces that have shaped what has become Asian Americanness.

In her book *Minor Feelings: An Asian American Reckoning,* Cathy Park Hong describes in depth the Asian American feelings of simultaneously fearing disappearing and worrying about taking up too much space.[15] Drawing from Sianne Ngai's concept of *ugly feeling,* Hong articulates *minor feelings* as the "non-cathartic states of emotion" that "occur when American optimism is enforced upon you, which contradicts your own racialized reality, thereby creating a static cognitive dissonance."[16] These feelings are *minor* because Asian American racial experiences have been framed by the mainstream as neither significant enough nor legible, especially compared to other racialized groups, and thus as not able to be properly expressed or resolved. They remain in the body of Asian Americans in small yet persistent ways until a new crisis lets them burst out. In a sense, Asian Americans are the exceptionalized subjects of *cruel optimism,* to use Lauren Berlant's term, where the assimilationist desire toward inclusion and upward class mobility as well as fantasies about the "good life" in fact have kept Asian Americans in neoliberal captivity, prohibiting them to fully flourish.[17] The governing principals of neoliberal multiculturalism have manufactured the diversity facade that racial minority members of the society can turn their race into commodities without making explicit the preexisting class stratification that deems some people's race profitable but others' burdensome.[18] Therefore, we continue to see how certain forms of racial outcry become legible in mainstream society, whereas others are considered an overreaction.

These excessive feelings largely constitute the unresolved identity of Asian Americanness. They create emotional, prediscursive bonds that are hard to enunciate but can only be felt, coming together in what are understood as Asian American experiences across ethnicity and culture. They are produced by the constant oscillation between discourses of oppression and assimilation taking place since Asian subjects have been in the North American imagination starting in the late nineteenth century, a phenomenon that I call *racial flexibility* in this book. Rather than conceptualizing Asian Americanness through the often-linear description moving from the stigmatizing "yellow peril" to the assimilating "model minority," I demonstrate how both tendencies have indeed coexisted throughout history, and the affective investment in positioning Asian Americanness as either an oppressed or assimilated subject continues to give life to its subject formation. As a result of the unresolvable Asian American subject position in the singular articulation of "the oppressed" or "the assimilated," the uncontainable, paradoxical emotional excesses become a dominant feature in how Asian Americans describe themselves. Echoing what Hong writes about minor feelings, "the racialized range of emotions that are negative, dysphoric, and therefore untelegenic, built from sediments of everyday racial experience and the irritant of having one's perception of reality constantly questioned or dismissed," these affective excesses challenge the authenticity and political legitimacy of one's racial injury.[19]

Asian American feelings are rarely intelligible in day-to-day life but function as a form of minor neurosis, or what Frantz Fanon in *Black Skin, White Masks* terms a "situational neurosis"[20] experienced by colonized subjects, which manifests as a perpetual conflict between a psychic impulse or wish to "become white" and the necessity to continuously repress such a desire. Drawing on Fanon's description of the unconscious urge of "dreaming of turning white," critical psychologist Derek Hook articulates how for colonized subjects, such a wish is impossible within a racist society and thus they frequently experience symptoms of neurotic disturbances, repeating psychical traumas in their minds, such as witnessing the lynching of one's father.[21] The symptoms of racial neurosis emerge from multiple analogous and repeated traumas and sometimes manifest themselves in dreams.[22] More importantly, trauma does not need to be experienced personally or based on an actual event. Trauma can be fantasized and curated from the existing cultural forms. It can be adopted as fantasized experiences by colonized and racialized subjects as a response to make sense of the violent world. Yet when the feeling of distress becomes excessive and unbearable, it can turn into a form of neurosis where one's intrapsychic conflict with the environment is no longer bearable. For Fanon, collective catharsis is the moment in which the unresolved feelings of rage are channeled into violence against the colonizers and colonial society, such as in third world liberation movements, where the colonized people have rebelled against European and American imperialists.[23] He states that "in every society, in every collectivity, exists—must exist—a channel, an outlet through which the forces accumulated in the forms of aggression can be released."[24] Fanon advocates for such forms of catharsis because he believes that this is the only way the colonized can reach psychic freedom from the neurotic state, but he also suggests that it creates new forms of culture, disrupting the negative images and stereotypes that the colonial societies have produced, where the colonized people can finally see themselves in a new light. This theorization of trauma and racial conflict has made a critical leap from mainstream psychology, which tends to conceptualize psychic disturbances of racial identity as symptoms of individual dysphoria or pathology. Fanon's conceptual move addresses neurosis through the social psychological scale of "epidermalization," connecting noncathartic feelings in the historical and political context, and points to its dialectical drive in racial and cultural identity formation, rather than it being an individual clinical condition.[25]

Whereas the ambivalence of Asian American identity is frequently framed in psychology as an issue of incomplete acculturation or integration, the noncathartic feelings from Asian American experiences accumulated in a racist society point toward further analysis of how trauma informs the solidification of a collective identity. The iterations of Ngai's ugly feelings and Hong's minor feelings all point out the problem that not all racialized subjects can achieve what Fanon describes as the state of collective catharsis. Asian American scholars and activists have embraced the late-1960s radicalization—particularly 1968, when the Asian-American Political Alliance was formed at the University of California at Berkeley—as the birth of Asian American subject formation without much contestation, and the minor disagreements seem to be located around when this movement ended.[26] Some scholars focus explicitly on the brief period of the late 1960s to the 1970s regarding Asian Americans' connection to third world internationalism and close ties with organizations such as Third World Liberation Front, the Red Guards, and Black Panthers, which have explicitly anti-imperialist and anti-capitalist ambitions,[27] whereas others include the mobilization around the Vincent Chin murder in 1983 as an extended period of Asian American radicalization.[28] We can understand the Asian American historiography, in a sense, for coining the late 1960s as a moment of collective catharsis, where the accumulated rage found an identity framework to express and actualize itself, confronting the neurosis and despair that one had had to endure as an individual previously.

However, borrowing Wendy Brown's words, when does this continued referencing back to the 1960s become a form of wounded attachment for Asian Americans? Brown is critical of the 1970s identity-based movements in the North American and European left that deviated from a structural analysis of class and a critique of emergent global capitalism. She contends that these politicized identity movements based on the categories of gender, race, and sexuality were subsumed under the liberal "logics of pain" to justify one's political position. Under the new liberal hegemony, the diverse proliferations of new identity groups had to articulate their subjectivity through specific histories of suffering. Brown asks, "Where do elements of politicized identity's investments in itself and especially in its own history of suffering come into conflict with the need to give up these investments in the pursuit of an emancipatory democratic project?"[29] Particularly, the failure of identity politics to address global capitalism has led to naturalizing it since the 1970s, replacing structural class analysis with feelings of class resentment in which the wounded subject no longer has emancipatory goals but is invested in mourning the loss of privilege and even turning toward bourgeois white male privilege as the sole object of desire.[30]

Asian American activists' repeated iterations of the Chinese Exclusion Act, the internment of Japanese Americans, and the Vincent Chin murder—these spectacular events of suffering—are now a common form of Asian American politicized historiography. That is, by recalling and revisiting these past traumas and the specter of violence, the prediscursive feelings of alienation and rage from heterogenous communities facing various forms of structural violence can be rearticulated and invested in *the* Asian American subject formation. A protester at a Stop Asian Hate rally at Foley Square, New York City, in March 2021 held an iconic sign that read, "Chinese Exclusion Act 1882 / Japanese Internment 1942 / Trump Calls Us Kung Flu."[31] These three rows of text address this popular iteration of the historiography of Asian American suffering in liberal circles, despite these historical events being produced by different mechanisms of racial state power and the wounded subjects of the historical events not seeing themselves through the same category of identity. This specific narrative of Asian American injury is also highly dependent on the visibility of East Asian body—especially Chineseness—as the primary holder of the racial pains. Although Asian American politicized identity was a radical project in the late 1960s, we must also confront how it may turn into a wounded attachment, holding the noncathartic feelings as sources of subject investment rather than releasing them for other forms of radical potential. As US society began to fixate on the successful image of the model minority, Asian American activists and scholars felt that the emphasis on historical suffering to claim Asian Americans' rightful political position was perceived as increasingly urgent. However, moving away from the 1960s anti-war and anti-imperialist radicalism that were supported by the global conditions for decolonial revolt, the professional class of Asian Americans mobilizes these feelings toward more cultural and ethnic ends, rather than toward the previous vision of internationalist solidarity.

Michael Liu, Kim Geron, and Tracy Lai have labeled the late 1970s and the 1980s as the "Mature Movement," where Asian Americans focused on the long-term development of different ethnic communities within the United States.[32] If one traces the inward folding of Asian American movements, starting in the late 1960s and proceeding into the professionalization following the 1980s, the current wave of Asian American politics ignited by the anti-Asian violence during the COVID-19 pandemic is notable as a moment of reinternationalization, where Asian Americans in the United States and in diaspora have shown up in mass numbers in the streets. On the one hand, there is an emergence in Asian American radicalization claiming anti-imperialist and anti-capitalist politics that sees itself alongside the rising Black struggles. On the other hand, under the new challenges of neoliberal capitalism, there is a growing professional class of Asian Americans who are invested in the politics of injury and putting forth assimilationist, and sometimes anti-Black, agendas. The solidarity that the Stop Asian Hate[33] movement has called for, between the middle-class Asian Americans who experience microaggressive verbal assaults and the Asian immigrant massage workers who were killed, can be misconstrued without making explicit how these racial injuries are connected to crises created by global capitalism, border control, heteropatriarchy, and US militarism.

In the global context of the rise of China, this book invokes Shu-mei Shih's Sinophone critiques[34] that problematizes the hegemonic influences of Chineseness in the diaspora and articulates the political consequences of the singular focus on anti-US imperialism as the primary, if not, the only empire to be critiqued. This approach, still prevalent in Asian American studies, is paradoxically US-centric and oblivious to the ways in which the United States and China energize and sustain their competing imperial projects through interimperial rivalries.[35] It highlights how the Stop Asian Hate campaigns that called for solidarity within Asian American communities yet rarely considered how Asian racial injury has been appropriated by the Chinese state as a tool of the new Cold War competition with the United States, justifying its image of victimhood and obscuring its authoritarian violence inflicted on dissidents from Hong Kong, Xinjiang, Tibet, and Taiwan who refuted the Chinese ethnonationalist narratives. These geopolitical conflicts have intensified and created ideological and political fault lines in contemporary Asian American politics especially since the outbreak of the COVID-19 pandemic. As Shih effectively argues, the issues of empire and imperialism are not subjected to the West.[36] The lingering leftist romanticism of China as a socialist and anti-imperialist force, especially among Western intellectuals, has ignored the hegemonic and destructive power that the Chinese state can bring and influence diasporic communities. By drawing on Sinophone studies, the book aims to contest the overwhelming presence of Chineseness in Asian American racial politics—that is, critically illustrating the problem of the dominance of Chineseness in Asian American subject construction. Sinophone critique as a framework breaks down the conflations and forced equivalence of language, culture, ethnicity, and nationality often exaggerated under the Orientalist and self-Orientalized views of the East versus the West. By centering the question of geopolitics and uplifting the scale to the transnational, this book emphasizes that contemporary enactments and understandings of Asian American politics must confront with not only US imperialism but also the growing Chinese imperial forces in the diasporic communities especially in the post-2010 era.

Furthermore, in the liberal arguments for "protecting our community," mainstream Asian American politicians have mobilized the rising anti-Asian violence to consolidate more state control and police presence across cities in the United States. The COVID-19 Hate Crimes Act—a legislation that is defined based on the idea of Asian American vulnerability during the pandemic—also neglects the fact that Asian Americans (excluding Pacific Islanders) have the lowest infection and death rates compared to all other racial groups, including white Americans. The politics of injury that Asian American liberal anti-racism frequently invokes, without being placed under broader material analysis, can individualize racism as "bad feelings" that can be replaced by "woke consciousness." Whereas Asian American feelings have the potential to bridge communities with distinct cultures and histories, they can also be misplaced and used as a form of racial transcendency, class resentment, and neoliberal multicultural sensibility that are detached from a broader analysis of racial injustice.

Aligned with what Paolo Virno articulates as sentiments of disenchantment as well as Ngai's ugly feelings under neoliberalism—where privilege is no longer assigned based on clear racial lines but instead is convoluted by circuits of global capital where one is encouraged to seek any opportunity for class mobility—these negative affects can be utilized toward feelings of a specific kind of class resentment that do not seek to change the structures of competition but rather reinforce their legitimacy. Virno notes how these affects of alienation have been perfectly integrated into the system of wage labor by being transformed into "an operational requirement: a special tool of the trade," where "insecurity about one's place during periodic innovation, fear of losing recently gained privileges, and anxiety over 'being left behind' translate into flexibility, adaptability, and a readiness to reconfigure oneself."[37] Although neither Virno nor Ngai speaks directly about Asian American subjectivity, the recent conservative efforts in consolidating Asian American feelings of injury into neoliberal post-racial agendas (as evident in the anti–affirmative action lawsuits as well as anti–Black Lives Matter (BLM) and anti–critical race theory mobilizations) are some of the explicit ways in which these sentiments of disenchantment can be turned into a politics of injustice.[38]

This book thus argues that the injured affect is as easily mobilized by the left—to unite a widely diverse and ideologically heterogenous community—as by the right to portray Asian Americanness as an exemplar subject in the politics of racial color blindness. Specifically, psychology as a scientific discipline has given shape to these noncathartic feelings by setting the boundaries of what constitutes the "Asian American subject" as well as placing them into seemingly different figurations that encompass this subject's racial flexibility. As I will describe in detail in chapter 1, from the initial formation during the first waves of labor migration as the convertible Oriental, Asian Americans have been constructed as the wartime captive, the acculturable minority, and the post-racial ideal throughout the time since World War II when the category began to appear in the field. Each of these figures absorbs and disciplines these feelings into particular psychological objects of investigation in different historical periods: convertibility to Christianity as an immigration issue in the nineteenth century, captivity as a geopolitical problem during wartime, becoming a model minority as a cultural phenomenon in the postwar period, and the undefined racial position of the Asian American subject as a question related to the racial unconscious in the neoliberal era. Although the psychological investments and interests in Asian Americanness have changed along with the field's paradigmatic shifts, this book demonstrates that the injured affect has never been properly resolved and thus has continued to drive the construction and identity politics of Asian Americanness. In other words, despite the figuration of Asian Americanness having shifted across time, the underlying drive of racial sentiments remains inconclusive and frequently exists in the collective unconscious of racialized Asian subjects. Only in the event of visible racial injuries are there brief moments of collective catharsis, when Asian Americans are able to see the reflection of themselves as subjects of racial trauma and form a temporary coalition across their heterogenous ethnic, class, and national differences.

The feelings are curated to imitate and hold together an imagined population of Asian Americans who have shared biological traits, cultural roots, and historical experiences. The continued desire from both inside and outside of Asian American communities to animate such population claims despite internal inconsistencies and structural heterogeneity, I argue, is driven by prolonged noncathartic affective injuries. These injuries have created the collateral of Asian American emotional subjects as being apolitical, dispassionate, unsettled, or even confused that are common in the public imagination. The negative affects wait and seek opportunities to slip out of their containment to intensify under new political goals. Although this book does not overemphasize historical accounts of injured affect or sociological events wherein it has occurred, it does articulate how the injured feelings have adapted to neoliberal racial configurations, seizing new opportunities for racial class advancements by portraying Asian Americans as wounded subjects. At the same time, drawing from Silvan Tomkins's well-known articulation of affect as capable of moving in multiple directions rather than being predetermined by a specific cognitive course or essentialist drive,[39] this book captures the desire of diasporic Asian American subjects to channel injured affect toward anti-imperialist and anti-nationalist aims.

From Representation to Assemblage

This book undertakes a critical interrogation of the category of Asian American, motivated by both its elasticity of multiple transfigurations as well as the stickiness of staying intact as a racial group since World War II. Moving away from the construction of Asian Americanness as a truthful population that can be scientifically measured and examined, the book aims to rearticulate Asian Americanness as a raced, gendered, classed, and sexualized biopolitical assemblage that produces physical and imaginary boundaries of nation, geography, and citizenship. Specifically, it highlights the entanglements between Asian Americanness and dominant figure of the racialized Chinese subject since World War II in psychology. To theorize Asian Americanness as an assemblage is to recognize its relations of exteriority to other converging structures of global capitalism, wars, and racialized immigration policy; its interiority of specific and irreducible qualities of the overdetermined "yellow" body and industriousness; and its temporal emergence as a social whole at different periods of history.[40] The concept of Asian Americanness as an assemblage rejects the characterization of a racial population as an entity of accumulated individuals who share essential properties. An assemblage is fluid and changeable when interacting with other macro and micro social entities. It does not always exist and has never been fully formed, yet at times it emerges as an "irreducible social whole"[41] with salient contents and properties. This book argues that the task of racial analysis is not about revealing the irrefutable internal qualities of what constitutes Asian Americanness but identifying the traces of its exterior and interior relations that give rise to its emergence within a given temporal and spatial configuration.

To *feel* Asian American within this new scale of global relations is thus to sense an intense change of spatial reorganization toward the expansive and complex webs of the geopolitical landscape. Borrowing Manuel DeLanda's analogy of water, the once-solidified assemblage of Asian Americanness can be seen as a piece of ice, mobilized by decades of racial liberalism and cultural citizenship to define its clear boundaries and properties. Yet spurred on by a burst of energy generated by the catastrophic event of the pandemic, Asian Americanness as a body of water has reached certain physical thresholds and started to melt and flow into a larger space, changing its interior molecular arrangements and thus its exterior shape. To understand a thing is to give it a shape and to hold it to a certain quantity and quality so we can approach it ontologically. Contemporary Asian American politics necessitates a framework, from the scale of US domestic politics to the global geopolitical scale. Although the term *perpetual foreigners* has always been understood as a racial assault against Asian American communities—which it certainly is when it denies the rights, citizenship, and belonging of Asian Americans—we may also think of it as one form of the inevitable attachments of Asian Americans with their foreign Other. To feel foreign warrants a perpetual critique against the insistence on loyalty by the nation-state and the consequences of imperialism.

The transnational scale of the Asian American assemblage is an unstable one. It has been expressed historically as both anti-imperialist struggles against American imperialism and a political contingency for civil rights within the United States, which illustrates the inherently contradictory relation of Asian American subjectivity, particularly since the end of World War II.[42] Asians were also associated with the Cold War divide between the aggressive "Oriental Communists" and the obedient citizens of developing nations in need of strong-arm American capitalism, democracy, and military. Similarly, Asians were portrayed as both foreign security threats and "honorary whites"[43] in the postwar American nation building to strengthen the leading ideology of meritocracy and the United States as a liberal, multicultural nation. These polarizing images illustrate how Asian Americanness has never been a uniform construction and has been positioned only referentially to the US nation-state, slicing off the Cambodian, Hmong, Vietnamese, and Filipino communities from Chinese, Korean, and Japanese, for instance, in higher education access debates. As I will argue in this book, Asian Americanness can only be intelligible geopolitically. Unlike mainstream multicultural discourse that attempts to depict Asian Americanness as a legitimate and cohesive US-based population that represents a set of minority interests and concerns, deployed often in contrast to African Americans, my analysis in this book proposes that these interests and concerns about rights, autonomy, prosperity, sexuality, family, and freedom must be understood as the desires and struggles between the competing yet interconnected nationalisms of the United States and the Asia Pacific. By examining the unresolved tensions of Asian Americanness as the "foreign within"[44]—the simultaneously foreign Other and model minority—in the textual accounts of psychology, in the bodily protests for and against racial justice, and in the psychical struggles around belonging, I aim to provide a conceptualization of Asian Americanness as a critical location that unsettles the binaries of exclusion and incorporation, opposition and assimilation.

The analysis of Asian Americanness from the perspective of the assemblage is also critical in that it does not privilege either the structural or the subjective aspects of the social whole. Whereas scholars in critical race and ethnic studies have focused on group-based discrimination and racial construction, the study of Asian American affective subjectivities are left undertheorized or dominated by the discipline of psychology, except for minimal recent scholarship that has attempted to bridge critical race theory and psychoanalysis through the conceptualization of Asian American racial melancholia and racial dissociation, most notably by Ann Anlin Cheng,[45] David Eng and David Kazanjian,[46] and David Eng and Shinhee Han.[47] Psychology as a scientific discipline and a totalizing discourse in North America, since its professionalization during World War II, has created the laboratory experimental subject of the individual that can be measured outside of their social context.[48] The psychological has been split off from the social and created a set of scientific and public discourses, ways of knowing, and social practices of understanding and regulating the self. The technology of subjectivity[49] facilitates the formation of Asian Americanness as a legible racial population in that Asian Americans subjugate themselves under the confines of this temporal and spatial formation and perform their race through these discourses. In other words, the function of the technology of subjectivity is to keep the relations of interiority intact within an assemblage, which then expresses its properties as essentialized and natural characteristics.

By examining the assemblage as a whole, we are able to understand Asian Americanness as both macro-historical occurrences and micro-phenomenological subjects that have emerged and receded for specific purposes. Moreover, to invoke the framework of assemblage demands an elevation of scale in Asian American inquiry from the domestic and national to the transnational and diasporic. Particularly, in the current neoliberal landscape, multiculturalism has been successfully appropriated by the American nation-state to legitimatize its global capitalist leadership. How Asian Americanness is deployed to mediate not only US racial relations but also the geopolitical relations between the United States and Asia Pacific thus becomes a central concern in this book.

EXCEPTIONAL SUBJECTS UNDER NEOLIBERALISM

In the twenty-first century, the Asian body can now be seen as a superior subject of speculative capitalism—surviving the 1997 Asian financial crisis and on the curve toward the next phase of financialized profits and conspicuous consumption. The apparent economic success of the Asian body and Asian nations reinforces the triumph of American imperialist intervention and capitalist market logic. The story *Crazy Rich Asians*, a Hollywood romantic comedy film adapted from Kevin Kwan's best-selling novel that topped the box office for four consecutive weeks in North America in the fall of 2018, has won sweeping celebratory reviews by both mainstream journalists and Asian American communities.[50] As the only all-Asian-cast Hollywood film since *The Joy Luck Club* from twenty-five years ago, although *Crazy Rich Asians* tells a typical, if not cliché, Cinderella storyline of a Chinese American professor from a humble background in New York City meeting her billionaire boyfriend from one of the wealthiest families of Singapore, supporters of the film praised it for its racial representation and social significance. In an interview, Kwan attributes the film's enormous success to how the story "transcends race."[51] The narrative on the malleability and transformation of the Asian racial subject is certainly not new. The depiction of *Crazy Rich Asians* by all means does not reflect the majority of experiences of Asian racialized subjects globally, yet its popularity has marked a significant new phase of Asian racialization since postwar racial construction. The widespread discussions around the film, both the glorification and the rejection of its representation, drove a new iteration of Asian American subject production in the neoliberal era.

Yet quite opposite to Kwan's statement of how the Asian narrative is "beyond race," as I argue in this book, the growing power of Asian capital ever since the rise of the so-called Asian Tigers post–World War II and the narrative of ascendancy to whiteness precisely relies on the interconnectedness of Asian racialization with capitalism, white supremacy, and US imperialism. Flexibility as a racial capacity of Asian Americanness has allowed it to expand and enclose its boundaries of identity for not only survival and inclusion but also for accumulation and exploitation. These processes do not reflect the transcendence of race but posit a new articulation of Asian American raciality as an aspiring futurity of neoliberal multiculturalism.[52] As scholars of racial capitalism have pointed out, the post–World War II racial representation in the United States has withdrawn from the logic of racial liberalism and distributional equality through the welfare state and begun to disproportionally invest in upwardly mobile "multicultural" subjects that do not fit perfectly into the traditional color lines.[53] The marginalization of the Asian body is now both valued and exploited in stories of speculative success and ascendancy, where select groups of diasporic Asian and Asian American subjects are incorporated into the neoliberal regime as exceptions—of new forms of inclusion and citizenship.

This book locates Asian racialization and its particular manifestation of the Asian American body in the contexts of this neoliberal shift and the rise of China in the twenty-first century. The model minority discourse that was initially mobilized to suppress racial liberation movements in the 1960s has offered a selective class of Asian Americans the privileges of national protection and temporary racial relief. Yet, it has also created a fiction of Asian American as a population with enduring internal and external contradictions. Asian Americans are now the love-hate subject of the American psyche: at times adored as the exceptional, accomplished minority, and at other times hated as foreign intruders. Anti-Asian violence is not merely a product of the COVID-19 pandemic racism but a reoccurrence within US racial politics utilized by right-leaning politicians to instigate fear of Asian hyperproductivity and of the manufactured threat that Asians, especially the Chinese, have been "taking over American jobs" since the 1960s. As the 2016 presidential election approached and issues of immigration became heated, the heightened anti-Chinese sentiment shocked Asian American communities with hateful graffiti signs spray-painted in San Francisco neighborhoods that read "No More Chinese."[54] These xenophobic expressions, particularly against Chinese in the United States, are certainly not new. During the peak of the financial crisis in 2008, white supremacist groups and right-wing politicians framed Chinese immigrants and China the nation-state as the job stealers and the primary problem that contributed to the American economic downturn.

Meanwhile, mainstream columnists such as Nicolas Kristof of the *New York Times* continue to fuel the model minority myth through highlighting the educational and middle-class successes of Asian Americans. The present discourses of the model minority, highlighted in Kristof's article "The Asian Advantage,"[55] no longer solely rely on the racialized biological paradigm of the "smart Asian brain" or the eugenics of IQ test scores, the latter being too reminiscent of backward scientific racism. The newer discourses, instead, incorporate cultural ideologies such as hardworking Confucian values to stress the technical and cognitive superiority of Asian bodies, which has created a highly select population of "disproportionately doctors, research scientists and other highly educated professionals." This portrayal of the "Asian advantage" is often supported by empirical psychological studies of cultural differences and perceptions[56] to explain how success to Asians and whites is conceptually disparate, where Asians are taught to always strive toward higher academic achievement through hard work and never feel content with themselves, as in Kristof's own words: "Asian-American kids are allowed no excuse for getting B's—or even an A-. The joke is that an A- is an 'Asian F.'" These awfully familiar narratives in the contemporary discussion of Asian Americanness, though avoiding attributing differences to biological race, genes, or intelligence, are culturally essentializing and serving the Orientalist function of contrasting Asianness with Americanness, marking Asianness as the ultimate cultural Other.

The subject of neoliberal exceptions comes with its internal unresolved contradictions, where Asian Americanness is sliced up into subgroups and congealed as a collective when convenient for the selected argument. Although Asian Americans have the highest median household income compared to all the other racial groups and the overall US average, income inequality is the highest among Asian Americans. In 2021, Indian and Filipino Americans are the only two groups exceeding the Asian American average of an $86,000 annual median household income, earning far more than other Southeast Asian American communities such as Burmese ($44,000) and Nepalese ($55,000), whereas the median household incomes among the East Asian groups—Chinese, Taiwanese, Japanese, and Korean Americans—are not far from the Asian American average.[57] In a sense, East Asian Americans have defined what constitutes a normative Asian American experience ever since the category has been created. The structural differences among Asian American social classes—as a result of the distinct waves of migration and imbalance in the amounts of financial capitals that the immigrants have brought to the United States as well as the continually received support from their respective societies of origin—have produced unresolvable ethnic and class tensions among Asian Americans. The exceptionalization of Asian American success in mainstream discourse that serves as what Virno calls "abstraction of opportunity" has only created more sources for competition, opportunism, and ambivalence about one's futile attempt toward achieving the fantasy of the good American life.[58] It fuels the injured affect among Asian Americans as they encounter not material opportunities but empty promises, as well as the indispensable reality that their suffering, though cruel, is still not comparable to other working-class people of color, especially Black and Indigenous communities. As Claire Jean Kim argues, the unitary concept of "discrimination" that Asian Americans experience under an overachieving structure of white supremacy can obscure the "differentiated positioning" of nonwhite communities and even push Asian Americans further toward the politics of anti-Blackness.[59]

THE LIMITS OF REPRESENTATIONS

However, ever since the 1970s, progressive Asian American scholars and activists have usually attempted to tackle the model minority myth through the route of representation, emphasizing how Asian Americans are a diverse population, including the comparatively less economically and educationally advantaged ethnic subgroups of Cambodians, Laotians, Hmong, Burmese, and Vietnamese.[60] They rightfully criticize the term *model minority*, which was created by white American sociologist William Petersen in 1966,[61] as a misrepresentation of these communities that created the myth of the United States as a color-blind society.[62] Similarly, in psychology, the stereotypical portrayal of Asian Americans is often treated as a sampling error that requires a more accurate and diverse representation of the racial group, particularly around how the outcomes of high academic achievement are a result of not differentiating ethnicity and generation among the Asian American population.[63] The arguments on representation often end up becoming tautological and theoretically weak and contradict the liberal discourse of visibility and representation that sustains the category of Asian Americanness in the first place. One might argue that there are poorer Asian Americans, so the model minority myth is untrue, but another might say that there are successful Asian Americans and they deserve rights and citizenship. This paradoxical logic is particularly evident in affirmative action debates, where Asian American academic achievement becomes highly contested, with discourse split between different conceptualizations of who can rightfully represent the population. On the one hand, opponents of affirmative action often deploy color-blind rhetoric to argue that Asian Americans with high academic achievements should have the right to enter elite universities over other racial minorities who have lower academic achievements. On the other hand, proponents of affirmative action disagree with the simplistic portrayal of the population and highlight how Asian American subgroups, particularly the Pacific Islanders who receive lower levels of education, are entitled to the rights of admission based on the policy.[64] These contradictory discourses of Asian American success are not purely external but circulate within Asian American communities: polls of Asian Americans have consistently shown a fifty-fifty split in their views on affirmative action.[65]

The case of affirmative action illustrates how Asian Americanness is deployed as a moving target in US racial politics, used by the elites to reinforce color-blind politics and white domination, picking and choosing the appropriate ethnic subgroup to represent the entire population along the lines of ongoing oppression and successful assimilation. Although the liberal discourse that addresses Asian Americanness as racial and cultural representation has traditionally served to strengthen visibility and demand group-based rights, it also reveals the instability of the racial category itself. Furthermore, the culturally essentialist depictions of Asian values are perpetuated by not only white interests but also Asian American elites, who have spent a fortune in reproducing the stereotypes and profiting from them. The popularity of Amy Chua's *Battle Hymn of the Tiger Mother*, emphasizing the Chinese cultural values of success, shows the public's obsession with Asian Americans as the model minority as well as the communities' own investment in cultivating these archaic yet partially advantageous representations.[66]

Therefore, the myth of model minority is not an inaccuracy of representation but that there is such a coherent racial population to be represented in the first place. The abiding myth about Asian Americans serves as a powerful metaphor regarding the virtue of American multiculturalism: its tolerance, inclusion of differences, and absence of racial conflicts. Despite the progressive attempt to emphasize the diversity within Asian Americanness as a means to resolve the representational conflict, it may be theoretically and politically more productive to examine how the formation of Asian Americanness as a population is the function of racial capitalism itself, which demands racial integrity and racial differences to protect the logic of capitalist class hierarchy. Ruth Wilson Gilmore critically defines racism as follows: "Racism is the state-sanctioned and/or extra-legal production and exploitation of group-differentiated vulnerabilities to premature death, in distinct yet densely interconnected political geographies."[67] This dialectical process of differentiation and interconnection is key to the possibility of capitalist accumulation by truncating spaces and groups into abstract entities of existence. According to Jodi Melamed, ideologies of democracy, nationalism, multiculturalism, and identitarianism are means to reduce people into narrow categories of citizens and to confine of nations, as well as to regulate and obscure relations of power through symbolic recognition.

Rather than achieving and nurturing "social wholeness" and interconnections, the upholding of categories becomes an alienating form of capital accumulation and compliance to state management.[68]

Multiculturalism and its associated new hegemonic discourse of diversity have proved to be particularly profitable for racial capitalism. As Anna Tsing has pointed out in her analysis of supply chain labor, global capitalism no longer functions through the mid-twentieth-century McDonald's or Walmart model of standard production across space but requires new figures of labor that consist of unequal class formation made out of the arrangements of "culture." In other words, the "noneconomic" factors of race, ethnicity, gender, sexuality, nationality, and religion are drawn into the supply chains as raw materials for exploitation as well as marketing strategies that target an audience who looks for cultural uniqueness in the products.[69] For instance, citing Jane Collins's ethnographic work in *Threads*, Tsing articulates how immigrant entrepreneurs in the garment industries often employ workers from their own immigrant stream in the Global South and frame these women of color workers as simultaneously having superior sewing skills and lacking professional qualifications in the job market.[70] Here, cultural diversity has become a paradoxical term. It disguises exploitation with opportunity and rearticulates global class relations and division of labor as a form of cultural determinism (e.g., Asian women's nimble fingers make them better at sewing). After placing diversity in this neoliberal context, it is crucial to examine the problematic entanglements between Asian Americanness and cultural diversity and the strong attachment with representational politics from the Asian American left to right. As of today, diversity can be sold for exploitative practices, so we need to revisit our progressive pursuit of racial justice and make sure it does not depend on the same logic of exceptionalizing Asian difference.

In fact, the argument that is often employed by progressive racial justice circles that "Asian Americans are not monolithic" to defy the model minority myth misses the point. Specifically, the noncathartic Asian American injured affect, exclusion, and alienation will persist despite the shift in representation from the figure of the unassimilable Oriental to the acculturated minority. The structure of capitalist competition and Asianness as an exceptional form of hyperproductive labor is deeply entwined with Asian racialization in North America. Indeed, Claire Jean Kim famously put forward the "racial triangulation" model in the late 1990s that characterized the particularity of Asian racialization based on not only Asian Americans' superiority and inferiority in relation to whiteness and Blackness but also their relative degrees of "civil ostracism"—that is, as the perpetual national and cultural outsider.[71] Although such foreignness, no doubt, has served as a harmful stereotype against all Asian Americans regardless of their migration histories, it has also been associated with Asian subjects' cultural superiority and hyperproductivity in contrast to other racial groups. In her book *Alien Capital: Asian Racialization and the Logic of Settler Colonial Capitalism*, Iyko Day argues that Asian racialization must be situated in the settler colonial project in North America where Asian peoples and their labor are conceptualized as alien, abstract, and threatening. From cheap yet hyperefficient Chinese railroad workers in the mid- to late nineteenth century to "high-tech" overachieving model minorities post-1965, there is a continuous logic of economism that undergirds Asian racialization, figuring Asian people as foreign and excessive forms of abstract capital, alien to the lands of settlers and opposed to the romanticization of white concrete labor and the inferiorization of Black labor.[72]

Day's analysis points to why anti-Asian racism surges during periods of economic recession and heightened global capitalist competition, as was the case when Vincent Chin was murdered in 1982 at the tail end of the early 1980s recession and in the midst of the US-Japan trade war and is also the case during the current economic recession under COVID-19 against the backdrop of the ongoing US-China trade war. In both cases, physical and lethal violence launched against Asian people can be understood as an attempt to reconcretize Asianness in its inferior and racialized bodily form over and against the alien and abstract economism of the Asian body. Romantic anti-capitalism is in fact not anti-capitalist at all but rather a backward and repressive drive of (white) nativists to fetishize concrete labor as "natural" and "organic" while demonizing (Asian) abstract labor as "alien" and "immaterial." It associates the mobility, hyperproductivity, and intangible labor embodied by Asianness as threatening and ultimately destructive to the nation-state. In this sense, the street harassment, physical attacks, and even murders of Asians can be understood as forms of violence that attempt to "put Asians back" into their confined, racialized corporeal form—to make Asians less economically threatening in the eyes of the "romantic anti-capitalist" nativists.

The economic modality of Asian racialization emphasizes how Asianness has been made synonymous with (foreign) capital itself. Challenging the common approach of Asian American theorization that locates Asian racialization as comparable or analogous to anti-Blackness, the transnational and anti–settler colonial framework points to the specific functions of Asianness within global capitalism and how its foreignness is seen as simultaneously a source of injury and a perceived privilege. Asian laborers from the nineteenth to the late twentieth centuries were brought to North America not only as exploited alien labor but also as a superior and more efficient form of labor compared to other racial minorities, associated to the biopolitical capacity of Asian culture and physique. To put it bluntly, the perpetual foreignness of Asian Americans cannot simply be reduced to a "disadvantage" in racial positioning as it assumes a powerful, intact, and durable "cultural essence" of (often) Chineseness that is superior in some form.[73] Whereas mainstream Asian American politics since the late 1980s has often been fixated on the politics of assimilation and national inclusion, foreignness has been rapidly transformed into a form of transnational mobility and hyperproductivity that can be easily accessed and exploited as sources of neoliberal class advantages.

This book argues that we cannot simply rely on the polaristic frameworks of oppression and assimilation to understand Asian American subjecthood—the history has shown that it has continually occupied both positions. Specifically, Asian Americans' unwavering foreignness signifies a source of both its racial oppression and its alien advantage. From a representational standpoint, the change of dominant discourse from yellow perilism to model minority may seem drastic, as they illustrate two distinct classed and racialized images of Asian people. Following this logic, in protests against anti-Asian violence during COVID-19, the association of the Asian body to disease has generated a strong sentiment among Asian Americans that the aliveness of yellow perilism destroys the model minority myth, serving as a proof that "things have not gone better for Asian Americans." However, such an argument neglects that the underlying economic and spatial logics across the images of yellow perilism, model minority, and the recent *Crazy Rich Asian*–esque neoliberal citizen are, in fact, similar. The three figures all embody the indisputable characteristics of foreignness, mobility, and hyperproductivity and are thus a threat. The difference lies in the degrees of externalization and internalization in geographical imagination. Whereas yellow perilism and neoliberalism signify an alien force and external threat, the model minority represents an internal and domestic interracial competitiveness. Across time, the noncathartic feelings regarding Asian Americanness of being partially included and excluded have arisen from these accumulative historical turns and been carried through different figurations. The foreignness never goes away—it has congealed into a kind of class resentment and the politics of injury.

Structure of the Book

The primary argument of this book is that Asian Americanness is precisely produced through its flexible racial capacity to oscillate between the oppressed and the assimilable. Despite liberal Asian American politics emphasizing the necessity to counter both the negative racial stereotypes and the assimilative subjectivities via representational means, it is the tension between the two poles that continues to drive Asian American identity formation. To look at the Asian American subject as simultaneously oppressed and assimilated rejects the common narrative of linear identity politicization in which Asian Americans move from the historical figure of the yellow peril to the racially conscious political subject. On the contrary, the book illustrates how and why the injured affect persists in serving as a temporal bind and investment in Asian American identity production. To put it simply, racial injury consolidates a cohesive historical narrative of Asian Americanness from the nineteenth century to the present. To trace the continuous affective investments that bind these heterogenous narratives and subjectivities across time, this book investigates three movements of Asian Americanness on the textual, bodily, and psychical scale. Each chapter illustrates an example of Asian Americanness in relation to its flexibility across space and time. It does not aim to produce a totalitarian definition of Asian Americanness, but rather, locate it in the different conjunctures of wars, racial relations, geopolitics, migration, flow of capital, and diasporic attachment. My aim is to observe a repetition of norms and a series of acts through the text, body, and narrative that capture Asian Americanness as a performative assemblage of racial imagination on which the US empire has always depended. In this way, Asian Americanness is no longer an "afterthought" of Black-white racial binarism, nor an exceptionalism ("beyond" Black and white or race itself), but a *sideways* construction along with the interrelations of "Asia" and "America."

The book, in refusing to illustrate the concrete boundaries and measurements of what Asian Americanness is, expands on psychological knowledge production, nation making, and identity construction by elevating the historical and geopolitical tensions that have constituted such a term. I employed multiple qualitative methods including a textual analysis of psychological literatures, an ethnographic study on Asian American participation in BLM, and discursive analysis of the anti-imperialist diasporic Asian mobilization in the era of rising authoritarianism in Asia. I took on a "subjectless" position of Asian Americanist critique to examine the relationship between Asian American subjectivity and its representations.[74] By subjectless, I mean to foreground the discursive constructedness of a geographical, racial, and affective unit termed *Asian Americanness*, instead of assuming its internal, biological coherence as a predetermined population. Each case provides the descriptions of different Asian American enactments that unsettle the discursive construction of Asian Americanness either as a distinct racial population or as a psychically and culturally "confused" subject trapped between the hegemonic binary discourses of "East versus West" in diaspora. These discourses have dominated and coexisted in the public imagination of what Asian Americanness is and have even been taken on by Asian American elites to make claims about the political and moral legitimacy of Asian Americans' role in US society. My application of discursive analysis is not to prove how psychology has constructed a "structure of lies" about Asian Americans but to uncover what historical conditions make these discourses productive and intelligible.

Chapter 1, *Psychology and Racial Flexibility*, examines how the textuality of psychological research as a particular scientific genre is significant for how it corresponds with an array of institutional powers—policy, medicine, culture, morality, and the psyche. The colonial taxonomy that explicitly displayed phrenology and racial phenotypes has now been replaced by the tone of scientific neutrality and tables of descriptive statistical results in the recent psychological research, yet these still contain an organized series of presentations, as Foucault articulates: "a certain *style*" and "a certain constant manner of statements"[75] (italics in the original). The chapter consists of my examination of the shifting configuration of Asian Americanness from the 1940s to the 2000s across psychological literature and the different subjectification within the co-constructed narratives of oppression and assimilation. Beginning from the early construction of the Asiatic worker as convertible Oriental in the event of nineteenth-century Chinese immigration and exclusion, I demonstrate how the racial flexibility of Asian Americanness persists across time. The difference between periods lies primarily in the scale of external deterritorialization and internal territorialization, rather than in how Asian Americanness is seen: from the oppressive yellow peril to the assimilable model minority. To put it another way, tracing the psychological investments in Asian Americanness shows that it is precisely the ongoing and unwavering tension between being oppressed and assimilable that produces the Asian American as a unique psychological subject. In this chapter, I illustrate how Asian Americanness has been mapped onto a transpacific history of wartime political anxiety, the 1965 waves of immigration under the Hart-Celler Act, and the "post-racial" neoliberal era by specifically following psychology's subjects of preoccupation: the Chinese and the Japanese. The psychological analysis of these two racialized populations in the United States has informed what later becomes "Asian Americans" in the 1970s.

Even though Asian American psychology has experienced a tremendous growth since 2000, many scholars have noted that the knowledge is still saturated by East Asian experiences.[76] Although this book does not cover Southeast

Asian and South Asian American experiences, by contesting the hegemonic representations of Chineseness as intertwined with the transpacific geopolitics and war histories, I want to acknowledge the lack of non–East Asian representations is not accidental but a consequence of biased epistemology in psychology. Recently, there has been a rise in attention to the specific racialized experiences beyond the dominant East Asian representations—for instance, the formation of Filipino psychology and Indian psychology as in relation to different histories of colonialism and impacts of Orientalism.[77] Hence, the book aims to capture a particular passage of transpacific entanglements and Asian American subject construction in psychology from World War II to the present "new Cold War" between the United States and China that mainly concern Sinophone Asian subjects, which has dominated the discursive and imagination of contemporary Asian Americanness. To trace such history, in this chapter, the psychological texts selected thus go beyond empirical, descriptive statements on scientific discovery; the knowledge they produce also feeds back into public discourses and becomes part of our collective consciousness. One cannot simply treat psychological research about Asian Americanness as an inaccuracy of methodological application or scientific hypothesis. It is just as much about diplomatic decisions, ethical life choices, moral judgments of success and failure, clinical practices, and institutional regulations. With discourse analysis that pays specific attention not only to the shifting yet persistent notion of Asian Americanness but also to the particular function of the genre in which psychological research takes shape, my goal is to demonstrate how psychological science has always been an intimate aspect of our cultural and material life.

To contrast the dichotomizing and Orientalist portrayal of Asian Americanness in the literature, in chapter 2, *Black Lives Matter and Asian American Political Fracture*, I apply ethnographic method to understand how contemporary Asian American geopolitics operates on the ground. This chapter extends the neoliberal post-racial subjectivity that I demonstrate in chapter 1, where Asian Americanness is under a new period of deterritorialization in terms of geographical scale. Demographically, the rapid immigration of people from Asia—the numbers of which doubled between 2000 and 2019—makes the foreign-born population of Asian Americans exceed their US-born counterparts.[78] Currently, around six in ten Asian Americans were born in another country—a major shift in composition since the creation of the Asian American identity that is primarily rooted in US-born Asian American experiences. The change in national composition also signifies that Asian American political subjectivity cannot be confined to domestic US racial discourses. The mobilization of conservative pro-police Asian communities and the #Asians4BlackLives contingency are heavily influenced by their imagination of the role of China: whereas the former sees seeking "racial justice" for Asian/Chinese people in the US diaspora as a way to demonstrate Chinese nationalism, the latter desires a nostalgic anti-imperialist form of Afro-Asian solidarity against the US racial empire.

The site where I began my ethnographic work was in the context of the BLM movement since 2013, where racial awakening was not only occurring in the Black but also Asian American communities. Specifically, the role of Asian Americans in the BLM movement drastically shifted when Peter Liang, a Chinese American rookie police officer in New York City, shot an African American man, Akai Gurley, to death in November 2014. This incident happened during the height of the Ferguson protests, where both Asianness and Blackness became collateral damage of state-sanctioned violence and became quite controversial in the movement, instigating debates about racial justice and anti-Blackness in Chinese and Asian American communities in the United States and abroad. While color-blindness is appropriated by both white and Chinese American elites to bolster the state's investment in anti-Blackness and neoliberal interests, a multiethnic, multiracial, and multigenerational alliance is lifted up by progressive Asian American activities to demonstrate the possibility of solidarity across racial and national categories. My ethnographic work specifically follows the tensions between how the conservative and progressive communities employ Asian Americanness differently to advance their agendas, as well as how the "sticky engagements"[79] of this incident were intertwined in the US-China geopolitics over the definition of a global multicultural society.

My insistence on Asian Americanness as a flexible, mobile construct, rather than descriptive of a racial population, is motivated by the intimate ties between "Asia" and "America." Although the Asian American framework born out of the civil rights era underlined a pan-Asian political project to build a coalition based on shared experiences of racialization under US governance, this nationalistic framework inevitably ran into its limits due to its inability to address issues of American imperialism as well as the Asian subject's internal geopolitical conflicts projected into the US diaspora. In chapter 3, *Racial Loss, Diasporic Attachments, and Anti-imperialism*, I describe these geopolitical fault lines that cannot simply be attributed to a nationalistic framework particularly in the context of the rise of China. Amid the surge of anti-Asian violence events during COVID-19, Beijing authorities contributed Asian American injuries to the US Sinophobic foreign policy since Trump's trade wars in 2018. The US anti-war left, notably the ANSWER Coalition, quickly organized a day of action that fused "Stop Anti-Asian Violence" and "Stop China-bashing" into one slogan.[80] Asian Americanness has never been so clear as a proxy Cold War subject. The Chinese Communist Party (CCP) flag waving at an Oakland rally for Stop Asian Hate in April 2021[81]—without acknowledging what the present damages and political repression of the Chinese state have done to the people of Hong Kong, Tibet, and Xinjiang, and Chinese political refugees—shows that a selective anti-racism and anti-imperialism is far from the ethical vision of solidarity for Asian America in the shadow of China's growing global power. Rather than conceptualizing the positionality of the foreign within as immediately "racist," I argue that it may be turned into a productive framework to approach Asian Americanness geopolitically via Sinophone critiques.

In this vein, I examine the two different types of anti-imperialist Asian American subjectivities in the COVID-19 period. Especially, I argue that in the time of the intensification of racial injury and racial loss, Asian Americans are split along the lines of their geopolitical positioning. The anti-Asian racialized attacks have pushed some Asian Americans to express stronger loyalty as Americans to be more fully included as minority subjects, while others question the legitimacy and violence of the United States as a hegemonic superpower globally. Among the latter anti-imperialist Asian American political milieus, I discuss two distinct forms of diasporic attachments through Muñoz's use of counteridentification and disidentification.[82] In terms of counteridentification, a desire to break free from the hegemonic identity, I illustrate the rise in anti-Americanism among left-leaning diasporic Asian Americans who see the rise of Chinese power as an object of attachment that can fill their racial loss. Alternatively, another milieu of diasporic Asian Americans embodies a position of disidentification, indicating an ongoing negotiation between the majoritarian and minoritarian identity, which does not consider their critiques of both the United States and China as well as their attachments to their home of origin in Asia as contradictory.

With critical analysis across a temporal scale, from the postwar period to the current phase of neoliberal globalization, and a geographical scale, from US domestic to transnational race relations, with this book I hope to offer an intersectional framework to conceptualize Asian Americanness as well as to challenge the dominant image of Chineseness in psychology, grassroots movements, and activist narratives. The book is divided into three parts based on the different scales of the investigation as illustrated above. The multiple methods are not separate elements in my analysis but together create momentum that leads to understanding how Asian Americanness circulates, diverges, and congeals in the transnational circuit. While the Asian American subjectivities I describe in the book are attached and formed through the affect of racial injury, even the left-leaning anti-imperialist camp, in the epilogue I indicate another possible subjectivity that can adequately contend with the global conditions and geopolitics, which is termed transnationally Asian.[83] Transnationalism is certainly not new to Asian American identity formation. Yet distinct from the typical iterations of progressive Asian American politics that tend to incorporate global perspectives and geopolitical critique into domestic US racial politics, the transnationally Asian political milieus do not see the United States as the only place of resolution of radical politics but rather, build and extend multiple commitments across the Pacific.

I describe this alternative path toward Asian America as a sideways approach of queer growth, borrowing from Kathryn Bond Stockton.[84] The sideways approach is a queer mode of accumulation and accretion, where vertical progress over time is not the primary object; rather, the term alludes to a horizontal and lateral movement of building networks and connections. Rachel Lee elaborates on this analytical strategy as "key to understanding Asian/America as a multispecies assemblage" that reorganizes agency as distributed across body parts instead of locating it in a singular identity.[85] My reading of Asian Americanness across history through the notion of the sideways is not to craft out a singular narrative about Asian American progress or the strengthening of group identity. Rather, I aim to highlight the continued tensions and conflicts over Asian American representations across ties, especially under the shadow of hegemonic Chineseness. My training as a critical social psychologist also indicates that I am attuned to the fractures and counternarratives of established group identity, where the analysis emerges from "lines of difference and power" that challenge the "representational coherence, integrity, and stability."[86] These fault lines of group identity are indeed not only the antiestablishment forces but also the openings of radical possibility. In short, while the making of Asian Americanness in this project is historically situated, it is not historically determined. Given the group's deep entanglement in geopolitical history, the sideways analysis also means attending to how Asian Americanness has come to be formed across lands, borders, nations, and wars, as well as within complex webs of intersectional subject formation, instead of due to simply the linear development of immigration *into* the United States.

Although the process of psychological knowledge production often flattens out the "thick descriptions"[87] of histories, politics, and affects in the name of objectivity, this book aims to uncover and make explicit the events that give life and meanings to what we understand as Asian Americanness today. By exploring the tensions between the construction of Asian Americanness and the establishment of the US nation-state and how immigrants have made sense of their racial, gendered, sexualized position in the host society, we can understand that subjectivity is neither developed intrinsically nor imposed structurally, yet it is a contested and politically charged process. One of my central arguments is that the flexibility of Asian Americanness emphasizes not only the Asian American subject's tendency to oscillate between the poles of oppression and assimilation in the US racial formation but also their elasticity and resilience in surviving and thriving under decades of imperialist and racial violence.

CHAPTER 1

Psychology and Racial Flexibility

The becoming of a subject holds an unbearable weight. Michel Foucault's critical analysis of the transformation of homosexuality into a "new species" shows the regulatory power of psychiatry in the nineteenth century in actively creating the subject of its own discipline.[1] Modern psychology has been particularly instrumental in crafting categories of personhood and defining the boundaries of a given subject via measurable notions of personality, character, and performance.[2] Nikolas Rose has articulated "psychologization" as a power of discipline that turns its subjects into quantifiable problems: the delinquency of a child, the mental illness of a patient, or the unproductivity of a worker are to be solved by psychological techniques of punishment, cure, and regulation.[3] Psychologization turns something into truth and offers the authorities legitimate discourses to make claims about the subject. The psy disciplines have been instrumental in disciplining Asian Americanness and containing it within a specific spatial scale since World War II. Here, the psy disciplines refer to the industrial complex of psychologically related fields including but not limited to psychology, psychiatry, and psychotherapy and how they dominate practices and knowledge production about the self, the mind, and human behaviors. Although there is an abundance of psychological languages that are used to describe Asian American thinking and feeling in cultural and popular texts, Asian American studies—a more humanist focus area of studies—lacks engagement with the psy disciplines itself and vice versa. It misses the opportunity to investigate how the "Asian American psyche" is not only culturally and historically constructed but is embedded with loaded scientific assumptions about race, gender, sexuality, intelligence, and human cognition.

This chapter offers a genealogical account of how certain forms of affect become associated with Asian American body and identity. It traces the historical developments wherein the Asian American subject becomes the epitome of a modern psychological production that demonstrates an exceptional capacity of racial flexibility to move across the triangulation of whiteness and Blackness as well as the geographical scale of the East and the West as an alien subject to the occupied Indigenous lands in the United States. My aim here is not to provide a "psychological reading" of Asian American experiences but to analyze the psychological texts via a Foucauldian method of genealogy by looking at the turns and emergences that shape Asian Americanness vis-à-vis historical and political events. By employing the critical impetus of genealogy as a counterintuitive way of reading, we may decode the psychological process of "making truth" about Asian Americanness as a population and understand it as connected to what Foucault terms as "a circular relation with systems of power which produce and sustain it."[4]

Prior to World War II, Asian Americanness was not considered a panethnic racial category; rather, disparate ethnic populations were marked external to the US national imagination despite the already existing immigrant communities in the country. The creation and inclusion of Asian Americans in psychology has been considered a celebratory progress toward advancements in racial equality. Specifically, psychologist Stanley Sue and Derald Sue's essay "Chinese-American Personality and Mental Health,"[5] published in 1971, gave birth to the concept of "the Asian-American" not only as a racial minority but also a personality type. Although their formation was groundbreaking and generated decades of research in Asian American psychology as a significant subfield, following Nikolas Rose's insistence on doing a "critical history of psychology," we need to consider how the psychologization of Asian Americanness has turned the subject into regulatory regimes of inspection, problematization, and minoritization. In what ways has it become "a personage, a past, a case history, and a childhood, in addition to being a type of life, a life form, and a morphology,"[6] as was Foucault's homosexual under discursive power? Tracing the psychological production of Asian American subjecthood from its historical figure as a convertible Oriental in the late nineteenth century to the post–World War II era, I illustrate how Asian Americanness is created through the constant oscillation between an oppressed and assimilable racial subjectivity. In this chapter, I employ the concept of racial flexibility as a mode of analysis to map out the parallel developments of Asian Americanness as simultaneously a subject of racial exclusion and a symbol of racial progress. Examining the period toward the end of World War II, as panethnic Asian Americanness begins to form, I trace the different figurations of Asian Americans from the wartime captive to the acculturable minority and the post-racial ideal. The noncathartic affect of racial injury serves as a perpetual affective drive that produces flexible narratives of racial oppression and assimilation, consolidating the widely heterogenous Asian American becoming and crafting a cohesive narrative of historical development—for a community that does not share common ancestors, ethnonational origins, or even migration history. The lens of racial flexibility rejects the linear discourse of politicized identity "from the yellow peril to model minority" and instead points to the intrinsic capacity of Asian Americanness to shift between the racial Other and the post-racial ideal.

The psy disciplines have utilized this racial flexibility to experiment on the psychological malleability regarding racial identity, cultural adjustment, and political ethics of Asian Americans. During World War II, both the Japanese and Chinese were attributed distinct psychological elements—the former being the "enemy Japs" and the latter the "friendly alien"—in relation to the geopolitical conditions of the war in the Pacific. In the 1970s, the emergence of the Asian American Psychological Association (AAPA) constructed Asian Americans as a racial subject with distinct psychological interiority—that is, consisting of unique cognitive, cultural, and emotional characteristics. The geopolitical wartime epistemology of understanding the Asian race became rapidly internalized as a domestic US national project in the postwar period. This psychological technique of population measurement, based on the logic of containment and internalization, requires the Asian American injured affect to create new categories of differences and at the same time ensures a collective catharsis will never be reached but instead tamed. Therefore, under the dominance of the color-blind and neoliberal multicultural discourses in the early 2000s, Asian Americans were portrayed as both the exemplar victim of microaggression and the post-racial ideal, and the discussion of Asian American racial experiences was gradually detached from the material reality of structural racism and shifted to the realm of "the unconscious," such as in the popularization of psychological paradigms of modern racism and unconscious bias. Undertaking an anti-essentialist reading of Asian Americanness via the framework of racial flexibility, I conceptualize psychology as a technique of cartography that has shaped the multiple articulations of Asian Americanness across different historical moments of external deterritorialization and internal territorialization, synthesizing various political concerns and motivations regarding the Asian American feelings of racial injury.[7] In other words, the categorization of Asian Americanness is made legible through the psychological techniques of geopolitical boundary work and affective management from a wartime epistemology of the enemies abroad and the domesticated aliens at home. These techniques enable psychology to subjectify what was thought to be an external threat to a racial minority within the US national imagination. During the COVID-19 pandemic, we see another push toward rapid external deterritorialization, where Asian American racialization is mapped onto the US-China geopolitical conflicts once again, which I will discuss in chapter 3.

With the terms *territorialization* and *deterritorialization,* I indicate that psychology is not only a temporal technology of constructing modern subjects along the time frame of Eurocentric civilization but also a spatial technology of differentiating the distance of subjects from the imperial centers. Borrowing from Manuel DeLanda's concept of assemblage, the psy cartography draws boundaries of each racial assemblage to either solidify or destabilize the cohesiveness of a group identity through its scientific measurements and discourses about similarity and difference. Here, the process of territorialization is the tendency toward ratifying the spatial boundaries of related parts and increasing the internal homogeneity of the emergent entity. This process occurs through both the exterior pressure toward cohesion such as the forces of racial fetishism and the interior capacity of identifying similar patterns of expression such as politicization through common experiences of oppression. The creation and psychologization of Asian American as a racial identity is, thus, an outcome of territorialization itself, where the congealed affect of racial injury and resistance consolidated the assemblage of panethnic identification in the 1970s—becoming a "new species."[8] On the contrary, the process of deterritorialization is expressed through the bursts of destabilizing energy surrounding any given assemblage. It decodes the standardized and normalized parameters, such as the rituals, languages, cultures, laws, and rights of the social entity, and exposes its internal heterogeneity that is no longer containable. The two processes are equally constitutive of the assemblage, and their constructing relations continue to drive the formation and deformation of the entity. To view Asian Americanness through the lens of assemblage, race is an expressive outcome in any given temporospatial arrangement, not an essentialized property.

The Racial History of Psychology

Although Asian Americanness in the scientific field of psychology has only a short history, the psychologizing of Asian and other racialized bodies has a much longer one. Psychology has a long history of involvement in scientific racism, providing the empirical, rational, and moral justifications for domination over the racialized Other since the late nineteenth century.[9] Psychology has been a key instrument in distinguishing the civilized from the savage, the superior from the degenerate, and the reasonable from the emotional through the rationale of Galtonian eugenics.[10] Cognitive traits such as intelligence, memory, and reflex time were measured to essentialize the categorical differences of race starting in the mid-nineteenth century. While scientific racism conveniently marked the superiority of white races over nonwhite races through a temporal privileging of European advancements in reason, modernization, and industrialism, the psychological construction of race is as much about time as it is about space. Whereas the Negro race has consistently been placed on the bottom of the evolutionary ladder, the rankings of the Asiatic—Chinese, Indians, and at times the Arabs—have been much more fluid and contested.

As a modern discipline that claims its expertise in the science of the individual, psychology has joined with other natural sciences to consolidate the notions of race with techniques of differentiation and quantification of the interior cognitive life. In order to distinguish itself from other disciplines, psychology must establish its object of study within the individual, whereas social hierarchies and conditions are merely expressions of variables within that the individual should fulfill. To put it another way, under the doctrine of liberal humanism of modern psychology, racism is conceptualized as a casual negative consequence of human cognitive bias rather than a central process of human hierarchical stratification. Therefore, many critics within the discipline—from the consolidation of Black psychology[11] and feminist psychology in the 1960s and 1970s[12] to the emergence of critical psychology in the 1980s[13]—have long pointed out the problem of psychology that conceptualizes race as a category that separates populations and signifies the different mental process and cognitive abilities between Westerners and non-Westerners, whites and nonwhites, where the line of normality and pathology is determined. These critics emphasize that race should be considered as a social construct established by the technology of regulation and imperialist ideology that was part of the problematic foundation of the discipline, rather than an essentialist feature that distinguishes populations.

Conceptualizing psychology as a scientific discipline built on the necessity of constructing the individual subject allows us to understand it as a scientific discourse, rather than a discipline that provides scientific truths about the mental life. The Foucauldian notion of discourse[14]—as a set of practices and knowledge formation that reinforce existing dominant ideologies and subjectivities—points to the underlying cultural constructions and power constellations that constitute assemblages of psychological scientific texts about race and normality. Throughout history, these discourses of psychology have been shaped by the social anxiety about population management and a defensive projection on the Other. The psychological techniques of population control, deeply rooted in the European colonial histories of the nineteenth and early twentieth centuries, became central to the tactic in the United States of social control starting during the World War II with a drastic increase of military funding in psychological research.[15] Between the 1940s and 1970s, the number of "psychological experts" increased exponentially—from 2,739 to 30,839 people with American Psychological Association (APA) membership—while they remained largely white and male.[16] The military involvement in US psychology has been to deal with the war-torn soldiers' mental health needs and mitigate racial conflicts domestically, and to influence the so-called third world through international mass persuasion techniques and anti-communist ideology starting at the beginning of the Cold War.[17] Since then, psychological expertise has been included in military practices, from selecting and training soldiers in the battlefield to soliciting the cultural knowledge in underdeveloped nations abroad by the Central Intelligence Agency (CIA).[18] Continuing this military engagement after the Cold War, the APA supported and engaged with the US military in the War on Terror through developing interrogation techniques, until internal pressure led to the adoption of a resolution against torture in 2007.[19] Nonetheless, the financial and symbolic bond between US psychology and the US Army has created a state of perpetual war in the continuous expansion of the US empire and militarism in Asia Pacific and the Middle East since World War II.

The psychological techniques of diagnosis and behavioral prediction must be built on a measurable subject or population; categorization thus becomes psychology's most important tool. As psychological historian Kurt Danziger articulates, psychology's scientific findings rely on constructing an individual subject that can be studied across contexts and experimental conditions. Identities such as race and gender were treated as interfering factors, and thus even the experimental subjects have been largely white male college students since the establishment of the discipline in the early twentieth century.[20] The emergent interest in the study of racialized populations during World War II, particularly in Black communities, became central to the way that modern psychology conceptualizes intergroup relations and racial subjects domestically. Since the postwar period of liberalization, psychology has moved from its early diagnostic and pathologizing impulses toward creating "natural subjects" that are viewed more positively yet still with distinct identity boundaries, psychological orientations, and bodies. In particular, psychology's treatment of Black subjects had primarily focused on domestic racial containment through analyzing the psychosocial phenomenon of self-hatred prior to the 1970s. One example is the famous doll study led by pioneering Black psychologists Kenneth and Mamie Phipps-Clark that influenced the *Brown v. Board of Education* decision toward school racial integration.[21] Another analysis of Black people's inner conflicts is the psychopolitics of "Black rage" by psychiatrists William Grier and Price Cobbs after the assassination of Martin Luther King Jr. in 1968, when racial distrust in US society grew exponentially.[22]

In contrast, before the 1970s, as Asianness was marked as "perpetually foreign," the psychological concerns associated with the category were primarily cultural and projected outside of the US national boundaries. The perpetually foreign state of Asians as national outsiders is intimately connected to the "permanent war" that has been taking place since 1945, as the Cold War propelled the institutionalization of a large network of national security apparatuses[23] still present today as the United States continues to exert its neo-imperial influences globally through military presence and neoliberal trade. As the perpetually foreign, Asians have been the subjects of psychological preoccupation as national security threats and the Communist red scare abroad as well as potentially disloyal suspects domestically. In the paranoia-driven Cold War era, when the boundaries between military and civilian were blurred, Catherine Lutz argues that the establishment of military psychology in alignment with American security interests was based in the belief that "it was disloyal *feelings* rather than seditious *acts* that required direct state monitoring" (emphases original).[24] The psy professions thus became the main theater of the Cold War specter and anxiety around Communist threats, where the ideological and geopolitical conflicts were channeled into the battle between Communist (Russian and Chinese) psychology, which emphasized the Marxist doctrines of societal influences, and Western psychology, which privileged the subjectivity of the individual and Freudian psychoanalysis of family dynamics. This era coined Oriental foreignness as suspicious, psychologically malleable, and morally flexible and thus in need of special psychological disciplining and conditioning; it also established the warfare epistemology in constructing these psychological subjects.

The psychological concerns over Blacks were primarily about domestic security, whereas Asians embodied foreign threats. The distinct spatial cartographies of Black and Asian racialization are not merely a Cold War geopolitical effect but also due to their different spatial economies in relation to settler colonialism. Based on Iyko Day's analysis of the triangular framework of race, both Blacks and Asians are considered an alien labor force that is destined to transform Indigenous lands and turn them into white property for settler colonizers.[25] Whereas the racialization of Blacks was primarily connected to the plantation-based slavery economy and Black subjects have been considered unfree yet indisposable to the settler state, the racialization of Asians was dependent on the more flexiblized industrial economy, and Asian subjects were deemed to be relatively more disposable through the means of migration policy across cycles of economic expansion and recession.[26] In other words, the indisposability of Black labor and Indigenous lands makes Blackness and Indigeneity a central domestic concern and object of anxiety for racial integration, with different degrees of the power of blood to "contaminate" or to "erase."[27] On the contrary, while the foreignness of Asians may make them appear to be "neither Black nor white" or only capable of standing up as a racial category in comparison to others, as in the framework of racial comparison,[28] the flexibility of Asianness becomes the very characteristic that the settler colonizers valorize and discipline via mechanisms of border control. The vast interest in Asianness as a psychological category and distinctive culture in postwar psychology highlights how the discipline adopts the technique of spatialization to manage Asian populations mainly as a geopolitical concern to US society.

Therefore, to make sense of how psychological discourse is implicated in assembling the foreign and racial Other, we must understand that the Asian subject is not only constructed within the chain of racial hierarchy but also distributed across the geopolitical landscape to fulfill colonial fantasies about Western superiority. Edward Said identifies the forceful geopolitical distinctions between the "East" and the "West" by means of scientific technology and cultural hegemony.[29] By invoking Antonio Gramsci's idea of hegemony[30] in the analysis of Orientalism, I highlight how Western power works through consent rather than domination. That is, under Orientalism, the Western form of life is understood as not only superior to Oriental backwardness but also normative in its way of governing the definition of humanity. Said elaborates that Orientalism is a "flexible positional superiority,"[31] where Western interests are invested in producing and maintaining a geographically distinctive "Orient" through sociological, psychological, historical, philosophical, and aesthetic descriptions where the "West" can be positioned flexibly and in relatively advantageous terms to such a construction. In a sense, Orientalism is neither a set of colonial lies that mystifies the "reality" about the Orient nor scientifically inaccurate depictions about "Oriental populations" but a system of knowledge that makes the Orient into a being; through that, the West acts as a sovereign consciousness at the center of the colonial cartography, projecting its fear and desire onto the Orient. Communist threats, the hyperproductiveness of labor, and cultural superiority over other racialized groups have created seemingly distinct Asian figures across time, yet they are all driven by the same logic of foreignness. For an alien subject, the borders of the settler colonial state are the key to its conditional livelihood through the opening and closing of the borders. This is why the struggles over immigration reforms have been crucial to Asian American subject formation and politicization. However, as Day argues, immigration is about the changes in not only Asian demography in the United States but "Asian aliens'" relationship with the settler colonial economy. The settler colonial mechanism not only allows Asian subjects to be conditionally excluded from full citizenship but also naturalizes white settler labor as essential and morally superior for the colonized lands.[32]

Overall, this chapter argues that Asian Americanness has turned into a symbol of not only a psychological problem of a racial population's political, cultural, and moral instability but also the field's very solution to the problem by constructing the Asian American subject as containing an interior flexible capacity to be molded and shaped by the psy discourses. To put it simply, the Asian American subject has been created precisely to demonstrate a racial population's flexibility between simultaneous conditions of oppression and assimilation. The frameworks of both racialization and settler colonialism are crucial for us to trace the colonial mentality in psychological techniques, as well as to enable a spatial analysis of Asian Americanness beyond psychology's confinement to the scale of individual identity and racial population. This chapter traces how psychology has attempted to contain the Asian subject at the periphery of the nation-state as well as to transform the subject's sentiments of unbelonging attributed to the Cold War societal panic to the inner psychic conflicts of the individual. In this view, we cannot avoid the issue of space because the definition of Asian Americanness as a population has always been about drawing boundaries regarding race and solidifying loyalty of national belonging. Returning to a global scale of spatiality allows us to reexamine the noncathartic feelings that continue to be carried out through different Asian figures. The common sentiment about Asian Americans as "neither Black nor white" within mainstream US racial discourse is based on Asian foreignness in the settler colonial triangulation. However, as this sentiment frequently gets absorbed into the liberal politics of representation, it becomes a convenient demand for visibility of the Asian category "beyond Black and white."[33] Nevertheless, neither the move toward exceptionalizing Asian racialization nor subsuming Asianness entirely within the US domestic racial paradigm allows us to unpack the geopolitical scale embedded in Asian racial construction. To the contrary, the liberal impulse that attempts to resolve the problem of Asian American invisibility or exclusion by representing Asian Americanness authentically often falls into the Orientalist trap of reproducing the Euro-American colonial projection and solidifies the US settler colonial triangulation, where Asian cultural superiority and hyperproductivity is juxtaposed against Black, Indigenous, and other marginalized racial subjects.

Racial Flexibility as Method

The flexibility of Asian Americanness has led to disparate feelings in the public: awe, for its hyperadaptability and hyperproductivity, but also fear of it always being an external threat to the nation-state. Since the 1950s, the psy disciplines have attempted to manage and make sense of the excessive feelings toward Asian Americans that cannot be fully explained and contained by depicting them as the "Oriental Other" or loyal minority subject in the United States. The changing signifier of Asian Americanness between the concepts of race, ethnicity, citizenship, geographical region, and nation illustrates how Asian Americanness can be thought of as transpacific flows that sustain the codependent, constructed regions of Asia and America, as well as embodied subjectivities over geopolitical struggles that harness both imperial fantasies and the possibility toward deimperialization. With such an analytical approach, I do not intend merely to offer a critique of the enactments of scientific racism and Orientalist epistemology in psychology through Asian Americanness but hope to address how these scientific discourses reflect on "our collective *psychological* history"[34] (emphasis original) of the societies we live in and which are still very much part of our conscious and unconscious lives.

As I articulated in the introduction, racial flexibility as a mode of analysis allows us to trace the constant oscillation of Asian American construction between being a subject of racial exclusion and a symbol of racial progress. Indeed, this flexible capacity is not just a product of the postwar history in which Asian Americans have become the exemplar of racial model minority; it can be traced back much further, to the mid-nineteenth century. In the mid-nineteenth century, large waves of Chinese migrants came to California for gold mining. Yet as the gold rush faded, many Chinese migrants became servile laborers on the

Central Pacific Railroad construction projects. Anti-Chinese sentiments grew, as the Chinese migrants were thought of not only as an inferior race but also as "dangerously industrious, cunning, and resilient."[35] Anti-Chinese riots spread among white settlers who believed that Chinese labor on these construction projects was driving down wages in the United States. The concern over US white racial purity, fear of continuous racial conflicts, and outright refusal to integrate the Chinese eventually led to the Chinese Exclusion Act, passed by Congress in 1882, and additional waves of suspension of Chinese immigration for the next several decades.

The Chinese Exclusion Act is often marked as the initial systematic "anti-Asian" event in the United States, wherein the Chinese, in the racialized figure of the yellow peril, due to their distinct race, culture, language, and beliefs, were largely considered "unassimilable" to the white, Anglo-Saxon, and Christian nation.[36] This event has somehow become representative of the foundational historical oppression of the entire Asian American population; however, the historical conditions have seldom been carefully articulated in contemporary liberal Asian American discourses. As Manu Karuka argues, race at this time was considered to be one's capacity of property ownership, distinguishing whites, those who possessed the natural right to own property, from the racial Other, such as Chinese, Black, and Indigenous peoples who could not own properties.[37] Similar to the Indian Appropriations Act of 1871 and the Fugitive Slave Act of 1850, the Chinese Exclusion Act not only established the territorial claim in the United States of the Chinese as excludable racial aliens but also created the infrastructure of racial boundaries interior to the nation-state strictly for white citizens.[38] Whereas this form of continental imperialism largely subjugated Indigenous and Black populations under the interior control of the US territory, Chinese bodies were deemed to be manageable through control over their circulation in space—that is, exterior to the domestic territory. In other words, the Chinese were not so much racialized as second-class citizens unprotected by the Constitution but alien bodies to be kept at the borders, which could be valorized when necessary and discharged when no longer profitable. The regulation of the Oriental subject was deemed to be a spatial concern over mobility and flow.

However, the story of anti-Chinese sentiment and racial exclusion has a different side that is seldom examined, which has the capacity to complicate the simplistic narrative of "anti-Asian violence" and its history. Outside of the overwhelmingly bipartisan consensus for passing the Chinese Exclusion Act, many US business traders and missionaries saw Chinese migration as key toward US political and cultural expansionism in the Asia Pacific. To the "cosmopolitan expansionists," China as a new market for trade and religious conversion was too big to miss.[39] The Protestant Christian leaders in the United States were among the more vocal pro-Chinese advocates in the 1870s and 1880s. Their interests in supporting the Chinese came out of their hope that the Chinese were potentially "convertible Christians." There was a strong belief among Protestant clergymen that "God Himself had brought the Chinese to California to be Christianized" and the missionary project would not stop at the borders of the United States but help bring Christianity to the "Far East."[40] As economic antagonism over jobs and wages rose between the Chinese and newly immigrated Irish Catholic communities in California, Robert Seager articulates how the Protestant clergymen began to depict the Chinese as convertible, civilized subjects and identified them as their new hope for Christian expansion: "The clergymen attempted statistically to minimize this fear of the 'Yellow Peril,' and they energetically defended the Chinese against the charge that they were an immoral, racially inferior, incurably heathen, crafty, low, lascivious, and generally debased race of people whose continued presence in the United States threatened the very structure of a well-ordered, moral, Christian society. On the contrary, the Reverend Messrs. Brier, Loomis, Deal, Francis, and Shearer all maintained that the Chinese were sober, polite, thrifty, quiet, and inoffensive; that they were eager to learn English and read the Bible."[41] Even though the pro-Chinese clergymen eventually were unable to exert real influence over policy changes in the 1870s and 1880s as anti-Chinese sentiments grew exponentially, this episode of history nevertheless marked an initial characterization of the Oriental figure as a convertible Christian. Different than the perspective brought to the early colonization of the Indigenous peoples through Protestant Christianity as a civilization program for the "savages"—to transform their "Indian character" and institute civilized ideas "already possessed by the Americans"[42]—Oriental subjects were considered already partially civilized and convertible, yet their cultural differences were too large to overcome.

The figure of the convertible Oriental allows us to map out the historical predecessor of the flexible racialization of Asian Americanness, triangulating between Black, Indigenous, and settler relations, rather than reifying a singular narrative of yellow peril racial exclusion as the only possible historical outcome. The convertibility, elasticity, and malleability can be productive modes of analysis to trace other potential becoming of Asian Americanness and to understand why psy disciplines have taken a particular interest in constructing Asian American subjecthood. In the wartime era between World War II and the Cold War, convertibility was demonstrated again by the psy discourses around

Japanese and Chinese populations—who were at times constructed as the racialized, evil enemies or brainwashed Communists abroad, and at other times depicted as "self-governable" internees and "friendly allies" domestically.[43] The poles of oppression and assimilation from the original figure of the convertible Oriental continue to oscillate across time and space and have become a scientific concern for the psy disciplines.

In mainstream US psychology, the emergence of Asian Americanness is often understood through the inception of the AAPA in 1972, riding the waves of the Asian American movement and the civil rights movement that inspired it as well as the largest increase in immigrant populations of Asian descents after the 1965 Hart-Celler Act for immigration reform (aka the Immigration and Nationality Act of 1965). The formalization of Asian American identity in psychology can be understood as an early territorializing effort to participate in the emergent racial liberalism in postwar US society, where the accumulated racial conflicts were directed toward state inclusion as a solution. In order to crush the popularized Black revolts across US cities and repress left-wing ideologies due to the rise of Soviet influences internationally, through this 1965 immigration reform, massive waves of skilled laborers were recruited from Asia—as the "alien labor force"—to generate more surpluses and suppress domestic labor union movements.[44] The American public's concerns over domestic social and economic stability as well as foreign ideological threats were expressed through the psychological investments in cross-cultural differences, where Asians as a homogenous biocultural group across nations and geography was thought to contain a distinctive set of cultural values in contrast to Westerners. The earlier invention of the factor analysis method employed by American psychologists in 1949, most notably by Raymond Cattell, allowed scholars to measure and compare group-level behavior and personality based on the unit of nationality by grouping similar traits into a cohesive "type" of group behavior, such as "conservative, patriarchal vs. ferment of release" and "thoughtful industriousness vs. emotionality."[45] In particular, this new technique enabled the shift of scientific interest from the body to the inner mind as well as from the visibility of race to the plasticity of culture postwar. Cattell states, "The [factor analysis] method is a radical departure . . . which has already proved so valuable in dissecting out the functional unities of the individual personality—in the field of group study."[46] Thus, the earlier categorization of Asians as the "Mongoloid race"[47] based on physical attributes and intelligence migrated to more sophisticated grouping of nations. Cattell's predictions of national psyches were also valuable to serve as a basis to determine the country's culture, economic growth, political strength, and war behaviors. Asianness is no longer a racial body but an external set of cultural values and personality styles that can be classified quantitively.

Cattell's comparative study paved the way for Geert Hofstede's "Culture's Consequences: International Differences in Work-Related Values,"[48] which maps out the four key dimensions of national differences at the height of the Cold War—namely, power distance, uncertainty avoidance, individualism, and masculinity—and has been one of the most cited sources in the Social Science Citation Index until today. In its 1991 revision, Hofstede added a fifth dimension of "Confucian dynamism" to the national culture variation with the new data from the Chinese Culture Connection's 1987 Chinese Value Survey.[49] Hofstede and Michael Harris Bond attributed the economic successes of the "Asian Dragons"—Singapore, Taiwan, South Korea, Hong Kong, and Japan—to their Confucian cultural influences.[50] The identification of this Confucian variable, in a way, has contributed to the formation of the success discourses about Asia, previously unrecognized at this global scale, as the economic successes of East Asian societies—largely through US financial aid to build anti-communist bases—are considered cultural. Hofstede and Bond's *Confucian dimension*, though later revised to *long-term orientation*, has remained a rather Orientalist cultural framework, examining the "Chinese minds" across Asian societies.[51] This cultural framework for national comparisons, in a sense, facilitated a cohesive image of the so-called model minority nations of East Asia and the influx of Asian immigrants to the United States, together creating the Asian American population as always situated in the position of the foreign within. In other words, both a collective regional geography and a cohesive racial imagination of Asian Americanness were thus conflated and solidified during the Cold War period.

In the 1970s, US psychologists attempted to respond to the activist demand of a new collectivity of Asian Americans by producing knowledge through a common racial identity. Similar to the cultural variation research on East Asian nations based almost exclusively on the Confucian dimension, ethnic Chinese psychologists and subjects at this time were overrepresented in the earlier discourses of Asian Americanness. This claim of Asian Americanness despite the lack of diverse Asian American subjects shows exactly how Asian Americanness is a discursively constructed subjecthood, meaning that it is not simply a reflection of the aggregated results of all Asian-raced populations in a given context. Rather, how Asian Americanness is studied and measured is always done with specific political intentions and national objectives. In psychology, it can only be constructed as a subject through discourses of delinquency and difference.

To put it another way, the population is only as real as it can be identified as a "problem."

In a search of Asian Americanness across psychological literature from the 1950s to the present, Asian American has never been a consistent racial category or a coherent concept. The "subjectless" position I employ allows me to look for Asian Americanness through the multiple signifiers of *Asian, Asia, Chinese, Japanese,* and *Asian American* in each decade since the 1950s because they are the most visible subjects of study in psychology. I used these terms in the literature title search to limit the articles to those whose primary concerns were about the given population, rather than just a comparative sample to other racial groups, to gain a deeper understanding of how psychological representations of Asian Americans map onto public perceptions and anxieties across time. I traced how the primary signifiers shifted through the decades and analyzed the different scientific preoccupations with the subject by highlighting the dominant theoretical paradigms and concerns in each decade. The distinct tensions of the Asian American racial construction in each period highlights the ongoing contested forces in the making of Asian Americanness that speak to racial anxiety and social preoccupation.

My review of the literatures does not claim to provide a complete representation of all Asian American ethnic groups or history. The selection of my archive follows a particular thread of postwar geopolitical developments between the United States and the Asian Pacific nations that have constructed the representations of the foreign within and model minority and thus emphasizes the two key ethnic groups of Japanese and Chinese Americans, who are arguably the primary figures that have established the racial prototype of Asian Americanness in this period. They are the primary obsession of American psychological investigation and are studied extensively more than the other groups, and thus created a more coherent historical genealogy to follow. By using this selection process, this chapter will not go into the discussion on the representations of South Asian, Southeast Asian, and other East Asian groups. Rather, I am interested in analyzing how Japanese and Chinese Americans solidify the psychological portrayals of Asian Americanness since the mid-twentieth century. Given the limitations, in this chapter, I will outline my analysis of the dominant discourse of Asian Americanness at three postwar periods with distinct patterns of scholarship in relation to the broader changes in Asian American politics: (1) the wartime tensions of the 1940s and 1960s, (2) the minoritizing of Asian Americans of the 1970s and 1980s, and (3) the rise of color-blind politics of the 1990s and 2000s that I argue have subsequently relied on these discourses of the wartime captive, the acculturable minority, and the post-racial ideal to illustrate

Table 1: Racial flexibility of Asian Americanness demonstrated in psy discourses across time

	Forms of oppression	Forms of assimilation	Racial figuration	Spatial scale
19th century	Exploited coolies	Convertible Christians	Convertible Orientable	External deterritorialization
World War II	Enemy Japs	Friendly aliens	Wartime captive	
Cold War	Brainwashed communists	Liberal Westerners		
Postwar	Politicized race	Model minority	Acculturable minority	Internal territorialization
Post-1990s	Unconscious microaggression	White ascendancy	Post-racial ideal	

these malleable psychological figures. The psychological cartography of Asian Americanness across these three periods demonstrates the spatial elasticity of the category as well as the geopolitical implications of the expansion and shrinkage of the scale. Despite the changes in Asian American figuration, the affective preoccupation over its racial injury not only changes shape but also remains a major source of anxiety for those racialized. Table 1 demonstrates the lines of oppression and assimilation Asian American subjecthoods oscillate in between, the dominant racial figures consolidated by the flexible racial capacity, and the spatial scale that these subjects operate through from the nineteenth century to the 2000s in psy discourses.

1940S–1960S: THE WARTIME CAPTIVE

> Because they collaborated in the making of the war, and because they're yellow and have different beliefs.[52]

The knowledge production of "race" and difference in psychology in wartime was more preoccupied with the question of "Who is American?"[53] than the previous blatant scientific racism on the attributes of biological differences across racial populations; for example, "war enemies" such as the Japanese were thought to be unassimilable to American nationalism in contrast to the relatively more upwardly mobile Jewish and Chinese populations. The focus on "national character" in the culture and personality school of psychology became dominant during the 1940s and 1950s as the United States was mobilizing its global appeal during wartime. In fact, the stance on *anti-racism*—the rejection of the nativist race-differences research from the discipline's previous work based on concepts such as intelligence (aka IQ)—became a central agenda. In the early 1940s, many psychologists who published studies that invoked an anti-racist take against the racial differentiation in IQ performance between Blacks, Native Americans, and whites stressed the significance of unequal environmental factors.[54] In 1943, Ruth Benedict and Gene Weltfish along with their colleagues in the fields of anthropology and psychology published a Public Affairs Committee pamphlet, *The Races of Mankind*, cautioning scientific communities that in the collective pursuit toward ending fascism, people of the United States must resist the irrationality of racial prejudice and the seduction of claiming the racial superiority of any group, as the "science" proved that all differences found in intelligence could be attributed to environmental factors: "In our country men of different color, hair texture, and head shape have lived together since the founding of our nation. They are citizens of the United States. Negroes and whites, Indians, Mexicans, Chinese, and people from the European nations are all taxable, subject to the draft and to the other laws of the land. They are part of our great national community. History today is only bringing together on a world scale races which have been brought together on a smaller scale here in America."[55] In a sense, the stance against fascism as a central national character that the United States wanted to project facilitated a rapid paradigm change toward how race was studied from the previous biological essentialist approach, where the nativist positions came to be seen as right-wing and unscientific.[56]

FROM ENEMY JAPS TO GOVERNABLE CITIZENS While this liberal anti-racism that was co-constructed with American exceptionalism was a useful discursive tool against European fascism, it reached a conceptual blind spot when it came to Asian populations, especially the Japanese, who were placed on the periphery of the US nation during wartime. Ellen Herman notes how the Japanese internment between 1942 and 1945 became a large field experiment of developing human management techniques by psy professionals, where a navy psychiatrist, Alexander H. Leighton, led the sociological research project in the Poston War Relocation Center for Japanese Americans in Arizona.[57] Following the model of the Bureau of Indian Affairs, which had deployed social scientific techniques to discipline Native American peoples, Leighton and his team were instructed to "make useful" the psychological techniques of group relations, psychotherapy, and cross-cultural research to manage the distress and group conflicts at the camp. Leighton's report, with intensive interviews and observation of dynamics at the camp, was published in an ethnographic form titled *The Governing of Men* in 1946.[58] From the perspective of the present, it is hard to imagine how a nation that claims to be anti-fascist can also implement authoritarian and racist policies of forced relocation and internment at home and see no moral conflict. Yet from Leighton's book, it was clear that the psy professions did not question the legitimacy of the internment but instead focused on how to make the conditions manageable. Social psychology, especially, was treated as a set of scientific tools that could provide interventions to the internment populations under stress, and thus provide "best practice" recommendations to the US government.

In the midst of wartime chaos and uncertainty, Leighton argued that the Japanese evacuees must "feel some security and some acceptance as *fellow Americans* and *friendly aliens*. A program of self-government was envisaged that would develop gradually and enable the Project Administration to withdraw" (italics mine).[59] Despite the horrors of internment, the tone of the writing was overtly sympathetic and even culturally sensitive toward the Japanese Americans to the extent that they were seen as the key toward the scientific discovery of administration and human behavior—the perfect subjects for a self-governance and democracy experiment—that is, unlike the "fascists," the United States portrayed itself as a benevolent state even in the face of foreign threats and potential enemies. The overall goal of the psychological program was to Americanize the Japanese internees and transform their anger and fear toward the US government into positive drive for self-governance in the camp. Leighton recommended the following: "Communities under stress, with their labile but intense emotions and shifting systems of belief, are *ripe for change*. While this is a situation fraught with danger because of trends which may make the stress become worse before it gets better, there is also opportunity for administrative action that is not likely to be found in more secure times. Skillful administration may be able to seize the moment not only to guide spontaneous shifts in constructive directions, but even to achieve extensive changes that would otherwise be impossible or extremely difficult"[60] (emphasis mine). As he illustrated, the insecure circumstances made the subjects particularly malleable and thus provided the perfect opportunity to experiment on psychological techniques of shaping social organization and belief systems. To put it another way, the extreme conditions and emotional stress that the internees faced made them more prone to psychological molding.

Certainly, none of this seemingly neutral "scientific discovery" could justify the tremendous traumas and violence enacted on more than one hundred twenty thousand Japanese Americans who lost their homes, families, and dignity and were being stripped off their basic human rights at the internment camps. What is interesting about Leighton's report is how he turned the event into psychological experimentation on the concept of anti-racism and self-governance. Throughout the report, he denounced some camp administrators' racist stereotyping of the camp residents that became counterproductive to establishing governing structures among the residents. Like the Chinese who were thought to be convertible to Christianity and Western civilization, the premise of the psychological exploration was based on the idea that the Japanese had the capacity to be "convertible" to democratic and self-organized principles. Leighton wrote in the conclusion that the administration must understand and accept the complaints of their constituents and turn them into advantages through communication and organizational techniques. At the end, he strongly argued for greater integration between scientific experts and state administration "to form a common body of thought and action which is not only realistic in the immediate sense of dealing everyday needs, but also in the ultimate sense of moving forward in discovery and improved practice."[61]

CHINESE BRAINWASHING During World War II, the allyship between the United States and China allowed the Chinese to be seen as "friendly aliens" domestically. However, these dynamics started to shift during the Cold War when China faced a drastic regime change to the Chinese Communist Party, and red scare was rampant in Washington, DC. The intimate engagements between the psy disciplines and the US military continued in the Cold War period and became especially instrumental to curating the distinctions between the American/Western and the Soviet/Eastern psyche. At the center of the Cold War specter, modern techniques of psychology were seen as both a problem and a solution to issues such as brainwashing as it was being conceptualized and used. Some psychologists at the time turned their investigations toward the essential differences between Soviet ("Eastern") psychology and Western psychology. Especially in light of Russian psychologist Ivan Pavlov's behavioral conditioning methods, Western psychologists generally viewed Soviet psychology as aggressively Marxist, mechanical, and privileging the structural over individual, whereas Western psychology established itself as safeguarding the principles of capitalist democracy and individual autonomy. Amid the brainwashing scare, the battle of the paradigms was then partially channeled into the convertibility of the brainwashed subjects. A series of studies on mind conversion was published during the 1950s and 1960s across the psy fields and the notion of "Chinese brainwashing" became a pivotal concern of the US psy disciplines as well as the public imagery of racialized foreign threats. Providing a more sensational account of the subject, British psychiatrist William Sargant's 1957 book, *Battle of the Mind: A Physiology of Conversion and Brain-washing,* directly traced the brainwashing technique to Pavlov's 1944 publication, *Conditioned Reflexes and Psychiatry,*[62] and called out the West's earlier failure to dismiss the Pavlovian behavioral training method because he experimented on dogs and not humans.[63] The book received great public praise and sold over two hundred thousand copies in ten years, as it tapped into people's fear and curiosity over the rising Soviet Union in the beginning of the Cold War.

After the heated debates about the Chinese Exclusion Act, the conversations around convertibility of the Oriental appeared again during the Cold War period, when the militarized psy professions became preoccupied with the technique of brainwashing perfected by Chinese Communists in the 1950s. Initially, the "Chinese brainwashing" was an unscientific rumor assisted by Cold War propaganda and paranoia. Yet, through state funding and research infrastructures, psy professionals began to produce an even larger stage for the Cold War specter. The "brainwashing scare" in fact offered an opportunity for psychological theories and methods to appear and circulate in the public realm and even in popular culture.[64] In 1952, US Marine colonel Frank Schwable and thirty-five other air force personnel were captured by the Chinese Communists during the Korean War and publicly made confessions to committing bacteriological warfare on their mission. Even more controversial, in 1953, one British and twenty-one American soldiers who were prisoners of war refused to return to their countries of origin and chose to relocate to Communist China instead.[65] The public fixation on the brainwashing scare prompted the CIA director at the time, Allen Dulles, to recruit psychologists to understand the underlying mechanisms of the technique. Lawrence Kinkle and Harrold Wolff's detailed survey, "The Methods of Interrogation and Indoctrination Used by the Communist State Police," published in 1956, was a crucial documentation not only of Russian and Chinese Communist interrogation tactics via emotional manipulation and physical deprivation but also of how psy professionals came to play the role of war experts during this time.[66]

Furthermore, in *Thought Reform and the Psychology of Totalism*, published in 1961, US psychiatrist Robert Jay Lifton interviewed twenty-five Americans and fifteen Chinese nationals who fled China and went to Hong Kong after the Chinese Communist takeover. It was one of the earliest books that examined the brainwashing techniques from a psychoanalytic perspective with clinical interview data. Rather than focusing on Pavlovian behavioral conditioning, Lifton attempted to apply psychoanalytic methods, particularly Erik Erikson's concept of ego identity, to rearticulate the ego dynamics that made thought reform possible beyond Pavlovian theory. Unlike Sargant, Lifton rejected the commonly held hypothesis: "Pavlov—Russian scientist—supported by Soviet regime—Soviets use his theory of conditioned reflex for propaganda purposes—they taught his techniques to the Chinese—result, thought reform."[67]

Rather, Lifton viewed the Chinese as more culturally complex and resilient but also more susceptible to thought reform due to their distinct tradition of Confucianism. The Confucian principles of self-cultivation, respect of reified societal roles, and pursuit of collective harmony, he argued, echoed the thought-reform mechanisms of authoritarian control and emotional manipulation. He stated,

> The Chinese family, with its characteristically complicated inner maneuvering, has been an excellent psychological training ground: in order to be "proper," Chinese children have had to learn to be aware of the emotional currents in their milieu. And this personal emphasis has extended from the family into the rest of Chinese life: whether performing official duties or seeking personal objectives, Chinese have always put great stress on exerting influence upon the people involved—and there is only a fine line between influence and manipulation. These human-centered skills have been carefully nurtured over centuries, and emphasized at the expense of technical achievements (even the gods play psychological games). In this sense, thought reform is the modern totalitarian expression of a national genius.[68]

What was critical about Lifton's work on the Chinese "converts" in this period is his framing of the Chinese subject as a flexible figure who has the potential to be molded between the ideologies of "Eastern Communism/Confucianism" and "Western democracy/individualism." In one of his case studies, a highly educated man in his thirties, Mr. Hu, who graduated from a revolutionary university in northern China and fled to Hong Kong later, grew an immense sense of guilt when disobeying the Communist reform. Lifton diagnosed that Mr. Hu's previous submission under Communist leadership as well as his guilt for leaving came from having a dominating mother figure from a psychoanalytical perspective. As Mr. Hu developed doubts about Communism, his struggles were understood not as political but as a psychodynamic rebellion against his father and the internalized resentful feelings of an "unfilial" child.[69] Lifton also noted how sexual desire was largely repressed under the thought-reform process, which further added to the internal turmoil of the Chinese subjects and led to a wide range of psychosomatic symptoms such as "fatigue, insomnia, loss of appetite, vague aches and pains, and upper respiratory or gastrointestinal symptoms."[70] These inner conflicts caused by excessive uncathartic feelings, according to Lifton, must be dealt with through psychoanalytic principles of transference—rearticulating the infant-parent authoritarian relationship with the therapist—and reintegrating the subject's core identity and desire. Whereas Lifton argued that thought reform was much more successful on converting the Chinese than the Western subjects due to the cultural imprint of Confucianism, experimenting on the Chinese subject's emotional and ideological flexibility was a more significant task for modern psychology, as that was when the discipline was attempting to exert its capacity for psychic conversion beyond repair or cure.

Although Lifton's work on Chinese brainwashing seems to have no relevance to the contemporary discourse of Asian American psyche, it has paved the historical trajectory of centering the Asian American experience in inner family conflicts, cultural plurality, and uncathartic pains. Furthermore, the wartime psychological preoccupation with the Cold War tensions shifted from a blanket discourse of the Communist scare toward a specific attention on the psyche of the Chinese and the distinct cultural structure of Chinese society. The Chinese subject was no longer a strictly distant, threatening, or inferior Oriental figure but a potentially productive candidate on whom to explore the "human-centered psychological skills" through Western psychological knowledges. Indeed, following this logic, to convert or reform the Communist-influenced Chinese toward liberal democratic thinking became one of the keys to Western psychological triumph of the individual mind over the Marxist-Leninist emphasis on structural determinism of human behavior. The ego-oriented approach of Freudianism that emphasized individual psyche versus the behavioral approach of Pavlovianism that stressed societal influences mirrored the Cold War rivalry itself, where individual autonomy and free thinking were believed to be the primary defense of Western capitalist democracy against the Soviet model of conformity and totalitarianism.

WARTIME EPISTEMOLOGY OF RACE The psychological exploration of the Oriental capacity of flexibility did not stop at the US national border but on the contrary, was central to the wartime cartography of conflict and alliance at home. While the postwar American deployment of military power and economic resources expanded westward along the Pacific Coast and recruited Asian Pacific countries, most notably South Korea, Taiwan, and Singapore as the exterior of the US empire, domestically, Asian subjects were marked by their different degrees of political affiliation and national loyalty to American values. During this immediate postwar period, Asia or Asianness had not been recognized as a coherent racial population in psychological scholarship, partly due to how the Pacific War on the stage of World War II divided the region by the competition between imperial interests; as part of the Axis forces, the Japanese as a race were particularly marked by anti-Americanism and put down as the "enemy Japs," whereas the Chinese were constructed as the "friendly" ones who were more "tolerant."[71] The self-proclaimed immigrant leaders in these different communities also used these contrasting representations of different ethnicities to project their group's respectability and civility in their own race making—that is, to reassure the American public that they were "*not* like the Chinese"[72] or vice versa. In a sense, Asianness became largely a geographical concept fueled by intra-regional and intergroup conflicts and the unwavering Orientalist ideas of difference, despite the imposed homogenization prior to the war.

As a result, the literatures on Asians as a coherent racial population either in the United States or abroad are absent from this period. There was an upsurge of interest in examining the personality characteristics of Japanese and Chinese populations that included the primary concerns about their psychiatric abnormality, motivation, values, and attitudes in comparison to the "normative subject," which was a white American. The first volume of *Psychoanalysis and the Social Sciences* in 1947 consisted of papers by scholars such as H. M. Spitzer that deployed the psychoanalytic framework to pathologize the Japanese national character.[73] These psychological evaluations were done with various assessment methods from the Rorschach test[74] to personality surveys[75] that aimed at differentiating test subjects from the normative subject. The depictions of the Japanese and Chinese, whether as immigrant populations based in the United States or abroad, generally conformed to the Orientalist stereotypes of being conformist, culturally traditional, and sexually repressed, as in lacking the Western romantic desire for heterosexual courtship. These representations were appropriated not only to show the inferiority of the psychological qualities of these populations but, especially for the Japanese, to explain why Japanese society was capable of waging wars against Western countries.

On many occasions, the Japanese and the Chinese were deployed in parallel comparisons with Negroes, Mexicans, Jews, and Italians regarding white Americans' perceptions of social distance and stereotypes of minority groups, where nationality was seen as synonymous to the concept of race, and the Japanese were separated from the Chinese as distinct racial populations.[76] Although these minority groups were treated as comparable on the same plane, their social positions were not seen as equivalent in any measurement. In Else Frenkel-Brunswik and Joan Havel's study on white American children's perceptions of prejudice through a series of vignettes and interviews, Negroes were consistently rated the highest on the white children's perceptions of prejudicial attitudes, and Jews were rated the lowest, while the ratings of Chinese, Japanese, and Mexicans sat closely in the middle.[77] This placement and differentiation should not come as a surprise, as the racial stratification based on the matrix of scientific racism at the time continually marked Blackness at the bottom of the temporal scale of civilization and at the farthest distance from whiteness. The Asiatic peoples, particularly the Chinese and the Japanese, fluctuated in the middle. The wartime epistemology segregated them by their assumed loyalty and disloyalty to the United States, and at the same time, their physically visible racial features—the yellowness—grouped them similarly on a racial ranking scale.

Although the Japanese and Chinese were placed on a similar racial rank out of the general prejudice ratings, the children in the study viewed the Japanese as more aggressive and treacherous, especially those who were from the West Coast and had witnessed the internment of Japanese Americans in the 1940s. One girl addressed the question regarding reasons behind the prejudice against the Japanese: "Because they collaborated in the making of the war, and because they're *yellow* and have different beliefs. It's so funny that many children say, 'the dirty Japs' and they don't even go over there and see them. So many people here hate them when they don't even know what it's all about" (italics mine).[78] Here, the "yellowness" of the Japanese race functions particularly as an effect of the war and is associated with the Japanese only. On the other hand, the Chinese were characterized by favorable middle-class values of "cleanliness, industriousness, thrift" as well as being "quiet, patient, and submissive."[79] Similar to the Jewish, the economic status and the hardworking morality of the Chinese were considered ways in which a minority could bypass their difference and assimilate into the mainstream society, freed from the visible, physical, and spatial segregation based on race that was particularly loaded for the Negro populations. The significant amount of Chinese Americans' participation during World War II in the military service and other wartime employment also became a major factor that enhanced American public attitudes toward the population, in contrast to Japanese Americans, and gradually improved their social belongingness in the country.[80] The wartime epistemology was deeply embedded in how race was constructed in this period abroad and in the United States.

Shifted from its early conception of the biological basis of race, modern US psychology's experimentation with anti-racism was key to distinguishing itself from the fascist and Communist Other. Psychology's anti-racism posits that there is no inherent racial difference but only psychological and cultural variation, and thus, racial subjects are considered ultimately moldable. The outcomes of *Brown v. Board of Education* for racial desegregation based on the doll study, which showed how Black children suffered psychologically from segregated environments, was a radical paradigm change.[81] It articulated a racial egalitarian vision of psychology that privileged the environment more than "innate differences" as leading factors regarding the achievement gap and psychological pain. As the discipline was trying to look past racial differences domestically and create a "psychological subject" that was a universal entity with fundamental, overlapping behavioral patterns, the Asian subject was considered to be the US front line of liberal democracy. Whether it was the Japanese internee or the Communist Chinese, the Asian subject was conceptualized as psychologically flexible, capable of being molded into various shapes suitable for consolidating a universal subject based on psychological interests. The Asian subject was not only culturally distinct enough from the normative white subject but also racially insignificant enough to be able to showcase the convertibility of psychological techniques, as psychology attempted to establish itself as a liberal anti-racist modern science between the 1940s and 1960s against the backdrop of World War II.

1970S–1980S: THE ACCULTURABLE MINORITY

> No other group has moved so quickly upward in the United States with the possible exception of the Jews.[82]

At the end of the 1960s, psychology in the United States had undergone a transformation on the subject of race, prejudice, and discrimination. The Society for the Psychological Studies of Social Issues (SPSSI) within the APA was the forerunner that began to publish on race-related topics such as policy issues around desegregation in its *Journal of Social Issues*.[83] In 1967, the SPSSI invited Martin Luther King Jr. to deliver the distinguished address on the topic of *The Role of the Behavioral Scientist in the Civil Rights Movement* at the seventy-fifth annual convention of the APA in Washington, DC. The irrefutable presence of the civil rights movement combined with the decades of Black psychologists' effort to challenge the apolitical stance and whiteness in the APA eventually opened up a space in mainstream psychological circles to address racial justice issues more directly. However, preoccupied by the previous debates of nature versus of nurture in intelligence, racial discourse was largely attached to the differences between the biogenetic-cognitive bodies of "Caucasians" and "Negroes." Even though by the late 1960s, the hereditarian racialists' arguments were found to have no solid scientific grounding and were considered lost to the environmental behavioralists, the turn to cognitivism left the door open for psychologists in the 1970s to consider racial differences through "innate programming."[84] Race remained mostly fetishized as a problem located in the bodies of Black Americans, while other racial minorities were rarely addressed in this Black-white binary paradigm.

The psychologization of Asian Americanness into a racial population only started to gain momentum in the 1970s. The formal establishment of the Association of Black Psychologists with Charles W. Thomas as its first president in 1968 gave Asian American psychologists a precursor to formalize the AAPA in 1972 with the leadership of Chinese American psychologist Derald Sue. Its initial interests were in dealing with mental health issues in the Asian American communities.[85] One of the primary reasons for the emergence of Asian American consciousness was the broader social context of changing immigration patterns. Since the 1965 Hart-Celler Act, the demographic profile of Asians in the United States has steadily shifted from a previously majority US-born population that came with waves of labor demands to a primarily foreign-born, highly skilled population due to the economic demands of postwar US society.[86] Other contributing factors were the civil rights movement and the anti–Vietnam War movement, which inspired widespread political participation across diverse groups, including Asian American activism across campuses on the West Coast that addressed specific issues of racial inequalities related to Asian American experiences. Finally, entering into the Cold War, the geopolitical relations along the Pacific had been reshuffled and realigned. The postwar emergence of "Pan-Asianism," developed through the wave of third world national independence struggles against Western colonization, was solidified into formal organizational structures such as the Association of Southeast Asian Nations in 1967, which led to the Asia-Pacific Economic Cooperation in 1989 as an attempt to redefine Asian regionalism on the global stage through strategies of economic interdependence.

The dramatic economic developments in the Four Asian Tigers of Hong Kong, Taiwan, Singapore, and South Korea since the 1970s, through alignment with the postwar free market economies of the United States and the United Kingdom, gave birth to the idea of "Asian values" as synonymous to Confucian ethics of hard work, discipline, and respect for authority.[87] As mentioned earlier, Hofstede's fifth dimension of Confucian dynamism, published in 1991, introduced a psychological justification of Asian cultural cohesiveness based on the phenomenon of economic bloom, including a positive relationship to the values of (1) persistence, (2) ordering relationships by status and observing this order, (3) thrift, and (4) having a sense of shame.[88] These ideas about the psychology of East Asian nations echoed the depiction of the Asian American success story prevalent since the 1970s. The psychological technology of cultural measurements allowed Asian Americanness to travel across ethnicity, migration history, and national boundaries to formulate a cohesive image of the racialized Asian subject.

All these domestic and global factors combined made the notion of Asian American possible but also subjugated its definitions to discourses of cultural essentialism and the Western vision of capitalist success. Moreover, this widespread social, cultural, and political transformation of the notion of Asia as a region eventually led to its separation from the previous Orientalist conception of Asia as merely external and exotic to the West. Rather, Asia, as a region, had formed intimate economic and military partnerships, particularly with the United States, that together facilitated the establishment of the United States as the global superpower and dominant economy on the world stage. In a sense, Asian Americanness has always been a transnational and transpacific construct and cannot only be examined as a category within US domestic relations. The seemingly separate and disconnected geographical regions of Asia and America have become an integrated part of the global political economy as well as a new form of entangled racialized subjectivity. As the image of the foreign within continued to define Asian Americanness, the assimilable possibility of the Asian subject to US racial citizenship also initiated conversations on the Asian racial distance from whiteness and Blackness.

NORMALIZING A MINORITY During the 1970s of rapid immigration expansion and Asian economic successes, new questions of assimilation and integration had arisen with this multigenerational and mixed socioeconomic status group that were roughly lumped into the category of Asian. Scholars from psychology, sociology, and the new fields of ethnic studies and Asian American studies formed through civil rights activism started to be concerned with how the Asian population could be integrated into American cultural citizenship. Vocal Asian American psychologists were particularly concerned with the establishment of Asian American as a racial minority in the United States. In psychology, there was an emergent production of literatures that addressed Asian Americans (or Asian-Americans) as the primary research subjects during the 1970s and 1980s. While the ethnicity-specific articles engaged with the ongoing issue of assimilation and acculturation of these immigrant groups, the articles on Asian Americans illustrated two new and distinct discourses: Asian American common racialized experiences and the success story. Although these discourses of discrimination and success seem divergent and unfitting, they in fact work together to accomplish the construction of Asian Americans as a legitimate racial minority group in the US racial paradigm. The psychological knowledge production particularly emphasized the homogenization of different ethnic groups by demonstrating the evidence of cultural similarity and shared oppression, creating a new psychological category of Asian Americans that now can be measured, compared, and aggregated with data about race, culture, and biology.

The key psychologists in the AAPA, Stanley Sue, Derald Sue, and David Sue, published the paper "Asian Americans as a Minority Group" in *American Psychologist*, which set forth the notion that Asian Americans are in fact not only a social group but a racial minority group that faces distinct forms of oppression and thus develops unique racially injured feelings in the United States.[89] The authors pointed out the controversy that surrounded the qualification of Asian Americans as a "minority group." They asserted that on top of their race, Asian Americans had to demonstrate "evidence" of oppression by proving that they were "poor or raised in the ghetto," whereas "[members] of more 'recognized' minority groups were not asked for such information. Their disadvantage status was assumed."[90] The authors called out the visible problems seen in the ethnic enclaves of Chinatowns and Manilatowns such as "poverty, unemployment, ill health, suicides, youth gangs, crimes, sweatshops, and immigrant survivals" as the shared experiences of discrimination, instead of separate ethnic issues.[91] The high attrition rates in mental health services among Asian Americans was also demonstrated as one of the urgent issues of racial discrimination as well as the limits of the psychotherapeutic paradigm in fitting Asian American needs. In a way, Asian Americanness posed an unresolved dilemma for psychologists during this period because it demanded a new paradigm of racial theory that was capable of addressing ambivalent and incomplete minority inclusion, which called for the recognition of Asian American as a coherent racial minority group instead of a scattered and separated foreign Other.

By the 1970s and 1980s, Asian Americans as the model minority had become a permanent fixture of the national racial imagination. From the earlier wartime construction of race where Asian immigrants were understood as separate social groups that were foreign and threatening—that is, "*definitely not-white*"—the model minority discourse solidified Asian Americans as a distinct racial group that were "*definitely not-black*" (emphases in the original).[92] Indeed, Asian American cultural values and the Confucian ethics of family honor were often used to demonstrate the racial distinctiveness of Asian Americans in contrast to not only the statistical national average of white normativity but also the relatively poorer performances of other racial minorities.[93] Nonetheless, the Asian American success story via the route of Western assimilation is not without a cost, and the consequences were framed as largely psychological. The formative essay "Chinese-American Personality and Mental Health," written by Stanley Sue and Derald Sue in 1971,[94] defined three typologies of Chinese

American men in relation to value adoption—the Traditionalist, the Marginal Man, and the Asian-American (see figure 1). Whereas the Traditionalist conforms to Chinese cultural values and is responsible, loyal, and yet looked down by his white peers, the Marginal Man absorbs Western values and is accepted by white society yet possesses a high level of self-hatred. For Sue and Sue, there is simply no possibility of finding a balance on the hyphenated identity of Chinese American, unless one develops a new identity and, ultimately, a unique personality type—the Asian-American.

According to Sue and Sue, the Asian-American carries a portion of the cultural and emotional baggage from both the Chinese and the American side. However, because of his[95] emphasis on self-growth, he finds limits in merely adopting his parental (Chinese) and societal (white) values and defines a new sense of pride through a collective identity and unity with other groups of Asian descents: "More than anything, society is to blame for his present dilemma and must be changed. Emphasis is place on raising group esteem and pride, for it is only through collective action that society's perception of the Asian-American can be efficiently altered."[96] The Asian-American is not only a politicized group identity, where the individual's "political and social awareness is more fully developed," but also a personality type different from the shame-laden, reserved Traditionalist and self-hating, defensive Marginal Man. To the opposite, "the Asian-American must be assertive, questioning, and active in order to develop in his present environment," "may become extremely militant in his reaction to racism," and even has a "tendency towards long hair."[97] Beyond a statistical number or accumulative data set, the Asian-American is now characterized with defined personality traits, interests, and appearance.

As Foucault argued in the late nineteenth century for emergence of "homosexuality" as a scientific category that is no longer just a sexual behavior but "a species,"[98] during this period, the psy disciplines at large were undergoing a wave of rapid normalization of previously pathologized subjects. For instance, the APA removed the diagnosis of "homosexuality" from the second edition of its *Diagnostic and Statistical Manual* in 1973, which marked the beginning of official depathologization of homosexual subjects.[99] Around this time, Asian Americanness was minoritized as a measurable category, a racialized psyche, a political agent, and an embodiment of societal and cultural conflict, rather than a scattered, unintelligible quality among the differently ethnicized immigrant populations. To put it simply, it became normalized as a domestic minority.

Significantly, Sue and Sue argued that the Asian American is not just a culturally influenced personality trait but an affectively charged political construct:

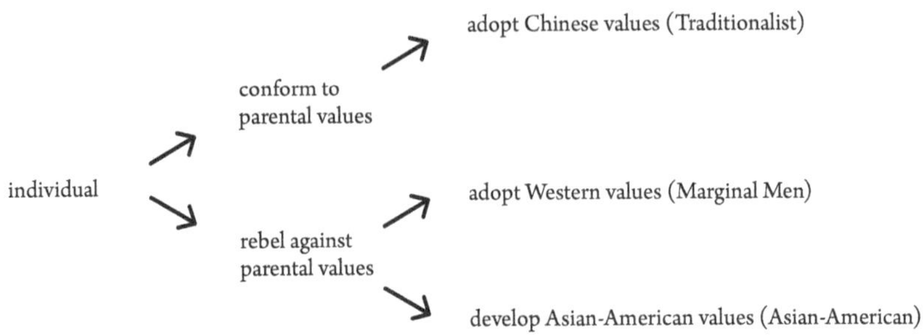

FIGURE 1. The personality conceptual scheme of Chinese Americans. Redrawn from Stanley Sue and Derald W. Sue, "Chinese-American Personality and Mental Health," *Amerasia Journal* 1, no. 2 (1971): 38.

> Asian-American may become extremely militant in his reaction to racism. While militancy may have valuable contributions in gaining civil rights, feeling of self pride and power, it may also make the Asian-American obsessively concerned with racism. He may become extremely sensitive and suspicious. . . . The Asian-American may experience a great deal of guilt and frustration in his relationship with his parents. His parents tend to view his disobedience, assertiveness, tendency towards long hair, and deemphasis on academic achievement as signs that he is disrespectful to them and to traditional values. He finds it difficult to communicate that he is attempting to gain self respect; that his parents have not failed in raising him; that he is, indeed, growing and achieving in his *own way* [emphasis original]. Thus the Asian-American may feel a real sense of loss. He is trying to help his people, many of whom do not understand his efforts.[100]

The Asian American now synthesized through this specific psychological profile is a subject marked by a male-centered racial injury. The injured feelings are a result of not only the Asian American's experience of facing racism from the outside but, more significantly, his inner turmoil struggling toward self-recognition and against guilt while facing his parents and disagreements from other Asian Americans, including the Traditionalist and the Marginal Man.

Queer theorist David Eng argues that the Asian American subject is formulated through a sustained psychical injury of racial castration and thus the understanding of Asian American as a racial category is inseparable from such sexual and gendered analysis.[101] This dynamic of insufficient masculinity has made the Asian American subject, in a sense, perpetually queer. Eng's analysis of "racial castration" anxiety clearly depicts the (Chinese, male) Asian American psychologists' preoccupation in the 1970s at the moment of the formulation of Asian American subjecthood. That is, as white male heterosexuality remains inaccessible for the Asian American men, inner racial and sexual anxieties arise and create tremendous psychic burden for the Asian American male subjects. Sue and Sue highlighted the differences in dating patterns between the Traditionalist, the Marginal Man, and the Asian-American to illustrate the distinctively affective responses and personality type of the Asian American from others. While the Traditionalist Chinese American completely submits himself to Chinese family values and thus faces anxiety and negative interpersonal relations with whites, the Marginal Man, who defines his success by degrees of assimilation to the white dominant culture, is likely to sense frustration about his emasculated status and get rejected by white women. Sue and Sue observed, "the Marginal Man may hate himself for possessing 'Chinese' characteristics. . . . He is frequently disgusted by his own physical characteristics such as shortness of height, round-flat nose, narrow eyes, and lack of a 'manly' physique.'"[102] Unlike the Marginal Man, the Asian-American, in the clinical profile of "Gale K" that Sue and Sue described, he would not feel a particular kind of intense self-hatred, but he would likely feel guilty for abandoning his parents' wish that he marry a white woman. To put it another way, the capacity to turn one's injured feelings from shame and deprecation outward to discontent with societal discrimination or concern about generational difference is a key marker of the distinctiveness of the newly emerged Asian-American psyche. Whereas the masculinist-centered racial injury and white desire persist as one of psychology's central concerns around Asian formation in the 1950s, the Asian American is someone who can turn self-hatred into "anger and militancy" against the racist society and even achieve self-pride through this specific form of masculine racial becoming.[103] This configuration of Asian Americanness, nonetheless, remains hypermasculinist and heteronormative. It turns the loss of masculine power into a form of racial injury rather than pursuing broader gender justice beyond the heteropatriarchal narrative. The Asian American man, in Sue and Sue's personality formulation, in a way, becomes the embodiment of racial castration anxiety instead of alleviating from such anxiety.

"JUST LIKE THE JEWS" Although scholars at this time did not have a consensus on what Asian Americanness is as a race, the discourses of both discrimination and success achieved the homogenization of Asian Americanness in contrast to the previous wartime race making. Whereas the sociological analysis of migration dominated the theorization of Asian Americanness, and there was only a glimpse of subjective analysis of so-called Asian American consciousness and psychology in the 1970s and 1980s, it was not until the early 1990s that the cultural and hereditary arguments emerged as two contrasting and dominant theoretical paradigms that attempt to theorize Asian American success.[104] The former emphasized Confucian teaching and discipline and the latter the cognitive functioning of the Asian American mind toward success, where Asian Americanness began to undergo a new process of internalization at a biologically essentialist level. Interestingly, Sue and Sue's psychological profiles of the different kinds of Chinese and Asian American identification were largely established through the personality typography of Jewish Americans, described by the works of the influential social psychologist Gordon Allport. They quoted an example from Allport's description of Jewish racialization to illustrate the racial hypersensitivity of the Asian American: "One day in the late 30's a recently arrived refugee couple went shopping in a village grocery store in New England. The husband ordered some oranges. 'For juice?' inquired the clerk. 'Did you hear that,' the woman whispered to her husband, 'for Jews?' You see, it's beginning here, too."[105] The 1970s psychological profile of the Asian American was unironically inspired by the newly assimilated yet still racially traumatized Jewish Americans. This link was made not only due to the strong influence of Jewish emigrants from Europe in the creation of postwar American psychology but also the emergent interests of psychology in analyzing the effects of racism in its disciplinarily specific terms. The disciplinary division between sociology and psychology was practically indistinguishable in the early 1900s, and scholars from the two disciplines worked under interdisciplinary programs funded by the military all throughout World War II, such as Kurt Lewin, who understood "social psychology" in the broader and cross-disciplinary relational terms.[106] By the end of World War II, many of the interdisciplinary centers had not survived. American psychologists gradually moved away from their sociological roots and adopted a more positivist and empiricist method to develop psychology's modern research aesthetics and disciplinary specializations. During the same period, psychologists attempted to craft a unique psychological framework to understand the newly emerged subject—the Asian American.

On the one hand, in sociology, the formation of the Asian American model minority was largely explained by the post-1965 immigration patterns, drawing from the "middleman hypothesis" of migration originally developed by sociologist Edna Bonacich.[107] Everett S. Lee and Xue-lan Rong argued that similar to Jewish American experiences, Asian American success was an accumulation of social and economic resources by the previous generations, the "middlemen" who were not invested in the host society yet heavily invested in their next generations. Consequently, the psychologists depicted Asian American success as part of a general framework of selective migration, where structural opportunities, the accumulation of capital, and emphasis on education led to the story of success that was "like Jews" in many aspects.[108] On the other hand, the psychological scholarship emphasized the hidden "psychological wages" underneath the success story. For instance, both Sue, Sue, and Sue's[109] and David Crystal's[110] work consecutively utilized nationwide comparative statistics of median income, education level, and mental health rates to illustrate the questionable success image of Asian Americans in order to establish Asian Americans as a legible "racial minority." Both studies pointed out that although Asian Americans' median income was higher than the national average, it did not account for the number of dual-wage-earner families that were above the national level. Moreover, educational achievement did not necessarily guarantee Asian Americans job security. Finally, the lower level of psychopathology as measured by hospital admission rates was highly misleading because it neglected Asian Americans' cultural attitudes toward Western psychiatry and medicine. As Crystal stressed, this success image of Asian Americans was "only the deceptive shimmer of a mirage—the dreamy gossamer arising from a mathematical bog," and he warned the readers that "a superficial reading of the statistics suggests that not only peoples of color but the white majority, too, may very well envy the material and psychological wellbeing of Asian Americans."[111]

This paradoxical and flexible racial capacity of Asian Americans as simultaneously oppressed yet assimilable allows them to be included in the state as an injured minority. This transformation mirrors the trajectory of racial formation postwar from racial repression to racial hegemony—that is, the racial strategies of the state have moved from the enslavement, segregation, and violent disruption of racial movement to coercive, inclusive tactics of neoconservative color blindness.[112] This "Great Transformation" of racial politics post–civil rights, as Michael Omi and Howard Winant name, rearticulated the racial meanings and identities that emerged in the movements to an ideological form of liberal governance based on equality and redistribution but not necessarily in any substantive form. Viet Thanh Nguyen points out that part of the hegemonic governance was done through the "bureaucratization of race,"[113] where Asian Americanness was integrated into the state via newly developed bureaucratic measurements such as the census and affirmative action, producing statistics of opportunities and inequalities. Riding the waves of modern psychology's drive to normalize its subjects of study and its unique disciplinary tool, the Asian American at this time was coined as a conscious racial subject who rejected racism yet had an appropriate amount of injured racial feelings. This minoritization of race making allowed the transition of Asian Americanness from a foreign subject in wartime toward a racial subjectivity driven by institutional inclusion and survival—that is, the desire to be fully incorporated into US society.

1990S–2000S: THE POST-RACIAL IDEAL

> Compared with other racial minorities, perhaps Asian Americans are less likely to psychologically differentiate feelings of confusion with feelings of idealization for whites.[114]

The representational paradox of the Asian American subject post–civil rights era, to define its own position neither as a raceless population "like whites" nor as a racialized population "like Blacks," was an opportunity for the professionalization of Asian Americanness in the 1970s through a rearticulation of the racial formation in the United States beyond the Black-white dualism. The discourse and the position of the "beyond" has also pushed the psychologization of Asian Americans further away from the initial comparative racial reference to Blacks. In the early 1990s, the post-racial neoliberal regime started to dominate US racial discourses. Driven by the neoliberal need to generate profits in the increasingly globalized market as well as to expand the consumer base and to cut down social services, color-blind racism, Omi and Winant have argued, was adopted to recategorize low-income people of color as the new consumers.[115] US racial politics was marked by the rearticulation of racism as a "race-neutral matter"—that is, racism as detached from its structural roots and considered a rhetorical object that can be deployed by any subject, including whites. The popular discourse of reverse racism that punishes people of color for getting "unfair advantages" shows the shifting meaning of the racial ideology beyond the Black-white logic that demands a defensive response to contain racial equality progress from "going too far."[116]

This post-racial Asian American political consensus occurs through what Nguyen calls the strategy of "territorialization,"[117] where the previously segregated ethnicities are constructed under the language of nationalist identification and assimilation as well as the commodification of racial identity that can be integrated as part of the now-acceptable US multicultural regime. Moving away from both the "not whiteness" of the 1950s and 1960s and the "not Blackness" of the 1970s and 1980s, Asian Americanness has been articulated through the emergent racial discourse of "beyond Black and white." To achieve this racial particularization, psychologists must demonstrate its exterior distinction and interior consistency. The susceptible race of Asian Americans during this period emphasizes the internal war of racial identification and racial struggle. On the one hand, Asian Americans demonstrate vast psychological similarities with whites; on the other hand, the popularization of the microaggression framework as the quintessential Asian American experience focuses on the specific experience of racialization and racial discrimination that is "not like Black." Both of these conceptualizations bring racialization from a structural and sociological analysis into the realm of the unconscious.

As a result, the flexibility of Asian American racial capacity that enables subjects to traverse the borders between "like white" and "like Black" is the most visible during this period, when the group is compared to other racial groups in psychological literature. When compared to other races, Asian Americans are often considered the most similar to whites, especially when socioeconomic class is considered as a factor in terms of parenting and academic achievement.[118] However, to justify the minority status and experiences of Asian Americans, there has been a continued effort to include Asian Americans in the framework of people of color in psychology. For example, in Justin Perry, Kristen Vance, and Janet Helms's study, they applied exploratory factor analysis of the People of Color Racial Identity Attitude Scale (PRIAS) among a sample of Asian Americans to understand how "the racialized experience of Asian Americans . . . may not be different from other POC [people of color]."[119] The fact that whether Asian Americans should be included in the category of people of color is a question of investigation is in itself an interesting phenomenon. The authors also dealt with this paradox in the study's rationale in which they argued that "no sweeping statistic of 'success' should overshadow the continued nature of racism and prejudice that Asian Americans still experience today" and "a historical legacy of being treated as 'non-white' binds them together."[120] The results, however, were inconclusive. Although the sample of Asian Americans displayed similar patterns of racial pride and white anger to other racial minorities, they showed a distinct characteristic of racial identity formation and conformity to the white race: "Compared with other racial minorities, perhaps Asian Americans are less likely to psychologically differentiate feelings of confusion with feelings of idealization for whites. Said another way, ambivalent or anxious thoughts about racial group membership might represent a natural starting point of racial identity development in concert with traditional aspects of Conformity."[121] To put it simply, the authors found that Asian Americans are prone to white idealization in the PRIAS. Although Asian Americans were normalized as a racial minority group, they still demonstrated a distinct pattern of racialization that was not "quite Black." As the study illustrated, their ambivalence or anxiety over their racial group identification led to a stronger affiliation with the white ideal. The authors suggested that the focus on acculturation, particularly for foreign-born Asian Americans, instead of racial pride or anger and white anger at whites, may be factors that contribute to a weaker sense of racial identity among Asian American communities. The key to facilitating a sense of cohesiveness, to the psychologists, is internalization—integrating "a shared historical legacy of oppression, whether they are aware of that legacy or not."[122] In other words, although the distinctive migration and class patterns since the 1990s of Asian Americans poses a problem in racial identity development, this could be overcome if a common sense of racial injury was recognized.

FROM MINORITIZATION TO PARTICULARIZATION The centering of racial feelings in studying Asian Americans became a useful strategy for psychologists to craft new discourses of racism of the unconscious. What is specific to the psychological construction of Asian Americanness as a racial category in this period can be found in the rearticulation of racism from the previous outright exclusion and blatant prejudice to the subtle and unconscious harmful exchanges of microaggressions. Derald Sue, Christina M. Capodilupo, et al. define microaggressions as "brief and commonplace daily verbal, behavioral and environmental indignities, whether intentional or unintentional, that communicate hostile, derogatory or negative racial slights and insults that potentially have harmful or unpleasant psychological impact on the target person or group."[123] Initially identified in the clinician and client interaction in the therapeutic setting, racial microaggressions have been broadly applied to practically all aspects of life where racial minorities experience invalidation and depersonalization by seemingly inconsequential racial comments. Derald Sue, Jennifer Bucceri, et al. emphasize how Asian Americans experience qualitatively different forms of racism that can be better captured through the framework of microaggressions due to the model minority stereotype that views Asian Americans as a group that has already "made it" and is "immune to racism," unlike African and Latinx Americans.[124] Verbal statements such as "You speak such good English" or "Where are you really from?" can be incidents of microaggressions that invalidate the identity of Asian Americans by treating them as aliens in their country. Whereas concepts including modern racism,[125] symbolic racism,[126] and aversive racism[127] have all illustrated the shifting forms of racism that have become more difficult to identify and are qualitatively different from the "old-fashioned" expression of racial bigotry and hatred, microaggressions are considered even more subtle and covert, where the (white) perpetrators themselves are not even aware of their racist attacks—that is, racism as an unintentional and casual aspect of life.

In the microaggression framework, the Asian American racial formation that is portrayed as distinct and outside of the boundaries of Black and white racial conflict allows this paradigm shift in psychological prejudice studies toward the unconscious and unintended "mishaps" of racist acts. As Sue, Bucceri, and colleagues argue, "Because microaggressions often occur outside the level of conscious awareness, well-intentioned individuals can engage in these biased acts without guilt or knowledge of their discriminatory actions."[128] Removed from the structural roots of dominance that have established the racial hierarchy of exploitation and spatial segregation, racism is further disembodied from a particular subject location—it is simultaneously everywhere but nowhere and could be committed by any person without explicit motivation. The concept of microaggressions, distinct from the claims of Asian American racial discrimination that was still largely rooted in structural inequalities such as income level and access to resources in the 1970s and 1980s, becomes an exemplary expression of post-racialism, as it is more concerned with regulating people's performance rather than examining the whole of racial relations. Through the psychological popularization of the microaggressions framework, Asian Americanness has allowed the production of a new paradigm of race that is no longer burdened by the definition of racism situated in the structural relations of anti-Black racism. It has curated an assortment of feelings that are specific about Asian American experiences in which class resentments are framed as racial injuries. It allows a flexible position of Asian Americanness that does not challenge the white supremacist effects of racial oppression but instead provides a position of Otherness, which is never completely inside or outside but always in between, triangulating the structural position of Blackness and whiteness.

The Problem of Visibility

With the normalization and particularization of Asian Americanness in the psy disciplines, another tension around the internal splits of this racial group also emerged post-1990s. Much scholarship has not only addressed the internal ethnic plurality and diversity of the Asian American category but also questioned whether the category could be unitarily applied for all Asian ethnic groups with drastically different cultures, languages, and histories.[129] Southeast Asian American groups were particularly constructed as "the Other Asians"[130] who faced a distinct process of racialization and forms of discrimination that were not comparable to the prototypical representation of Asian Americans as high income earning and high academic achieving.[131] Nguyen argues that ethnic territorialization of consolidating a singular Asian Americanness strips off the internal contradictions of the racial category and creates a class of Asian American bourgeoisie that assumes the political leadership of the communities.[132] In the psychological production of knowledge, while panethnic pluralism provides political and moral access, much of the scholarship today still focuses on the experiences of Chinese Americans—accounting for 15 percent of the population among the thirty-five different Asian ethnicities.[133] This racial flexibility is made possible by the conflation of race and culture under post-racialism. In other words, Asian Americanness is only solidified as a racial subject via the construction of a coherent affective racial injury, whereas the narratives of model minority success are largely justified by the lens of culture—the dogma of the "Asian values" of collectivism, Confucian ethics, filial piety, and authoritarian parenting that have continually dominated in psychological literature since the 1990s despite the rise of Asian American racial consciousness.[134]

Despite the efforts to expand diversity in Asian American representations, I wonder whether the disciplinary imperative of "being seen" as a race is fundamentally counterproductive to forming a truly intersectional and coalitional project of racial justice. The *American Psychologist* special issue published in 2021 in light of the anti-Asian violence in North America continues this discourse of demanding visibility: "Asian Americans remain marginalized and invisible in scientific endeavors and the public sphere."[135] The authors argue that this invisibility is largely due to the perceptions of "the perpetual foreigner stereotype" and not been seen as "true" Americans which "have been long held in US history . . . from the caricatures of early Chinese immigrants in the 1800s Goldrush to the incarceration of Japanese Americans during WWII to the current day xenophobia and anti-Asian rhetoric around COVID-19."[136] The desire to seek unity in racialized histories leads to the psychological curation of a particular Asian American subjecthood that is attached to injuries. However, this narrative not only flattens the distinct historical contexts and geopolitical nuances between Chinese coolies, Japanese incarceration, and racial violence under COVID-19 but also does not account for the changing structural relations of Asian Americanness to power, especially class power.

As is evident from the historical shifts since the 1960s, the psychological making of Asian Americanness has been a process of detaching racial claims from their geopolitical origins and war epistemology, first through remaking its foreign elements a "cultural phenomenon" of Confucianism, second via the legitimatization of Asian Americanness as a racial minority in the United

States, and third by projecting it as a flexible subject position regulating the domestic racial relations between Blackness and whiteness. Asian Americanness is simultaneously "just like" any other racial group yet surpassing its racial category with its distinct cultural traits—beyond Black and white.

As Asian Americanness is further removed from its colonial and geopolitical context and more depoliticized, it becomes easily recruited into the current neoliberal multicultural project, where long-standing cultural discourses have depicted the Asian American subject as the exemplars of immigrant work ethics and racial self-regulation. Although the rise of Asian American consciousness and resistance to white supremacist norms briefly crafted an alternative and broader racial justice framework, we must be cautious of the Orientalist epistemology of psychology that continuously constructs Asian Americanness as not just the racial Other but the cultural Other juxtaposed to white, Western norms. The analytical separation of race and culture that is prevalent in the psychological production of Asian Americanness can be dangerous when scholars selectively critique the homogenization of Asian Americans as a racial category but overlook the hegemonic assumptions about Asian values that are used to demonstrate the distinctiveness of Asian Americanness as a biocultural population superior to other racial minorities. The problem of visibility is not that Asian Americans are invisible but that they have only been seen in a certain way. As Jodi Melamed notes, neoliberal US racial relations are managed by cultural discourses that have replaced the centrality of race and realigned power beyond conventional racial categories, where certain racial minorities are granted access to white privileges through cooperating with elites of color and neoliberal values.[137] In other words, race can be demonstrated to be part of the neoliberal multicultural performance of governmentality whenever profitable and not be seen as threatening. Appropriating the revolutionary origins of Asian American political ideology as a broader racial solidarity movement against white supremacy, the dominant form of Asian American racial liberalism is unified to lessen racial discrimination to protect the accumulated class privileges and ensure the continuous path of assimilation into US society.

Therefore, the distinct Asian American racial cartography of "beyond Black and white" is certainly not a politically neutral depiction but has granted it proximity to neoliberalism. This paradigm shift of Asian Americanness from the foreign Other to a domesticated racial "species" is made possible through the psychological production of a distinct experience of racial victimization and the territorialization of Asian Americans as a coherent racial population, while overlooking the internal contradictions of class privileges and ethnic identities. The position of the beyond can be a seductive path because it readily assumes Asian Americanness' racial particularity without excavating how it has been carefully arranged to mitigate war crisis and domestic racial conflicts. To not fall into this neoliberal trap, we must understand the formation of Asian Americanness through the geopolitical and wartime psychological construction of Asian Americanness as the foreign within—a measurement of assimilability of US subaltern nation-states and racial minorities, the shifting space between Asia and America, and the political possibility between whiteness and of color, rather than a fixed racial position defined through a separate racialization process and distinct cultural traits.

The unresolved tensions from both within the Asian American category and between Asian Americans and other racial subjects have placed Asian Americanness in a constantly unstable yet flexible racial subject position—which could be easily appropriated by neoliberal governmentality but may also be the potential site for an anti-essentialist racial critique. As Kandice Chuh asserts in her strategy of Asian Americanist critique, to achieve the project of racial justice is not to neutralize the unsettled meanings of Asian Americanness to a uniform demand or simply to assert critiques of epistemological violence done to the Asian American subject but to highlight the limits on the liberatory potential that could be achieved through subject construction and representational politics. To deconstruct Asian Americanness is thus not to claim the internal diversity as yet another form of identitarian essentialism but to make explicit the technologies of imperial domination, assimilation, and neoliberal multiculturalism in the very formation of Asian Americanness.

CHAPTER 2

Black Lives Matter and Asian American Political Fracture

The seductiveness of the "beyond Black and white" arguments for Asian Americanness lies in not only their spatial position outside of the binary racial imagination but also in its temporal claim on the future. As I argued in the previous chapter, the emergence of Asian Americanness as a measurable population and a psychological concept has a specific temporality. It tells a story of US racial progress from wartime toward multicultural harmony. The discourses about race and racism always involve a certain amount of "time work,"[1] where social agents actively create representations of their racial subjectivities and experiences in relation to time. For instance, the claims of Asian Americans as either "beyond racism" or "continually oppressed" both involve racial time work in which the continuity and discontinuity of anti-Asian racism are pivotal to the construction and the status of the racial group. The post-2010 landscape of Asian American politics reached a new era of growing neoconservatism as the country was recovering from the 2008 financial crisis and racial inequalities soared. The enthusiasm of liberal multiculturalism achieved its peak at the same time as Barack Obama was elected as the first Black president of the United States the following year. The paradoxical conditions of both heightened class inequalities and hope for representational politics created two parallel developments in Asian American politics. On the one hand, by 2010, Asians surpassed Latinx as the largest group of new immigrants to the United States. The highly educated class of Asian immigrants—with at least six in ten college educated—believed that the United States provided better economic opportunities than their country of origin.[2] The massively diverse and transnational populations led to even more ideological heterogeneity among so-called Asian American communities. As I will illustrate in this chapter, the rise of Asian American neoconservatism was represented by part of this new middle class of immigrants—especially Chinese Americans—on concerns of meritocracy, color-blind racial demands, and diasporic ethnonationalism on an unprecedented scale. With geopolitical tensions between the United States and China on the rise, the conservative milieus of diasporic Chinese American communities channeled a sense of Chinese ethnonationalist injury into the racial conflicts vis-à-vis their discontents with the political aims of Black Lives Matter (BLM),[3] portraying themselves as the racial victims in the United States. On the other hand, the liberal Asian American politics of representation continued to focus on challenging the model minority stereotypes and called for a wider racial alliance. Prompted by the Ivy League affirmative action lawsuits largely organized by Chinese and Indian Americans, by 2016, community organizations began to call for data disaggregation between East Asians and the other Asian American ethnic groups that are more economically and educationally disadvantaged such as Southeast Asians and Pacific Islanders.[4]

The two seemingly parallel developments of Asian American subjectivities—post-racial color-blindness and liberal representational politics—came into direct conflict during a moment in BLM when the color-blind politics expressed strong ethnonationalist sympathies for Peter Liang. Liang was an Asian American policeman who was indicted for killing an unarmed Black man, Akai Gurley, in a stairway alley in Brooklyn, New York, on November 20, 2014, and became the first officer to be indicted since BLM's call for police accountability began. Asian American communities were torn between two racial positions following the post-2010 political landscape: a pro-police faction that accused the state for "discriminating" against a Chinese American police officer when other white cops were not made accountable for their anti-Black crimes, and a racial solidarity position where #Asians4BlackLives activists insisted on prioritizing Gurley's unjust death and the demands of the BLM movement at large. The former position, which centered on the discourse of "fair treatment" for Chinese American police, was mobilized by both an ethnonationalist politics within the Chinese American community and color-blind racial ideology that refused to recognize BLM's demands for overall police accountability; the latter radicalized the liberal faction of representational politics and emphasized the material basis of structural racism. As the BLM movement challenged the hypocrisy of the nation's post-racial imagery and demanded a new vision of justice that took into account the ongoing effects of racial capitalism, the Liang-Gurley conflict became a productive rupture that forced the two factions of Asian American subjectivities to come into direct contact for the first time at a national scale. It disrupted the decades of the interior consolidation project of Asian American subjecthood, which I described in chapter 1, that mainly intervened at the level of cultural representation. The two factions in the Liang-Gurley conflict represent not only the opposing ideologies but the two kinds of temporality that have simultaneously taken shape in the racial formation of Asian Americanness as fitting into a "raceless" future or reclaiming a historical cross-racial alliance. The case also captures a distinct moment of Asian American subjectivity where neoliberal class interests, the American dream, and Chinese ethnonationalism coincide to establish a new racial order and reorganize the privileges and stigmas previously assigned by racial liberalism, assembling new political subjectivities apart from the preexisting racial line.

The competing articulations of Asian Americans as either an oppressed or assimilated group are certainly not new. The intensified racial conflicts in the United States as highlighted by the BLM movements rearranged and rearticulated the existing contradictions in Asian American subjectivity toward a broader temporality, as either a racially injured minority or a radical subject of Asian-Black solidarity reminiscing about the initial formation of Asian Americanness in the 1960s. The framework of temporality I use in this chapter aims to highlight precisely how racial flexibility allows Asian American subjects to claim their position of oppression and assimilation by imagining and desiring nation(s) across time, where they identify and disidentify with the contested racial paradigms that have emerged in the United States at different historical moments. Under the waves of rapid neoliberalization that fracture traditional forms of racial solidarity politics, the theorization of Asian Americanness has been moving toward acknowledging the ideological heterogeneity within Asian American communities. This growing body of scholarship particularly attends to the intra-racial (divisions between East Asian, Southeast Asian, and South Asian), interracial (Asian-Black), class-oriented, and transnationally shaped dynamics.[5] For instance, Claire Jean Kim's formative work on Black-Korean conflicts in 1990 in Brooklyn, New York, has shown how racial power operates to reconstitute racialized immigrant groups and exerts white dominance through bodies of color.[6] More recently, Rowena Robles has illustrated how the Chinese Americans appropriated the stereotype of model minority based in the ideology of meritocracy for color-blind policies against affirmative action in the educational context, which ultimately benefits neoconservative interests.[7]

The "neither white nor Black" and "near white and Black" racial ambiguity has allowed Asian Americanness to transcend the meanings of race, as a simultaneous victim and success story.[8]

Whereas in the previous chapter I emphasized the shifting geopolitical placements of the Asian American subject, in this chapter, I examine the "*temporalized* invention of the subject," to use Elizabeth Freeman's term,[9] particularly in relation to Asian Americanness' proximity to post-racial discourse. Asian Americanness, like other hyphenated identities in the United States, is the exemplar of the American exceptionalist discourse of multiculturalism as well as of racial and ethnic national inclusion. It exists as both a theoretical and political contradiction because on the one hand, the racial and ethnic part of the compound term signifies the inclusionalist ideal, and on the other hand, the American represents the universal principles of democracy, human rights, and equality.[10] Because of this hegemonic universalism that obscures structural inequality and pushes for ideological integration, Asian Americanness is always "future-oriented," as Rey Chow[11] articulates, moving toward a day when universal ideals are fully realized and ethnic particulars are diluted to seemingly neutral cultural aesthetics. In this chapter, I argue that the racial time work of Asian Americanness neither supersedes nor is trapped in a relationship of racism but instead is beside the duration, frequency, and intensity in which Asian Americans' competing subjectivities emerge and accumulate, subjugating and resisting the total social control of racialization to become a population. As we see, the heightened racial conflicts expressed through the BLM movements in the past decade necessitated a new politics from racialized communities beyond liberal inclusion. Both right- and left-leaning Asian Americans emerged on the scene, with allegiances complicated by ever-more-diverse and transnational demography as well as new alignments in geopolitics under neoliberalism.

Unlike the blatant form of racism enacted through violent exclusion, neoliberal multiculturalism aims to incorporate populations, especially the racial Other, and capitalize on their differences as potential sources of profits. The shifting paradigm of race from violent exclusion to compartmentalized inclusion places Asian Americanness at a historical juncture—to either move forward toward post-racial neoliberalism and turn into a profitable cultural commodity or recuperate the nostalgic formation of Asian American nationalism and profess allegiance to US racial liberalism. Neither approach is driven by a simplistic recruitment of white assimilation or hegemonic patriotism. The push and pull on the temporal and ideological scales demonstrates a competition between multiple forms of nationalism and political affiliations that have constituted the flexible subjectivity of Asian Americanness as well as the conflicting racial paradigms in the United States today. I attend to the growing ideological heterogeneity and focus on the malleable corporeal visibility of Asian American body politics in the field of Asian American studies.[12] The concept of the body politic I use here considers not only this shifting representation of Asian Americanness in the political realm but also the political acts of the material body that cannot be easily dissolved into a single locus of racial representation. Asian Americanness is constantly struggling against the dominant white norms that attempt to represent it as a unified body. As Wendy Cheng articulates, the "body in politics" is a crucial site of analysis that intervenes in the previous preoccupation with "Asianness" as a symbolic representation of race that has been reduced to a US nation-based ontology on the Black-white binary.[13] Instead, the visibility of racial body politics makes it difficult to essentialize Asian Americanness and highlights its shifting operation via the analytical categories of class, ethnicity, gender, sexuality, and nationality.

A Contested Field of Splitting Asian Americanness

As a part of the diasporic Asian activist milieu in the United States, I was involved in a pan-Asian coalition of progressive nongovernmental organization leaders in New York City (NYC), API People's Solidarity (APIPS),[14] from 2013 to 2017, primarily working on facilitating anti-imperialist dialogues and actions across the Pacific. The coalition became an entry point for me to begin my ethnographic fieldwork when the controversial Liang-Gurley case shocked Asian American communities in the greater New York area, where there are historically accumulated conflicts both between Asian and African Americans and between the fractured political ideologies within Chinese American communities, the latter of which have become increasingly visible due to issues such as gentrification, educational access, and nationalistic interests.[15] As a result of the geographical and historical particularities of the Asian American communities in NYC, APIPS member activists had worked on political projects attentive to the class and ethnic specificities as well as to the broader anti-imperialist goal in Asian American movements through campaigns around anti-gentrification, labor solidarity, anti-neoliberal trade, and anti-militarism in the Asia Pacific region. The ideological heterogeneity and transnational ontology of Asian American politics informed by the APIPS activist milieu, which joined the broader #Asians4BlackLives actions in NYC, became a crucial intervention and framework for my analysis as the Liang-Gurley case evolved. As my ethnographic notes highlight, the emphasis on Chinese nationalism in the pro-Liang mobilization drew out a new politicized sector of recent Chinese immigrants across class that included middle-class families from the suburbs as well as working-class immigrants from Chinatown in the city. This development could have been aggravated by the intense racial segregation in the geographical politics of NYC, which has suspended any substantial development of cross-racial class solidarity regarding anti-capitalist demands in the past several decades.

Due to the controversial nature of the event, during my fieldwork, I had seen my close comrades and friends divided on the issue around the political position of Asian Americans—one side holding on to the radical racial justice goal of Asian and Black solidarity and the other demanding an apology from the state for decades of Asian victimization and marginalization. To engage in fieldwork on the issue for me was politically charged as well as deeply personal and emotional. I thus employed a feminist activist ethnographic method precisely to counter the neoliberal tendency to individualize conflicts and neutralize differences, to reject the removed stance of the scientist on objectivity, and to make explicit claims of both sameness and difference within a seemingly homogenous community.[16] Feminist activist ethnography stresses making explicit neoliberal technologies of assimilation and regulation based on subjectification within the transitional and intersectional matrix of race, gender, class, sexuality, and nation, as well as the ways in which the neoliberal regime seeps through political ideology and policy decisions and into the everyday experiences of individuals and their narratives. It holds on tightly to the friction of the unstable encounters of subjectivities on the global stage, while providing a lens to understand the flexibility of neoliberal governmentality that recruits progressive political rhetoric into market logic.

The concept of neoliberalism I examined in my ethnographic context addresses several levels of processes. First, at the global level, I looked at how discourses of Xi Jinping's "Chinese dream"—that is essentially about class advancement and ethnic empowerment of the Chinese people through the continued market liberalization and expansion of Chinese capital and military power overseas—circulates in the diaspora.[17] Second, at the level of the color-blind ideology of neoliberal multiculturalism,[18] I examined how racial stratification is discursively rearranged and detached from its structural roots in colonialism, imperialism, slavery, and the prison industrial complex for profit accumulation. Finally, at the level of the construction of the neoliberal subject through the logic of "bootstrap" ideology and assimilation,[19] I looked at the dominant technologies in the racial formation of Asian Americans as the model minority. Considering neoliberalism in this way acknowledges transnational feminist concerns with how power disseminates across global and local borders and the ways in which all actors are implicated in neoliberal processes, including activist communities.

As part of the fieldwork, I attended numerous events and protests hosted by both sides of the Asian American political spectrum in NYC: the BLM multiracial activists and the pro-Liang Chinese American community. I have decided to focus my ethnographic analysis on several critical events because of the drastic contrasts between the demographics of the participants, the narratives put out by the organizers, and the level of affective intensity of the events from both sides of the conflict.[20] I am particularly interested in the performativity of Asian Americanness across these actions and how these groups utilize Asian Americanness as political leverage to claim legitimacy of representation. To be clear, the discursive analytical strategy I have employed here focuses on how Asian Americanness is performed, rather than how it is deployed as an identity politics. That is, even though many of the pro-Liang Chinese Americans may not strictly identify as Asian Americans, they are directly using Asian American racial discourses and histories to justify their claims of racial justice and oppression. Furthermore, a significant part of the battle over representation in this incident has also been online, via the transnational Chinese social network app WeChat as well as the bicoastal #Asians4BlackLives activist alliance on Twitter and Facebook. I have paid close attention to these online spaces to examine the scope and the effects of Liang's shooting and its aftermath and how the incident has incited critical debates around Asian Americanness in the United States and beyond.

My analytical approach draws from Margaret Wetherell and Jonathan Potter's discourse analysis that sees racial discourses as actively constitutive of both social and psychological processes.[21] Discourses are not merely reflections of reality but an agentive power structure that constructs the subjectivities of groups and individuals. Under neoliberal multiculturalism, racial discourses have become increasingly versatile and often adopt a seemingly political progressive rhetoric to disguise white supremacy and color-blind ideology by both white and racialized bodies.[22] My analysis started with an open coding process of my field notes of the selected key events and their related media exposure. The ideas of rights and representational legitimacy became salient for both of the groups. Visual signs, protest chants, and the contrasting ethnic and cultural demographics stood out and were incorporated into my codes regarding how each group attempted to demonstrate their justification of their own claims in the Liang-Gurley case. I then identified various discursive strategies used by each group, which are discussed in later sections.

ASIAN INJURIES AGAINST BLACK LIVES MATTER

Within the BLM movement across the United States, participants often use the phrase "Black and Brown Lives Matter,"[23] where an anti-state racial subjectivity is defined by not only shades of skin tone but also the disproportionate police violence against particular racialized bodies, including African, Latinx, and South Asian Americans. Although this political message expresses a sense of racial solidarity, it simultaneously operates to single out Asian Americans—especially East Asians—as a differently positioned group in US racial relations that is absent from racial struggles and often actively embraces racial assimilation. Statistically speaking, Asian Americans, particularly East Asians, are not as likely to be targeted by direct police violence in contexts such as stop-and-frisk compared to people of African and Latinx descents. However, it should not be interpreted that Asians have not been subjected to police violence throughout US history. The Atlanta spa shootings in 2021, where Asian migrant women were targeted, is a recent tragic event with highly racialized intent. Despite these acts of violence against Asian bodies, a "machinic assemblage" of statistics and information, which Jasbir Puar termed data bodies,[24] continues to produce the biopolitics of Asian Americans as high income earning, upwardly mobile, and ultimately apolitical. State violence against Asian bodies is actively erased to cultivate Asian Americans as legitimate citizen subjects under the beneficence of US multiculturalism. This mechanism of subject making obscures the ongoing racial antagonism in the United States, which is then granted cultural and moral legitimacy to continue dominating global neoliberal affairs in Asia Pacific.

This racial antagonism between Asian and African American communities, which resulted in accumulated transnational geopolitical conflicts, reached a peak in the aforementioned incident of Liang's shooting and killing of Gurley in November 2014. This incident, occurring during the height of the BLM protests in Ferguson, became a controversy in the movement. It created a division not only between African and Asian Americans but also within Asian American communities because Liang, a young Chinese American man, was the first among all police officers indicted, the others all white, who had abused police powers in the line of duty resulting in the deaths of many unarmed and innocent Black people. Most Asian Americans felt that the government was using Liang as a scapegoat to try to alleviate the national racial "crisis" highlighted by BLM activists and their demands to reform and abolish the police system built on the practices and ideology of white supremacy. This targeting of an inexperienced Asian American officer offended many Chinese Americans. Within a few months of the incident, two large-scale rallies and several press conferences were mobilized in support of Liang by Chinese American business leaders and local politicians, who accused the city's indictment of Officer Liang as racist. This seemingly defensive mobilization against Liang's indictment was quickly appropriated by conservative elites and politicians and turned into an offensive anti-Black critique of BLM's racial justice vision. I identified four distinct discursive strategies that the pro-Liang groups adopted to turn BLM's critique of the state's racism via police violence into racism against Chinese Americans: racial injury, ethnic empowerment and deservingness, the American dream, and anti-Blackness. These discursive strategies allowed the pro-Liang groups to shift the attention away from BLM's broader demand for racial justice and toward intergroup Asian-Black conflicts.

RACIAL INJURY The pro-Liang coalition mobilized Chinese immigrant communities not only in NYC and its surrounding suburbs but also transnationally. An online petition to the White House opposing Liang's indictment started by a Chinese American community member quickly reached almost one hundred twenty thousand signatures.[25] Within a day of the court's announcement, tens of thousands of dollars were donated to the campaign to withdraw Liang's indictment from Chinese people of all classes—restaurant workers, beauticians in hair salons, business managers, lawyers, retired elders, and so on.[26] Meanwhile overseas, the Chinese Communist Party's (CCP) central propaganda newspaper, *People's Daily*, not only reported the incident but also condemned the US government as "unjust" and argued that "the US legal system still has a long way to go,"[27] implying that the unequal treatment of Chinese Americans crushed the fantasy of egalitarian multiculturalism in the United States.

Due to the wide-scale response and interests in the case, a self-proclaimed "civil rights" organization called Coalition of Asian Americans for Civil Rights (CAACR) was quickly formed after the incident. The coalition organizers, mostly Chinese American businessmen, saw this as a chance to inject rarely visible Asian American agendas into mainstream politics and strengthen the community's ties with the police and the state. Thousands of Chinese American protesters gathered on the lawn of Cadman Plaza in Brooklyn on April 26, 2015, waving American flags and bilingual signs in support of Liang. The crowd largely consisted of middle-aged, first-generation Chinese Americans and their young children. Many people wore red clothes as a symbol of Chinese national pride. Although the event was set as a protest against the "unjust treatment" of the state and many were chanting "No scapegoats!" along with the organizers on the stage, the tone of the event was strangely celebratory. Some families brought picnics and speakers to play Chinese music in the park, as if it was an extension of the Lunar New Year celebration that had happened earlier in the month.

Because of the sheer amount of people present in the crowded space, it was difficult to hear the speeches from the politicians and business leaders on the main stage. The political content of the rally was not clear to me in the first place. My conversation with a Chinese woman in her thirties from a New Jersey suburb confirmed at least one segment of ambiguous political motivation of the participants, as she admitted that she was not familiar with the details of the Liang-Gurley case. The reason she had decided to come was because a message in her WeChat group encouraged people to show up to demonstrate "Chinese unity." The themes of Chinese unity and pride seemed collectively shared among the participants, who expressed a sense of urgency to show up and to "not get looked down on by the Americans"—in other words, the mainstream society that they felt had silenced their political views for too long.

The reason that the mobilization was successful and effective should not be attributed to the significance of the Liang-Gurley case alone but be examined in the context of a cumulative organizing effort within Chinese communities. Several precursor events contributed to the turnout at Liang's rallies. First, in October 2013, on the *Jimmy Kimmel Live!* segment "Kids Table Government Shutdown Show," ABC aired an episode in which four children were discussing how the United States should solve the problem of its massive national debt to China. One child suggested that the government should build a big wall, and another six-year-old child laughed and said, "Kill everyone in China."[28] The remarks infuriated Chinese American communities, a group of whom sent a petition to the White House's "We the People" online initiative[29] to demand that the US government investigate ABC's racial hatred. It reached a hundred thousand signatures in the three weeks following the show's airing. Although the White House used the argument of free speech to deflect the demand, a new online network of Chinese Americans was built and carried a sense of political purpose to challenge racism against Chinese communities in the United States and abroad, unaffiliated with the existing Asian American nonprofit networks formed after the civil rights movements, galvanizing a new Chinese American collective identity of racial victimhood.[30]

Second, this insurgent political consciousness of middle-aged Chinese Americans, traditionally thought of as silent in American mainstream politics, was mobilized due to their desire to preserve their children's educational privileges in higher education, as many institutions now do not consider "Asian American" a protected racial category. A coalition of Asian American groups filed suits against Harvard and several other Ivy League universities in 2015 and 2016 regarding their racial quotas in admission processes.[31] While progressive affirmative action activists have been adapting the category of Asian American to argue that not all Asian Americans fit into the high-achieving stereotype, especially when Pacific Islanders and Southeast Asian Americans are considered, the complaints around higher education admission from Chinese American communities in recent years are primarily based on the ideology of meritocracy regardless of one's race. This demand is about eliminating the "Asian American" racial category as a protected class that is no longer needed. A color-blind racial rhetoric packaged in discourses of rights and justice has emerged in conservative Chinese American communities.

These two political mobilizations together became the background driving forces for a solidified Chinese American subjectivity in the Liang-Gurley case, built on a form of racial injury. While the pro-police group is largely Chinese rather than typical "Asian American," the discourse of racial injury has only been effective because its members have invoked the long histories of Asian racial injury. The Chinese protesters, particularly the leadership, called out the state's scapegoating tactic against Liang and labeled the incident "racial discrimination," "unfair treatment," and "selective treatment," as many white officers have killed innocent people and have not been charged with manslaughter. Signs depicting Martin Luther King Jr. and speeches about the killing of Vincent Chin in the 1980s were highlighted in the rallies in March and April 2015, each drawing thousands of Chinese American participants.

ETHNIC EMPOWERMENT AND DESERVINGNESS Whereas the deaths of Gurley and many other Black victims of police violence were not fairly addressed by the state or mainstream media, many Chinese publications in the United States portrayed the Chinese American mobilization in a unilaterally celebratory tone. *World Journal* and *Sing Tao Daily* called the pro-Liang movement, which started in New York and spread across major US cities, a "historical" phenomenon and the "largest" Chinese American gathering in the United States, showing an "unprecedented unity" and "solidarity" as well as a "mature and rational" image of the community.[32] The Asian American rhetoric from the civil rights movement was largely appropriated by the pro-police crowd to manufacture a united front of the Chinese American body politic as racial victim and, again, a legible racial minority deserving of institutional access and apology.

This celebratory narrative of the newly emerged Chinese American "political unity" quickly became a political opportunity for Chinese elites to form a "rainbow coalition" with local Republican politicians, Asian and white, seizing the moment to condemn the current Democratic government and form stronger ties with the city's police department. For instance, Joseph Concannon, a white retired New York Police Department (NYPD) captain, failed Senate and city council candidate, and president of the Tea Party–aligned Queens Village Republican Club, was a major force behind the pro-Liang rallies.[33] Concannon, along with other Chinese American Republicans including Phil Grim and Doug Lee as well as *qiaoling* (僑領), overseas Chinese business leaders, worked together against police reforms as means not only to undermine the government of the more liberal-leaning mayor Bill de Blasio but also to unite Asian American voters for the upcoming local elections, as voter registration forms passed through the rally crowd.

In the March 9, 2015 "Support Your Local Police" rally to protest the indictment of Liang, Concannon implicitly condemned BLM activists as "racial arsonists" and "professional agitators" who were "turned loose" under de Blasio's leadership. He and other Republican politicians addressed the Chinese American community as the "natural ally" for the pro-police and conservative agendas. A right-wing alliance developed between conservative Chinese and white Americans, who share a deep investment in preserving class privileges and status, in the name of "racial justice." Far from being cross-racial solidarity, this alliance is white assimilation in disguise. Although securing Asian American voter blocs seemed to be the rainbow coalition's primary motive in participating in the pro-Liang rally, for many of the Chinese American participants, it was a rare opportunity to express pride in their long-overlooked ethnic and national identity. This intensified sentiment of Chinese nationalism became salient to me in the rally on April 26, 2015. Whereas the coalition leadership was drawing from a more multicultural, pan-Asian discourse to put forth their demands to drop Liang's charges, the conversations I had with the participants emphasized that Chinese people should stand up for themselves and not get "harassed" or "put down by the Americans" anymore—meaning not only the white Americans who occupy a superior position in society but also other racial minorities, particularly Blacks, whose demands seem to be taken more seriously by the state.

The Liang-Gurley incident has become another classic example of how Asian Americanness as a racial discourse is lifted up to perpetuate model minority success to deny the institutional access of other marginalized racial subjects, such as in the affirmative action debate. It is ironic that the coalition leadership monopolized the representation of "Asian Americans" as a way to reappropriate the current racial crisis for ethnic-nationalist concerns, as the coalition was composed of only Chinese American and white leaders. The discourse of Asian racial victimology was mostly present in the official rhetoric of the Chinese American leaders, but to the participants, especially for the first-generation immigrants, it was more of an issue about Chineseness. Their urgency to stand up and join the rally was to express political power as a people to the American public after decades of being silenced as a racialized population.

THE AMERICAN DREAM The discourses of the American Dream were everywhere in the pro-Liang rallies. Chinese American families waved American flags while marching across the Brooklyn Bridge on April 26, 2015. The American anthem played before the speeches. Interestingly, the participants, who were largely native Chinese speakers, seemed uninterested in the American anthem, and hardly anyone sang along. Most of the participants, Chinese families with young children, gathered in small groups to take pictures with the American flags given to them by the coalition leaders. Any pedestrian walking by that day would have had difficulty recognizing this gathering as a "political protest," as many participants treated the event more like a social celebration. Some participants were waving heart-shaped signs with the Chinese letter "love" (愛) in red along with the American flags. A thick, impenetrable, and totalizing force of Chinese nationalism was forged during the event. The collective political narrative of Chinese ethnic empowerment superseded the more nuanced ways the participants understood the Liang-Gurley incident. At one point, the redness of the American flags and the redness from the participants' signs, clothes, and banners, which symbolized Chinese unity, merged in the scene. It became clearer and clearer to me, as I marched "ethnographically" with the crowd, that the American dream was aligned with an equally powerful, affective Chinese dream and a neoliberal transnational dream of class advancement that requires exclusion and stratification of the classed and racial Other.

As a queer Taiwanese American observer in the march, my otherness was indeed quite apparent. Despite being ethnically Han, my queerness and nonconforming gender expression drastically singled me out from the crowd of middle-aged parents and their young children. When I spoke to the march participants, my Taiwanese Mandarin accent was also quite distinct from that of the Chinese mainlanders. I felt as though I was a "race traitor" and consciously distanced myself from the crowd so that they would not recognize my ulterior emotions. At the same time, I recognized the very flexible capacity of my Asian Americanness that blended into the collective expression of Chinese American body politic to the non-Chinese spectators. Yet my queerness continued to signify a stance of dissidence and protest—an opposition to the American and the Chinese ideal. However, without the presence of other dissidents, my race and ethnicity were quickly absorbed and territorialized by the collective body politic in the event—the ambiguous yet powerful signs of Chineseness, creating an impression of total consensus by the bodies, the chants, the redness everywhere on participants' signs, banners, and clothes. The collective political narrative of Chinese ethnic empowerment superseded the more nuanced ways the participants understood the Liang-Gurley incident.

The American flag in the event symbolized not only allegiance to the state but an aspiration to become successful as Chinese people in the United States. During my fieldwork that day on the bridge, another middle-aged Chinese woman told me that she had brought her son to the rally because she wanted him to "learn democracy" to be "successful in this country." As much of the Chinese press that covered the pro-Liang mobilization as a historical event has shown Chinese solidarity and Chinese people's capacity to participate in civic actions in a "mature and rational" manner,[34] the subjectivity that emerged in these events was less about a demonstration of American patriotism and more about Chinese modernity and desire for a new nation as a people. As the previous Asian American assimilationist politics in the post–civil rights period emphasized American national and cultural identity—that is, a liberal racial ideology of national belonging—the pro-Liang coalition expressed a qualitatively different kind of national belonging grounded in a moral and cultural ethic of economic advancement and civic respectability, as well as in a dream of Chinese modernity. Aihwa Ong has defined neoliberalism as a technology of governance that rearticulates the social criteria for citizenship for the purpose of optimizing the effects of the market and demoralizing economic activities.[35] Citizenship is thus no longer strictly attached to national identification but defined by economic productivity. In short, the participants' desire for US nationalism was less about being seen as "Americans" and more about a longing for continual economic prosperity and political opportunities for their communities and their next generations. Similarly, the discourse around Liang's "unfair" indictment focused not on his unequal treatment as an "American" but on how the promise of model minority advancement was temporarily shattered by a state-inflicted racial crisis.

Historically, post–World War II America as a place that signified freedom and liberty was in fact deeply connected to the rise of liberalism in China since the 1980s, where socialism was seen as a backward ideology as the Soviet Union regime deteriorated. As Deng Xiaoping's open-door policy started to welcome foreign investments when he took office in 1978, the Chicago school's ideology of neoliberalism significantly impacted the political economic directions that China undertook in the following decades. As Chinese New Left intellectual

Kuang Xin Nian observes, "Just like how the Chinese dream in the '50s was 'today's Soviet Union would be tomorrow's China,' 'today's America will be tomorrow's China' is the new Chinese dream since the '80s."[36] Indeed, while Xi Jinping's Chinese dream is far from a clearly defined or completely new ideology, its central concept is "national rejuvenation" from the "century of humiliation" through the continuation of economic liberalization and patriotic pride to restore its past global position and glory, as the CCP's mission is no longer about achieving communism.[37] As in the case of pro-Liang mobilization, the American dream and the Chinese dream in the diaspora are not at odds—they share the neoliberal desires for free market, individual freedom, and liberal democracy.

Although the racial victimology of Asian Americanness works hand in hand with Chinese ethnic nationalism to craft a new form of assimilationist body politic under the civil rights rhetoric to secure conservative agendas, the present body politic of Asian injuries expressed through the pro-Liang mobilization is distinct from the previous Asian American demand for institutional access, powered largely by American identity and US-centrism. Rather, the body politic that has emerged here must be examined under the rise of China and Chinese nationalism transnationally. As I stated earlier, the "success" of the Chinese American mobilization was due to not only a domestic but a transnational effort through online social media platforms. The Chinese media, both in the United States and within China, have carefully monitored the American racial conflicts since BLM unfolded. The CCP's major newspaper, *People's Daily*, published comments in an article on foreign policy that critiqued the failures of racial liberalism and multiculturalism as an American project: "Each time, when the hatreds old and new of US racial contradictions boil over . . . it clearly tells the world that the declaration 'all are born equal' in this so-called field of dreams still has yet to take root."[38] The Chinese state media were particularly cynical about the ongoing criticism from the West of China's human rights abuses. This episode of racially instigated "social unrest," to the Chinese public, signified the "vulnerability of American social structure" and thus reaffirmed the superior Chinese vision of governance, without problems such as the "racial inequalities" found in the United States.[39]

The shattering and betrayal of the American ideal in light of the US racial "crisis" reaffirms the larger Chinese state project of building a strong Chinese national identity that does not rely on the West or replicate the latter's problems. That is, the body politic in the pro-Liang mobilization is both allied with the American state and distanced from the state's racial burden. It presents a particular color-blind narrative of overcoming race as highly assimilable and upwardly mobile Chinese American subjects. This intensified Chinese nationalism through the state construction of the Chinese dream is particularly evident under Xi Jinping's leadership, which also allows for a transnational discourse of Chinese deservingness and ethnic empowerment in the diaspora. In Xi's speech in Seattle in September 2015, he described China's current prosperity as allowing millions of people to now enjoy a "better life" because of steady economic growth. More importantly, the Chinese dream is a driving force toward the population's advancement: As Xi said, it is "a dream of the people. We can fulfill the Chinese dream only when we link it with our people's yearning for a better life."[40] What the Chinese dream promises to accomplish is not only the sense of ethnic empowerment and being deserving of a middle-class life but also the leveling of Chinese national identity with Americanness in the consciousness of diasporic Chinese immigrants. The Chinese, as a people, whether in the United States or in China, are no longer inferior to Westerners but mutual partners at the scale of the nation and individual subjectivity. That is, the Chinese dream aims to transform the previous "humiliation discourse" to a "rejuvenation narrative" in the making of Chinese identity politics.[41] As China struggles to be recognized as a normative nation-state on the global stage, its

FIGURE 2. Pro–Peter Liang marchers encountering a "China friendly" tour bus. Photo by Brian Hioe.

people, too, urgently wish to move beyond the image of Oriental Other, striving to be an equal counterpart to Americans and specifically white Americans.

Overall, in the pro-Liang mobilization, what might be read as a moment of acculturation in which the Chinese American subject moves toward American cultural citizenship through civic participation and immersion in racial minority discourse needs historical and transnational articulations. The American dream is not just about crafting the American nation-state as an exceptional place upholding democracy and freedom; it is an imperialist ambition. What becomes more complicated is when the conservative Chinese American communities intentionally conflate a form of "Chinese racialized nationalism,"[42] which has been China's state propaganda of promoting Han-centrism over other multiethnic groups via cultural superiority and a sense of reparation to overcome the national victimhood, with Asian American injury. These ideologies indeed travel across national borders as transnational capital moves through geopolitical spaces, demanding an open market and culturally equipped consumers, building a parasitic ideological relation between the two nations. The racially injured body politic is fused with the model minority ethics of hard work and deservingness as well as anti-Blackness, and it treats any political outcry against racialized state violence as a performance of political correctness.

ANTI-BLACKNESS What mobilizes the highly nationalistic, patriotic pro-Liang rallies is not just the discontents of Chinese Americans' "not quite whiteness" but also anti-Blackness, which justifies Black criminality and Asian deservingness through the ethics of hard work. Anti-Blackness is not just a prejudicial attitude against Blacks but a performance of whiteness. The substitution of racial inequality with cultural difference allows Asian Americans to remove themselves from broader racial justice demands and functions effectively to reinforce white dominance. In other words, presenting as non-Black and thus not antagonistic to US nationalism allows Asian Americans to bargain for partial privileges that have previously belonged to whites. During Liang's trial, he was repeatedly painted by the media as the model minority, striving from his humble immigrant family origins, an inexperienced, harmless "rookie cop," whereas Gurley was criminalized as the "drug-dealing thug" who had a criminal record.[43] These racialized portrayals certainly fit into the stereotypes of Asians and Blacks and were intended to incite racial conflicts. However, in the scenes of the pro-Liang rallies, the politics of anti-Blackness followed a different kind of post-racial logic—not highlighting the difference in racial citizenship between Asians and Blacks but refusing to acknowledge the significance of race in the Black body politic. Indeed, the dominant narrative behind the pro-Liang rallies was the silencing of Asianness in relation to the hypervisible Blackness in US politics and anger toward this lack of visibility—refusing to be the "silent Asians" (啞裔).[44] This discourse is congruent with the post-racial discontents of BLM in which Chinese American protesters hold signs that say "All Lives Matter" in pro-police rallies, endorsing the white supremacist structure of racial hierarchy that is built on Black criminality.

The drive for profit, middle-class promises, and the post-racial ideology infused with anti-Blackness have assembled to formulate a kind of Asian American body politic that treats race as a flexible position from which to demand access to whiteness and participation in the neoliberal economy, erasing any internal contradictions of class, ethnicity, and skin color privileges. This new form of subjectivity has bypassed the previous bifurcated representation of Asian Americanness as either a foreign threat or a desire for domestic integration. It is neither threat nor desire yet both, and it is motivated by a neoliberal kind of elastic pragmatism instead of stubborn ideology. The United States, if anything, is a vehicle moving toward profits, a good middle-class life, and temporarily, the desire for Chinese modernity. The Chinese Americans who pledge allegiance to transnational capitalism, for which the United States is a signifier, do so not as a nation-state but as a corporate body.

The post-racial Asian American subjectivity is also heavily influenced by Chinese neoliberalism and must also be examined in its transnational context. As China has shifted from a labor-intensive production house to a venture capitalist investor in the past decade, Beijing is now heavily motivated to building an economic empire in African countries. Whereas Beijing has developed an official rhetoric of South-South cooperation that positions it as a developing country helping another developing country via its economic intervention, the anti-Blackness expressed in Asian American subjectivity is circulated transnationally and appropriated by Chinese capitalism to justify the devaluation of African laborers and ensure Chinese superiority and dominance on the continent. In other words, whereas the BLM movement signifies a failure of racial equality domestically, the Asian-Black conflicts in the United States manufactured and intensified by neoliberal elites produce anti-Blackness to be again circulated for capital accumulation on a wider geopolitical scale. The self-making and being made of Asian American subjectivity has come to a historical conjuncture that can be effectively used to optimize neoliberal capitalist goals.

Asian American Counter-Body Politic

The Asian American body politic is not a singular construction. As I have articulated, the pro-police Chinese American mobilization emerged precisely out of the crisis of representation of Asian Americanness in which the model minority promise of success is threatened and panethnic solidarity is crumbling. Whereas pro-police Chinese Americans seized the moment to insert a post-racial agenda, other Asian American community organizers aimed to repopularize historicized sentiments of Asian-Black solidarity and panethnic Asian Americanness to counter the ethnic nationalism of the Chinese American mobilization and support the broader racial justice demands of BLM.[45] This strategy effectively radicalized the previous liberal focus on cultural representational politics and galvanized multiracial and multigenerational alliances—reaching a new height of Asian American left-leaning identity formation. In the political milieus in which I was involved in NYC, young Asian American activists formed and joined small reading groups about prison abolition and racial capitalism. Chinatowns across American cities including but not limited to Manhattan, San Diego, and the Bay Area organized rallies and held vigils for the Black victims of police violence. Multilingual signs of #Asians4BlackLives spread all over the internet and in the streets. The vibrant cross-racial solidarity was something that had not occurred for a long time in Asian American history. In the meantime, #Asians4BlackLives framed the pro-Liang faction of Chinese Americans largely as a matter of misinformation spread by the Chinese media and thus an issue of cultural adaptability of first-generation immigrants.[46]

FIGURE 3. Flowers of solidarity in the #AsiansBlackLives vigil for Akai Gurley's family. Photo by Wen Liu.

Although the Chinese media was certainly invested in portraying a singular and biased narrative of the Liang-Gurley incident and affected the framing of the case, the emphasis on translations by #Asians4BlackLives activists as a means to overcome such ideological divides was incapable of teasing apart the transnational and geopolitical backdrop of the rising conservatism in Chinese American communities. The radical vision of #Asians4BlackLives, to an extent, was still confined to its domestic focus on racial politics at this time. Regardless, the fierce mobilization of #Asians4BlackLives has reinstated a cross-racial solidarity vision against neoliberal color-blindness for Asian American politics, which continues to expand and externalize in the political landscape during the COVID-19 pandemic as I will discuss later in chapter 3.

HISTORICIZING ASIAN-BLACK SOLIDARITY

Soon after Liang was indicted, a coalition of Asian American community-based organizations, led by CAAAV: Organizing Asian Communities, mobilized a vigil for Gurley's family in front of the Police Plaza in NYC on March 15, 2015. The number of participants at the vigil was small compared to the pro-Liang mobilization that would occur the year after, approximately forty people on a chilly, rainy spring afternoon, but the crowd was by all definitions a diverse group of individuals: members of Korean, Filipino, South Asian, and other Asian American nonprofit organizations; Gurley's family including his aunt, daughter, and partner; and other members of BLM, socialist, and anti-war leftist organizations also participated in the event. This multiracial and multiethnic gathering demonstrated an image of cross-identity solidarity in the time of tragedy.

This image of cross-racial and cross-ethnic alliance was intentionally delivered. In a speech, then executive director of CAAAV Cathy Dang called attention to the importance of standing in solidarity with the broader racial justice demands of BLM to counter the numerous deaths and unnamable violence through persisting in valuing lives, particularly Black lives. She drew from the organization's experiences of working alongside Black and Brown communities in the past twenty years to demand justice from the police and judicial system. Specifically, she referenced the case of an immigrant Chinese boy, Yong Xin Huang, who was killed by NYPD in the 1990s, and how the incident bridged activists across racial lines: "Black and Brown communities were the first ones there for the Huang family and, as our member said, I believe that the Chinese community should stand on the side of justice." This cross-racial representation is not just crucial but necessary to the Asian American body politic—to signify that Asian Americans, too, have had a history of violence inflicted by the state. It argues against the persistent image of model minority success and proximity to whiteness. It relies on the temporary shift back to the time of violent state exclusion to reinstate an Asian American racial position that is closer to Blackness.

Beyond the physical presence of a multiracial body politic, the #Asians4BlackLives contingency that emerged out of the Liang controversy organized a platform on Tumblr specifically to counter the conservative representations of Asian Americanness dominated by the Chinese American pro-Liang mobilization. They called out the anachronistic reference to Martin Luther King Jr.'s speech as being ignorant of Black history and the broader implications of the civil rights movement in the United States. The "Afro-Asian" solidarity images of Asian American activists protesting alongside Black Power activists in the 1960s against police violence spread across different #Asians4BlackLives blogs to stress the interdependent histories of the communities. King's and Malcolm X's speeches against the Vietnam War and calls for third world solidarity were repeatedly cited on these platforms to highlight the intersection of domestic racial violence and imperialist wars abroad.[47] Not only does historicizing Asian-Black solidarity serve to demonstrate that the perspective of #Asians4BlackLives is indeed temporally legitimate and morally justifiable; it brings a sense of urgency to rescuing pan–Asian Americanism from prior to the neoliberal disfranchisement of the category of Asian American itself. The widened class and ethnic divisions within Asian American communities in recent years have reduced the political power and racial legitimacy of the category as a whole. For the #Asians4BlackLives activists, only through claiming its proximity to Blackness can Asian Americanness move outside of the awkward position of neither white nor Black and continue to exist as a relevant and legible racial community. In other words, as the pro-police Chinese Americans are moving closer toward the pole of assimilation, the #Asians4BlackLives activists are reaching further toward the historicized idea of shared common racial oppression. Yet the fact that both of these subjectivities coexist simultaneously illustrates the nonlinearity of Asian American political subjectivity. Rather, it is the bidirectional oscillation that continually gives rise to the Asian American identity.

To historicize a sense of Asian-Black solidarity, the #Asians4BlackLives activists also needed to address the problem of anti-Blackness in Chinese communities in the first place. Some coalition members relied on the internalized racism related to uncritical acceptance by Asian Americans of the anti-Black messages circulating in the American public and the idea that the only way out of their own racial baggage is to identify with whiteness. As one Vietnamese American blogger noted, "Without making excuses, anti-Black racism by Asian Americans could be attributed to internalized racism from media and also the varying degrees of relationship to authority due to immigration and refugee backgrounds."[48] In a sense, there was a general belief on these #Asians4BlackLives blogs that if Asian Americans received the correct messages about their race and the truth about their history with Black communities, there would be possibility for a change in ideology. The Asian American activist group I worked with in New York also put a lot of effort into translation work in hopes that more accessible information in ethnic languages could counter the dominant pro-police, anti-Black narratives propagated by the Chinese media.

Nonetheless, almost none of the platforms addressed the drastic changes in the conditions of the so-called third world—that the old Cold War framework that allowed for the formation of a "capitalist West" and a "Communist East" has completely collapsed as global capitalism has taken over international relations. As Vijay Prashad, Gary Okihiro, and other third worldist intellectuals have noted,[49] "Afro-Asian solidarity" was built on a transnational anti-imperialist effort, where the national liberation movements throughout Africa and Asia struggled against Western colonialism and were inspired by an alternative vision of the world toward the end of World War II. These movements in turn very much inspired the Asian American identity and movement in its initial formation during the 1960s. However, several decades later, neoliberal capitalism has trumped the ideology of liberal racialism and recruits developing nation-states to the competition of multilateral free trade zones. China's trade expansion through the Association of Southeast Asian Nations Free Trade Agreement in Southeast Asia since 2010 and the Belt and Road Initiative in Central Asia and Europe are examples of the country's ambition to become a global capitalist center independent from the influence of the United States. Time will tell whether the Chinese empire can take over the US empire, yet China as a global hegemon through its economic power, diasporic networks, and diplomatic imperiousness has significantly altered the previous victimized discourse of being a colonized country.[50] However, some third worldist scholars have continued to idealize contemporary China as being at the forefront of anti-Western imperialism and a socialist alternative to the neoliberal West. Prashad's Tricontinental Institute exemplifies such a global-left contingency that links back to the Non-Aligned Movement. While exerting a seemingly radical vision, this political milieu that idealizes Maoist China has also faced criticisms for its blatant Chinese apologism on issues of authoritarian state repression.[51] It is in fact beyond a mode of affective nostalgia, and rather a politics, that reflects the crisis of the left at the moment.[52] To put it bluntly, China is no longer the Maoist China that stood as a socialist vision of alternative third world development prior to the 1970s. Such a drastic political shift necessitates a new articulation of the Asian-Black solidarity that was built on the collective resistance against Western colonialism and imperialism. Therefore, the anachronistic interpretation of the past is when the flexible position of Asian Americanness becomes troubling in that it has turned into an empty holder of time and been stripped of its original political contents. Beyond reductive nostalgia, diasporic activists have since organized transnational alliances and cross-racial and cross-regional solidarity as both BLM mobilization and anti-Asian violence has gone global since 2020, which I will go into in more detail in chapter 3. The 2016 event can be understood as a precursor that intensified the Asian-Black discourses across political milieus.

ANTI-BLACKNESS AS AN ISSUE OF CULTURAL ADAPTION

The obstacles that have faced #Asians4BlackLives activists are thus multilayered and messy.[53] I recall many times when my Asian American comrades were frustrated by their inability to properly communicate with the pro-police Chinese American groups. BLM activists made efforts to cross the linguistic and cultural barriers by doing bilingual outreach on multiple online social networks. However, there was a gap that seemed impossible to bridge—a gap that is beyond racial or ethnic identification, which I later realized is perhaps a fundamental difference between the dreams of these two groups. The activists who had worked on gentrification issues with residents in Chinatown, Manhattan, particularly, were saddened by the fact that the residents they worked and fought with chose the opposite side of racial justice to what they believed in on the Liang-Gurley case. Many decided not to mobilize any direct confrontation with the pro-Liang rallies, as they believe that it would only agitate the division that already exists among Asian American communities. In a phone conversation on national coordination for an #Asians4BlackLives mobilization regarding the Liang-Gurley case, an Asian American activist based in NYC expressed her concern: "I'm against counter-protesting in the Peter Liang rally. As frustrated as I am about the whole case, we can't see the Chinese communities as our enemies—the state is. We can't diverge from our real focus."

Although as a coalition, the #Asians4BlackLives activists in NYC reached a consensus not to mobilize officially against the pro-Liang actions, some went to the March 8, 2015, pro-police rally at the request of Gurley's family, and intense confrontations occurred between the multiracial BLM activists and the Chinese American protesters. The BLM activists reported that racial slurs were exchanged between some Chinese American protesters and counterprotesters, where both anti-Blackness and anti-Chineseness were violently expressed. An Asian American activist who witnessed the confrontation said, "I feel like we have retreated back in time . . . Black and Asian folks hating each other, and the white men just walk free." The feeling of going backward in time not only pierces through the illusion of racial progress but also illustrates that raw, blatant racial hatred coexists with the normalized discourse of civil rights.

Furthermore, the mainstream media, both English and Chinese, have framed this divide among Asian American communities as a generational issue. An immigrant who moved to the United States from Hong Kong in 1970 was quoted in an article by NBC News explaining the divided opinions on Liang's case: "The young Chinese generations do have local education, and they do tend to be taught more about police brutality and abuse. For the older generation, however, there's a lot more appreciation for law and order, particularly for people who have come from China who experienced older regimes that did not supply stability."[54] There was a clear disproportionate representation of older, first-generation Chinese immigrants whose primary language is Chinese at the pro-Liang rallies. However, the divide cannot be explained merely as a generational difference, thus naturalizing the ideological split as something that can be eliminated or repaired over time. In fact, the mainstream press such as NBC appropriates the discourse of the assumed generation gap to alleviate "(white) America" from this interracial conflict—that is, as immigrants become more integrated, they should naturally "grow out" of their racial biases or the lack of racial consciousness. In the same vein, a young Chinese American ethnographer in NYC, Christina Xu, called for Asian Americans to contribute to the multimedia project "Letters for Black Lives"[55] that aimed to communicate with their parents and older family members about anti-Blackness within their communities. The "letters" were produced as videos in different languages. Young, multiethnic, and mostly second-generation Asian Americans speak directly to the camera with concerned and sincere facial expressions. One woman opens, "Grandfather, grandmother, we need to talk." She sighs and continues, "You may not have grown up around people who are Black, but I have." Throughout the video, they talk about the hard statistics of how police brutality harms Black people, acknowledge discrimination against Asian Americans, and identify the same institutional target of racism: "We are all fighting against the same unfair system that prefers we compete against each other." The obstacles against such unity were clearly framed as "misunderstanding" or "disinformation" of racial issues because of a lack of access to education, English-language media, and Black communities, rather than a materially based class antagonism or ideological division. The assumption is that the first-generation immigrants just need to be "psychologically" transformed to get rid of their biases through becoming "integrated" into US society over time. Unfortunately, this perspective overly simplifies the complex dynamics of national affiliations and transnational geopolitics that are often unacknowledged in liberal Asian American milieus, especially within diasporic Chinese communities. The liberal approach sought to amend the division within Asian American communities by rearticulating the ideological divisions as a matter of domestic cultural and racial concern. Although it was a touching effort and galvanized support among second-generation Asian Americans, the effectiveness of the "Letters for Black Lives" project to address the core concerns of those who were driven by a diasporic Chinese dream was unfortunately limited.

However, the #Asians4BlackLives activists continued to mobilize. On May 20, 2016, they organized a protest in front of the headquarters of *Sing Tao Daily* newspaper in NYC. Frustrated and angered by the widened splits and heightened racial tensions provoked by the Liang-Gurley case, the group decided to target one of the major Chinese news sources and demand they cover an unbiased perspective on the case—that is, to include the voice of Gurley's family and the BLM critique of racialized police violence. The group consisted of mostly college-aged Asian Americans, who wrote bilingual messages such as "Akai Gurley's life matters" on top of the *Sing Tao Daily* newspapers and prepared to deliver them to the chief editor as a way to demand media neutrality and transparency about the Liang-Gurley case.

As the protesters were reading their demands in front of the headquarters in both English and Mandarin, the chief editor of *Sing Tao Daily* stepped into the crowd, interrupted the chants, and started a series of confrontation with the protesters. One of the Chinese American activists in her mid-twenties named Jen (pseudonym) stepped up from the crowd and addressed her confrontations in English. The editor first asked if Jen read Chinese, then pushed the question further: "Do you read every single article from *Sing Tao*? Why are you targeting us?" Jen responded that the activist group had read all the coverage of Liang's case by the newspaper, which had a biased representation on the issue. The agitated editor argued that they should also call out all the other Chinese press such as *World Journal* and not simply criticize *Sing Tao Daily* to be fair. Immediately after this exchange, the conversation took on an assumed generational split between the "Chinese immigrant readers" and the "Asian American readers":

EDITOR: Did you read the *New York Times*? Why don't you attack them, too?

JEN: We read the newspaper, too. Our parents read your newspaper. Your paper is influential in the Chinese community and so it's important for you to have a more diverse coverage.

EDITOR: Yes, the problem is that your parents read the papers because *they* [emphasis mine] are Chinese.

Despite Jen's efforts to stress that members of the group had Chinese reading capacity and many identified as Chinese, the editor used generation as leverage to claim Chinese authenticity and thus to reject any responsibility in including a different perspective on the issue. From the perspective of the press, the #Asians4BlackLives protesters' view did not represent the legitimate Chinese voice: it represented the *New York Times*, the Americanized version of racial reality, unlike the protesters' parents, who represented authentic Chinese subjectivity that did not contradict the viewpoint of the press itself. In this conversation, the editor used *Sing Tao Daily*'s cultural proximity to first-generation Chinese immigrants to demonstrate the paper's authenticity in comparison to its distance from the second-generation Asian American activists, despite their fluency in the language. The activists were portrayed as agitators attempting to disrupt the ethnic harmony of Chinese communities, whose acculturative viewpoints made them no longer suitable as legitimate actors of Chineseness, despite the fact that many of them had language capacity in Chinese and strong identification as Chinese Americans.

The issue of the generational divide must be interpreted not as a superficial result of the divergent perspectives on the Liang-Gurley case or of the different nationalist allegiances to China or the United States between first- and second-generation Chinese Americans but rather as a manifestation of the contrasting visions and understanding of "American values." Whereas the pro-Liang groups viewed the United States as a placeholder for hardworking meritocracy and minority advancement, the BLM activists prioritized issues of racial justice and cross-racial solidarity as fundamental to Asian American politics. These differences are no doubt partially the result of demographic differences,[56] but most importantly, they signify the present ideological rupture in the categorical conceptualization and the varied political deployment of Asian Americanness. The manufactured divide between the generations, similar to the split between Asian and Black interests, again projected racial antagonism onto the Asian American body, leaving whites untouched by the consequences of state-inflicted racial violence.

These counter-representations of the mobilization of #Asians4BlackLives activists also highlight the incompatible temporality of a future-oriented neoliberal Asian American subjectivity and the nostalgic Asian American subjectivity rooted in third world anti-imperialist struggles. Although both groups recruit the discourse of civil rights, the epistemologies they rely on are drastically different. The pro-Liang mobilization takes civil rights as the American promise of racial advancement, the model minority bootstrapping ideology that is built on hard work and merit. In contrast, the BLM activists demand a radical restructuring of racial relationships deeply rooted in anti-Black violence and minority complicity. The discrepancy shows how civil rights are also a dialectically complex assemblage that bends toward either co-optation or radical transformation. To counter the pro-Liang groups' body politic of Asian Americanness, the Asian American BLM activists deployed two distinct yet related discursive strategies: historicizing Asian-Black solidarity and cultural authenticity. These strategies were adopted by the #Asians4BlackLives activists not only to distinguish themselves from the pro-Liang groups but to signify an alternative vision of racial history and futurity against the dogma of color-blind neoliberalism.

Reclaiming Life, against Multiculturalism

During my fieldwork, I constantly sensed an intense frustration and hopelessness from my fellow #Asians4BlackLives activists. As I discussed earlier, many had organized and worked alongside Chinese Americans, yet on the Liang-Gurley case, they stood on opposite sides of justice. This was indeed a disheartening historical moment for progressive Asian American politics. However, the Liang-Gurley case is only a symptom of the larger process of transformation of Asian American subjectivity. As neoliberalism exerts its hegemonic power that shatters previous forms of solidarity and demands that nations and individuals express loyalty to the market, simply examining domestic racial relations and the intergroup level of anti-Blackness does not sufficiently explain the global geopolitical shifts that account for the changing subjectivity of the Asian American body politic. In a sense, the conflicting Asian American body politics are driven by not merely movement between the binary poles of assimilation and opposition but competing paradigms of US racial relations and multiple frames of nationalism at a transnational scale. Asian American racial construction is now at a new juncture of neoliberalism: either capitalize on structural racial difference as leverage for neoconservative interests or claim it as a critical point of racial solidarity. However, Asian-Black antagonism, whether imposed by white and Asian elites to instigate racial conflicts or reified by some activists as the "internalized racism" of the Asian American psyche, prevented us from asking more nuanced questions about the Liang-Gurley case. Although the violence against Gurley was simply erased by the former group, I found that the #Asians4BlackLives activists were also selectively silent around the state's treatment of Liang.

In a sense, the motivation to overcome the model minority stereotype has become so dogmatic for Asian American activists involved in this conflict that they have had to overlook the systemic racism—that also determined the state's manipulation of Liang as an easy target—to mitigate a national racial crisis perpetuated by white supremacy. I am not arguing that individual activists are not aware of how white supremacy acts in both directions, damaging and dividing Asian and Black communities. However, in the face of right-wing confrontation from both conservative white and Chinese groups, it was difficult to insert a more nuanced collective strategy that could bypass this binary position of for or against Asian American model minority representation. The #Asians4BlackLives activists' reclamation of the past, a time-space where Asian and Black relations were amicable, is produced through another problematic reliance on the unchanging geopolitical formulation transnationally. Each side of the struggle paints a contentious Asian American body politic that is constantly displaced, rearranged, and oscillating on the scale of temporality. To the current formation of American nationalism, Asian Americanness is either hyperfuturistic, symbolizing a kind of global class alignment where race no longer matters, or exceptionally backward, romanticizing the previous anti-colonial, cross-racial solidarity unfathomable by the current neoliberal capitalist order. In other words, Asian Americanness is a projection of the irreconcilable racial temporality of American nationalism itself.

However, I have begun to wonder whether holding on to the nostalgic sense of pan-Asian Americanness is still politically productive, as the access gap widens between East Asian and Southeast Asian communities. With the right-wing mobilization support, in 2023, the Supreme Court made a historical decision to reject affirmative action programs at Harvard and the University of North Carolina.[57] This decision will likely influence the vitality and legitimacy of race-conscious and inclusive programs in the entire nation. Although the majority of Asian Americans still favor affirmative action policy that help other minorities in higher education, it cannot disguise the fact that a strong faction of Chinese American conservatives has become the key allies to the color-blind political agendas, fueled by anti-Black and ethnonationalist interests.[58] During the height of the Liang-Gurley conflict, in a 2016 survey conducted by Asian and Pacific Islander Americans Vote on Asian American attitudes toward various policy measures, 63 percent of Chinese American participants thought that the "affirmative action programs designed to increase the number of black and minority students on college campuses" were a "bad thing," whereas other Asian American participants, especially of the Southeast Asian groups, including those who were Filipino (67 percent) and Vietnamese (78 percent), considered affirmative action a "good thing."[59] These phenomena necessitate a radical break from the liberal conceptualization of Asian Americanness as an intelligible racial population that shares similar experiences of racialization and immigration. The deterritorialization of ethnicity is an inevitable move in the context of changing Asian immigration and the polarization of class among Asian American communities. That is, the previous shared experiences of racialization, on which liberalism is built, are rapidly taken over by the disproportionate opportunities for mobility and survival—those who benefit from the flexible movement of capital and national borders and those who are further exploited by such flexibility. To speak of Asian Americanness without addressing the paradox of these material realities is to bolster the false imagination of multiculturalism, perpetuating the fantasy of politically neutral and culturally pluralistic racial relations. As Kim argued in her op-ed on the Liang-Gurley case, Asian-Black solidarity must be careful not to "assume the unity of all nonwhite interests."[60] Asian American politics must take seriously the continued effects of racial ordering on a transnational scale and how racial self-interest is complicit with anti-Black racism and racial capitalism.

In the midst of the controversy, nonetheless, the most pressing issue is not to debate the accurate or authentic representation of Asian Americanness but to return to the demand that the BLM movement calls for in the first place—that is, to reclaim what a livable life is. When one speaks of the value of a life, it is impossible to generalize all bodies across divergent material and political conditions. Instead, one must realize the politics in the body not in abstract projections but in their material manifestations. To denounce the political possibility of Asian Americanness is thus not to turn back to the dualist paradigm of Black-white racial antagonism or to speak for the Other as another self-deserving, injured subject. Rather, it is critical to challenge the moral and political legitimacy granted through Asian Americanness and to expand the narrow tunnel of survival that has become increasingly restricted by intensified racial profiling and surveillance. As an Asian American activist said at Gurley's vigil, "We must remain vigilant and not let systems divide our communities in what is right—valuing life. At the end of the day, it is about valuing life—Black lives—and finding humanity." The centering of "lives" is also about placing the racial time work in the present, to feel how our lives are inevitably bounded by connected processes of racialization, rather than seeking an idealized future or repeatedly memorizing the past. In recognizing our shared vulnerability to white supremacy and the unstable structures of privileges based on race, we can move forward from a racial politics and a national futurity that make life livable only for some and unlivable for the rest.

CHAPTER 3

Racial Loss, Diasporic Attachments, and Anti-Imperialism

On October 9, 2016, the *New York Times* deputy Metro editor, Michael Luo, was strolling through the Upper East Side of Manhattan with his family, when a woman suddenly yelled at them, "Go back to China . . . go back to your fucking country!" Luo protested, "I was born in this country!"[1] After this racist encounter, Luo started the Twitter hashtag #thisis2016 to describe this experience. The hashtag soon went viral on multiple social network sites, as Asian Americans came forward to speak about similar forms of racism they faced in their everyday lives.[2] The response publicly exposed the racism Asian Americans had been experiencing regularly. That it was directed toward an Asian American man with a prestigious job, which symbolizes literacy, intelligence, and the liberal values of multicultural America, and in one of the wealthiest neighborhoods in the country, makes this incident even more ironic, intolerable, and theatrical since his social status and cultural capital do not protect him from the kind of racialized assault that continues to frame Asian bodies as perpetual foreigners. Yet, the social effect of the incident would have been dramatically different for someone who carried a stronger signifier of foreignness, in that yelling at them would no longer be intelligible as an assault. For instance, if a Chinese immigrant had encountered such an attack, they may not even have protested it. Had they really been from China, they may have lacked urgency to refute their national affiliation and thus the assault would not hold the same emotional weight for both them and the yeller.

This common experience directed Asian American communities to claim belongingness in the United States as expressed by the #thisis2016 campaign. The Asian American respondents spoke about their common traumas of being seen as a foreigner, called by racialized slurs, and most importantly, challenged on their national loyalty to the United States. For instance, Cafaan Kim, an Asian American journalist, speaks in a video about his experiences while serving in the US Army: "When a fellow soldier called me 'Private *Ching Chang*' . . . we had to fight to convince them, we were as American as they were, we were willing to fight, bleed, and die for this country. That was the struggle we took on."[3] As anti-Asian violence surged during the COVID-19 pandemic, we began to see both the forms of attacks and affects of claiming national allegiance intensified in Asian American communities. For instance, just a few weeks after the Atlanta spa shootings, where six Asian women were killed in March 2021, Lee Wong, a Chinese American veteran and an elected official in West Chester Township, Ohio, removed his shirt in a board meeting to reveal red scars across his chest from military service to protest the nation's ambivalence toward violence against Asian Americans. Wong said, "Here's my proof. Now, is this patriotic enough?" The necessity to show the most extreme forms of patriotism is perhaps compelled by an equally intense feeling of foreignness, as evidenced by both the 2016 and the 2021 events.[4]

The COVID-19 pandemic, indeed, became a crucially global and historical event that further sharpened the splits of Asian American politics along the lines of not only racial ideologies but also geopolitics. On the opposite side of the usual rhetoric of liberal assimilationist Americanism, there is an emergent type of anti-Americanism in which on the contour expresses via the 1960s Asian American anti-imperialist sentiments yet in its essence contains mostly a sense of racial injury and loss as a minority subject under the context of US neoliberal racial politics. In other words, on the one hand, in the liberal assimilationist model, the racial loss of becoming American can be absorbed by the nationalist order and the class privileges that it offers such as the Asian American feelings expressed in the #thisis2016 video. The "wounded attachment," which is driven by the affect of class resentment that Wendy Brown theorizes, the accumulated feelings of loss of privileges, turns into the very source of identity formation.[5] On the other hand, the rejection of liberal assimilationism produces a different form of attachment toward another imperial center, which under the US-China geopolitical conflict—"China" as a rising global superpower, an "anti-imperialist center," and a "motherland" as it often projects to the Sinophone diasporas—can become the source of Asian American projection.

The Asian American process of racialization is inevitably intertwined with a loss of place, a lack of origin. In *The Melancholy of Race*, Anne Anlin Cheng depicts the unique racialized subjectivity of Asian Americanness as a "ghostly position" in which one is forcibly attached to the fantasy of the East yet constantly under pressure to pass as American and non-Black in order to sustain life.[6] Lisa Lowe articulates that this persistent tension between racial inclusion and racial erasure in the project of US nation making "requires the orientalist construction of cultures and geographies from which Asian immigrants come as fundamentally 'foreign' origins anti-pathetic to the modern American society that 'discovers,' 'welcomes,' and 'domesticates' them."[7] The uprooting of Asian origins must be understood as an intentional process of effacing the history of exploitation and colonial conquest. The subjectification of Asian Americans is therefore wrapped up with narratives of loss and mourning linked to histories of dispersal as well as a yearning for belonging. Anne Anlin Cheng coins this racial identity construction attached to the lost object as "racial melancholia," a process of becoming consumed by one's loss, "swallowing" the object, and turning into a subject defined by the possession of loss. The melancholic racial formation of Asian Americanness is constructed by its perpetual grief for the loss of place. Once consumed by their own melancholia, Asian American subjects are defined by their own grief and cannot afford an imagined or real return to the lost place.

This melancholic state is widely demonstrated in the psychological literature on the bicultural trauma and acculturative stress of second-generation Asian Americans,[8] who have supposedly lost their place of origin and are defined by the perpetual ghostly emptiness of racial positionality. The failure to resolve colonial trauma results in the ways that violence and terror linger in the present and continue to haunt Asian American subjects despite the relatively high rates of assimilation and economic advancement. Bicultural Asian Americans have reported higher levels of acculturative stress and depressive symptoms than white Americans due to the pressure to adopt both majority and minority cultures.[9] The hyphenated subject is haunted by a perpetual injured affect of being neither Asian nor American *enough*. The *bicultural blues*—as a specific psychological construction of Asian American injured affect—is thus tied to the sense of not fitting into either the host society or the "home country"—which is now a lost object, "Asia," that becomes melancholily devoured and internationalized. Ien Ang has articulated the absurd diasporic subject position of "looking Chinese but not speaking Chinese."[10] The bicultural Asian American subjectivity that feels alienated from both sites of belonging disrupts the naturalized immigrant linkage between culture and ethnicity, nation and allegiance.

Consistent with the theory of acculturation, the bicultural framework has identified the capacity of integrating the mainstream and ethnic cultures as the ideal for immigrant identity construction. The well-adjusted immigrant switches cultural frame depending on the context, as a sort of "double consciousness": "[These] biculturals do not perceive the mainstream and ethnic cultures as being mutually exclusive, oppositional, or conflicting. They integrate both cultures in their everyday lives, show behavioral competency in both cultures, and switch their behavior depending on the cultural demands of the situation."[11] Under this framework, being an ideal and healthy immigrant is to be *unstuck*—to let go of the object of loss and to embrace the banal multiculturalism in the host society. However, the biculturalism theory rarely recognizes the fact that the "mainstream culture" and the "ethnic culture" are not weighted equally in the host society. That is why to simply identify oneself as the hyphenated Asian American or Chinese American is never a satisfying answer to the Western spectators—it begs further explanations over one's foreignness and nonwhiteness.

The bicultural blues of Asian Americans as demonstrated by the literature thus produce many distinct styles of diasporic attachments. If the hegemonic assimilationist path of inclusion and acculturation inevitably creates the conditions of melancholia and ambivalent attachments to both the host society and homeland, how does one begin to mourn? As Anne Anlin Cheng asks, "How does an individual go from being a subject of grief to being a subject of grievance?"[12] These questions of racial melancholia arose from my larger ethnographic research on Asian American political participation in anti-imperialist solidarity activism in New York City with the API People's Solidarity (APIPS), a coalition of Asian American activists working to connect issues of militarism and neoliberal trade abroad to racialized violence in the United States, as discussed in chapter 2,[13] and my observation of the new Asian American political subjecthood that has emerged during the COVID-19 pandemic.

From Anti-Assimilationism to Anti-Americanism

As waves of anti-Asian violence took the stage in the mainstream press in the midst of the pandemic, I began to notice a new turn in racial and national discourses among Asian Americans. Whereas the Asian American political elites, such as those who pushed for the COVID-19 Hate Crimes Act, continued to advocate for an assimilationist path and US national loyalty, the left-leaning

Asian Americans—mostly among the younger, educated generations of both US-born and diasporic members—started to consolidate their ideologies around anti-US imperialism and China's rise on the global power stage as a "socialist alternative" to Western hegemonies. The online space, particularly Twitter, has loosely identified this milieu as "left diasporic Chinese nationalists,"[14] colloquially known as "tankies,"[15] a term originating during the Cold War to describe those hard-line Stalinists who unwaveringly supported the Soviet Union despite its authoritarian turn and violent crushing of revolutions such as in Hungary and Prague by Soviet tanks. Whereas the Cold War tankies are affiliated with a pro-Soviet position, the current milieu of "tankism" or "campism" is generally associated with support for the PRC and North Korea regimes. The rise of diasporic Chinese nationalist ideologies among Asian Americans can be marked by their "anti-Americanism" and strong desire and identification with China as the anti-imperialist center of global leftist politics.

Anti-Americanism certainly has a radical history when it is mobilized as a politics of anti-capitalism and anti-imperialism, particularly during the Cold War, when the third world decolonization movements perceived the United States as the hegemonic capitalist power and sympathized with Vietnam's resistance war against the United States.[16] After the attacks of September 11, 2001, the war in Afghanistan and the War on Terror marked another high point of anti-Americanism, when the progressive anti-war movements identified the United States as a form of racial imperialism wrapped in the banner of liberal democracy. State-based anti-Americanism, such as that in China, can be especially dangerous because it is often rallied by the political elites as a means to suppress any other forms of collective mobilization and solidarity from civil society. In short, it becomes another form of nationalistic identity politics that is ideologically conservative, rather than providing a robust anti-imperialist or anti-capitalist critique of US hegemony.

Since 2019, the anti-Americanism expressed through the diasporic Chinese campism emerged and intensified during Hong Kong's Anti-extradition Law Amendment Bill (Anti-ELAB) protests, during which the US-based left were split between supporting Hong Kongers' struggle toward democracy and self-determination and seeing the Anti-ELAB movement as another "colored revolution" instigated by a "foreign imperialist power" such as the United Kingdom and the United States.[17] The latter position inevitably turned into explicit and implicit support of the Chinese state for strengthening its party-state power by crushing down protests. Promise Li, a Hong Kong activist based in the United States and a member of the Democratic Socialists, points out that although those in this political milieu would not identify themselves as "tankies" and their politics may diverge from extreme left-wing sectarianism, their commonality is founded on identifying US imperialism as the primary, if not the only, political objective of the left, and thus they are willing to bypass a stronger position against China's rising authoritarianism and nationalism.

In March 2020, anti-Asian sentiments were on the rise as the COVID-19 pandemic hit the United States and Asian bodies were heavily associated with the virus known as being from Wuhan, China. On March 19, Stop AAPI Hate, a coalition of AAPI Equity Alliance, Chinese for Affirmative Action, and the Asian American Studies Department of San Francisco State University, was urgently launched in response to the escalation of racist harassment and attacks happening in the United States and to create a platform for self-reporting of anti-Asian incidents on the internet. The coalitional activism has been quite successful in the ways that Stop AAPI Hate has pushed state officials—from the state of California to the White House—to allocate funding to track hate incidents and even implement the federal COVID-19 Hate Crime Act in May 2021. Despite the coalition finding that a federal solution that centers on criminal law is insufficient to address the "root causes of systemic racism and oppression,"[18] it represents a long legacy of liberal Asian American activism that seeks the attention of the US state to resolve issues of inequality through its domestic civil rights infrastructure. However, Asian American liberalism is both indifferent to and incapable of forming a cohesive stance on the transnational and geopolitical implications of the burgeoning "new Cold War" amid the racially charged pandemic.

While facing transnational controversies, the liberal Asian American impulse is to retreat to the domestic agenda and concerns and defuse the international tension. For instance, when the Biden administration ordered a ninety-day investigation into the origins of the COVID-19 virus, effectively placing the World Health Organization and Beijing's natural origin hypothesis in question, Stop AAPI Hate issued a press release to urge the Biden administration to avoid hateful language when speaking about the Chinese government and divert the federal actions from the international to more state and local levels of civil rights and human rights measures in AAPI communities. Cynthia Choi, cofounder of Stop AAPI Hate, states, "The United States' relationship with China has long influenced how Chinese Americans, as well as others of Asian and Pacific Islander descent, are treated throughout the nation. . . . Regardless of the need to hold China accountable, when the US attacks China with words and policy, it puts our community in harm's way—and our data shows it. We implore the Biden administration to make good on his commitment to do everything within his power to protect the AAPIs, who now make up 24 million of the US population."[19] Although it states the inevitable implications for geopolitical rivalries on racialized minorities, where Asian Americans are unfairly projected as an extension of the Chinese government, Choi's narrative is about reinserting the priority of the US nation-state—protecting its citizens within its borders. It is a necessary political move from a US-focused standpoint, yet the lack of an explicit transnational stance on issues of the United States and China's geopolitical contestations has created the vacancy for a left, diasporic, and anti-American subjectivity to emerge among Asian Americans, as I have previously noted. Their anti-Americanism is not necessarily a rejection of their Americanness or simply a reidentification with Chinese citizenship but rather, a critique of the Asian American liberalism that ultimately seeks resolution in a US-centric worldview.

Qiao Collective, an Anglophone media collective of "diaspora Chinese people living in the West . . . including ethnic Chinese people from Southeast Asia, mainland China, Hong Kong, and Taiwan," is the exemplar of this newly formed diasporic subjectivity that fills the vacuum of Asian American geopolitical critique. It announced its launch on January 18, 2020 on Twitter, specifically framing its Marxist-informed interventions in the "intensification of U.S. antagonism towards China and the internalization of U.S. state talking points by the ostensible left," where it identifies that "critical analysis and resources for understanding China's positive role in the Global South is desperately needed."[20] On the one hand, this diasporic anti-Americanism grows out of a fundamental rejection of Asian American liberal multiculturalism, as members realize the curated cultural particularity of their Asianness will only be absorbed by the US nation-state to further its racial capitalist and imperialist project of American exceptionalism. On the other hand, they project domestic racial politics onto a binaristic framing of Cold War imperial rivalry between the United States and China and in turn identify with China as the global racial Other especially under the rising Sinophobia during the pandemic.

The emergence and consolidation of such left-leaning anti-American diasporic subjectivity has marked a new iteration of Asian American subjecthood driven by the injured affect. Whereas the Stop AAPI Hate political milieu emphasizes a reinclusion into the US nation-state and citizenship through racial injury, quite literally, the left diasporic anti-American position projects their injury as a racialized Asian subject onto the US-China geopolitical confrontation and sees the rise of Chinese power as an object of attachment that can fill their racial loss. The rise of right-wing white nationalism and the political landscape since the COVID-19 pandemic have extended the previous fissures within Asian American communities to a new spatial scale and a higher level of intensity. Whereas the liberal faction of representational politics has been consolidated into a legible minority figure through the COVID-19 Hate Crime Act initiative with bipartisan support, the anti-nationalist and anti-imperialist faction has departed further geographically, reaching a new era of Asian American identity deterritorialization. Beyond liberal multiculturalism, this chapter will investigate the multiple subjectivities of diasporic attachments among Asian Americans. Anti-assimilationist politics has been a familiar subject and centered critique within Asian American studies, but few have examined what the alternatives are in the realm of being able to "imagine otherwise," particularly from a diasporic perspective.[21] The rejection of US liberal multiculturalism and the refusal to be the ethnic particular in service of racial capital does not warrant a solid grounding in identity formation for Asian Americans to resolve their ambivalence with their ascribed foreignness. Therefore, to invoke the concept of "Asian diaspora" here is, first, to signify the entanglements between Asianness and its foreign remains and, second, to problematize the unidimensional boundaries of "Asia" and "America," including examining Asia beyond regional and geographical terms. Diaspora as a subjectivity space-time collapsing multiple geographical locations and migration histories describes how these subjects construct their identities with the multiple referents of "Asia."

Diasporic Attachments

The anti-imperialist political subjecthood, I argue, is a specific outcome of Asian American education and identity formation in the United States, which has stressed the importance of carving out an anti-assimilationist and anti-(US)-nationalist political stance. I, as a first-generation immigrant, have ascribed to such a political ideology and practiced it in the activist projects that I have been involved in, from the anti-Trans-Pacific Partnership trade agreement to the #Asians4BlackLives protests. However, anti-imperialism is not a singular politics but consists of various political trajectories and analyses. Among the left-leaning Asian American political milieus, a key differentiation is located in how the political actors comprehend the rise of China as a global hegemony. Some have seen it as a threatening event specifically relating to the political economic order in the Asia Pacific, and others consider the hawkish responses from mainstream US politicians, notably former president Donald Trump, as overreactions and even racist. These are certainly not mutually exclusive concerns—as left-leaning Asian Americans, we may feel both are accurate at the same time. Yet the question of China has since produced polarizing racial subjectivities among Asian Americans. In *Anti-Japan: The Politics of Sentiment in Postcolonial East Asia*, Leo Ching describes how one single concern has split East Asian activist youths. Whereas activists in Taiwan and Hong Kong during the Sunflower Movement and Umbrella Movement in 2014, both of which reacted to the expanded economic and political control from Beijing via neoliberal trade deals and anti-democracy measures, see the rise of China as a problem regarding peace in the region, others, particularly those on the "anti–(US and Japan)–imperialist" left, disagree with the anti-China sentiments in these movements and continue to see China as the beacon to countering US hegemony.[22] This complex sentimentality, in fact, is not specific to youths in East Asia but travels to the diaspora in Asian America and creates various types of what I call "diasporic attachments" among the racialized subjects.

During the #Asians4BlackLives protests in support of Akai Gurley between 2014 and 2017, there was a glimpse of similar nostalgic tendencies in longing for a return of the Asian-Black solidarity past under Maoist China as the model for a radical Asian American future, which I have illustrated in chapter 2, but the pervasiveness of the discourse and the intensity of Chinese nationalism has not been at quite the same scale since the COVID-19 pandemic. On the one hand, the Gurley-Liang event divided Asian American communities along the lines of racial politics—between the pro-police and the pro-BLM members—where the former was mobilized around a neoliberal color-blind politics of racial futurity and the latter around a desire for Asian-Black solidarity and racial equality. COVID-19, specifically, split Asian American communities in terms of geopolitical positioning in that the dissatisfaction with the US handling of the pandemic domestically as well as the racial attacks against Asians have pushed some people to express stronger loyalty as Americans, while others have developed stronger identification with the Chinese power as ways to express their anti-racism and anti-American radical politics. Both processes of identification are pathways to replace the psychic racial loss that Asian Americans experience. These two routes—"buckling under the pressures of dominant ideology (identification, assimilation) or attempting to break free of its inescapable sphere (counteridentification, utopianism)," to borrow José Esteban Muñoz's words—can be tempting and perhaps a survival strategy.[23] However, they can turn into another form of destructive nationalism and reinforce the "good-bad" dichotomies. As an alternative to this route, Muñoz conceptualizes disidentification as both a "working on and against" strategy where the minority subject reassembles the majority culture and recodes it for a new purpose.

Since the assimilation of subjecthood has been well researched and critiqued, in this chapter I want to focus on the divergent anti-assimilationist diasporic subjectivities among Asian Americans. Looking into textual and interview data of diasporic anti-imperialist Asian American activists, I will highlight two distinct types of diasporic attachments—an anti-American counteridentification as well as a queer of color disidentification. Although both parties subscribe to anti-US imperialist politics, they signify different ways of attaching to the concept of that nation-state. For this chapter, my analysis focuses on online discourses of various diasporic Asian American collectives as well as narrative interviews with activists who have been actively involved in racial justice organizing. The counteridentification narratives are specifically drawn from the public archives of Qiao Collective and China Is Not Our Enemy, both of which are online platforms that predominately aim at producing online political discourses against the so-called new Cold War between the United States and China.[24] The disidentification narratives, on the other hand, are drawn from loosely connected Asian American activists who belonged to various organizations in 2020—from the #Asians4BlackLives to the Justice for George Floyd campaigns—with whom I developed close connections during my fieldwork in New York City. I found that how they dealt with the sense of racial loss differently sparked distinct types of diasporic attachments.

COUNTERIDENTIFICATION

Although diasporic communities can productively intervene in the seductive assimilationist path in the host country that reproduces heteropatriarchal structures,[25] there seems to be an increasing caution around the right-wing turn of diasporic politics in the era of neoliberalism and neoconservatism. Daniele Conversi notes that state-linked diasporas, involving political actors who identify with a specific nation-state, as opposed to the stateless diasporas, that are actively looking for international recognition for their stateless nations, have contrasting characteristics in terms of nationalism.[26] There is abundant documentation on the role of ethnic diasporas in maneuvering US foreign policy through lobbies and connections with multinational corporate industries.[27] The powerful influence of the Zionist lobby in alliance with the Christian right for pro-Israel and anti-Islam policies in the United States is a prominent example of right-wing diasporic nationalism, which has outperformed other less resourceful and more dispersive Arabic states. As China dominates the world economy, diasporic activism has also gained more influence in the US lobby scene, attempting to counter Taiwan's long-standing foreign relations with the United States and promoting more American ties with Beijing,[28] while countering US influences over the recent controversies in Tibet, Xinjiang, and Hong Kong. By the mid-2000s, the explosion of social network sites and the new capacity to instantly communicate across national boundaries have intensified and multiplied the forms of diasporic politics. Chinese cybernationalism, for instance, has evolved from state-controlled media agents promoting patriotism toward much more diverse and scattered forms of ideological discourses.[29] The leftist diasporic Chinese nationalism from US-based Asian Americans is in fact quite distinct from the Little Pink, who are Chinese cybernationalists mobilized by China's state and consumer agendas and motivated by a protectionist ideal of China's national pride on the global stage.[30] It can also be differentiated from the mostly first-generation Chinese nationalists in North America and Europe, who appropriate the right-wing populist rhetoric of anti-Black, anti-immigrant, and pro-market ideals, prominent during the 2016 Trump presidential election and Brexit referendum.[31] The left-leaning Asian Americans who are sympathetic toward Chinese nationalism utilize discourses of racial injury of their own diasporic upbringings and map these onto the geopolitical struggles between the United States and China, advocating for an "anti-imperialist" vision of Chinese nationalism against the US empire. It is a specific form of Asian American feeling mobilized by accumulated racial injury and radical anti-multicultural liberalism. This affective politics does not reject its foreignness, unlike the Asian American liberals do who seek to ultimately integrate with the US nation-state. Unlike the Asian American neoliberals, it does not valorize its foreignness as a form of capitalized culture for upward class mobility; instead, it splits its foreignness between a negative attachment to the US colonial past in Asia and a positive attachment to the rise of China.

For a racialized minority subject in the United States, the search for identity can be a particularly politically charged process. Conversi notes that diasporic radicalization often occurs when the target ethnicity lacks immediate localized experiences to create more enduring bounds. In this instance, radical ethnonationalism might take over the process of intergenerational passing on of culture to otherwise reinstate national boundaries.[32] To put it another way, due to the host country's assimilative stress, the loss of culture may counterintuitively create vacuums for ethnonationalist radicalization toward the diasporic subject's nostalgic "home." Framing nostalgia as a "historic emotion," a "defense mechanism," and "a longing for a home that no longer exists or has never existed," Svetlana Boym theorizes how nostalgia takes the distinct forms of the restorative and the reflective in *The Future of Nostalgia*.[33] Whereas restorative nostalgia seeks to reconstruct the lost home, the *nostos*, and re-create the absolute truths about the place, such as in the practice of national commemoration and religious revivals, reflective nostalgia "thrives in *algia*, the longing itself, and delays the homecoming—wistfully, ironically, desperately."[34] The racial intensification during COVID-19 has produced a type of nostalgic futurity among Asian Americans who find frustration in and reject identification with US liberal multiculturalism and turn to projecting their racial injuries onto the geopolitical presence. It is a nostalgic form of futurity because it does not desire a return of a lost home but romanticizes the possibility of bringing back another nation-state to replace US global hegemony, specifically, a socialist China that no longer exists in the consensual reality. Although some militant nationalists may argue that China is still very much a socialist state that is oriented toward economic equality and poverty elimination, unlike Western capitalism, most people long for its potentiality and final actualization in the near future. In this sense, their sentiment is more similar to Boym's typology of reflective nostalgia, which presents a mode of flexibility that "cherishes shattered fragments of memory and temporalizes space."[35] It organizes assemblages of historic remains and future desires to formulate new forms of longings.

In a sympathetic reading of their politics, Qiao Collective grew out of the frustration with the limits of US liberal multiculturalism and the assimilationist narratives that often rely on the dichotomy between the United States as a symbol of freedom and democracy and China as a symbol of authoritarianism and despotism. Since their first appearance on social media in January 2020, Qiao Collective's presence has expanded drastically, perhaps more rapidly than any other Asian American–affiliated account. As of January 2022, in a two-year time span, they have garnered at least fifty-four thousand followers on Twitter and thirty-eight thousand followers on Instagram, becoming one of the most popular media platforms that articulates Asian American and diasporic politics. To understand their discourses on diasporic subjectivity in relation to US and Chinese nationalism, my analysis mainly focuses on three out of the twenty published articles on Qiao Collective's website that contain more explicit narratives about the role of the Chinese diasporic subject in rejecting what they refer to as the "Asian American representational tropes" and the US "multicultural empire." In "Can the Chinese Diaspora Speak," published by a US-based socialist magazine, *Monthly Review*, Qiao Collective cites the controversial commencement speech by Yang Shuping in 2017, a Chinese college student graduating from the University of Maryland, who contrasted the "fresh air of free speech" in the United States and air from her hometown in China that had questionable quality as a metaphor for her positive feeling for freedom of speech when coming to the United States. She describes, "Democracy and free speech should not be taken for granted. Democracy and freedom are the fresh air that is worth fighting for."[36] However, Yang's speech drew overwhelming attacks from Chinese netizens, accusing her of demonizing and insulting China's national dignity. *People's Daily*, the Chinese state-run newspaper, also accused Yang of "bolstering negative Chinese stereotypes."[37] The comments were so detrimental that Yang had to issue an apology online to clarify how criticizing China was not her intention. Although Qiao Collective's position is not necessarily about defending the Chinese nationalist attacks on Yang, they use Yang's case to explain the impossible position from which the diasporic Chinese subject must speak. According to them, the diasporic Chinese subject can only "affirm the universalism of Western liberalism in opposition to a Chinese despotism defined either by dynastic backwardness or communist depravity."[38] In other words, the diasporic subject's attachment to the United States in itself will always already be interpreted as a rejection of China, which reproduces the Cold War binarism; thus, the anti-imperialist diasporic radicalization is about rejecting such a version of Americanism.

In Qiao Collective's view, denouncing US multicultural liberalism is not only a racial justice goal in itself, toward obtaining a more material basis of structural equality rather than merely subscribing to symbolic speech, but also deeply connected to the project of rejuvenating a "socialist China," which has been unfairly criticized. They posit that Yang's narrative is dangerous because it has become "representative of a broader genre of multicultural empire that wields the confessional speech of newly incorporated Chinese Americans as part of a campaign to delegitimize China's socialist project." That is, they are connecting the racial loss of the diasporic Chinese subject who has to conform to US nationalism to the imperial advancements of the United States in countering the rise of "Red China" since World War II. Although the United States has demanded and continues to demand national loyalty from minority subjects and its systems have created countless forms of violence against those who have precarious citizenship status, Qiao Collective does not seem to consider the absurd political context in which an overseas Chinese student who supports freedom of speech has to face internet attacks and issue an apology to her fellow Chinese citizens. This tendency of subscribing all nuances of an event to Cold War binarism and all critiques against China as a form of "red scare" is a limit that Muñoz has warned us about regarding the politics of counteridentification. He points out that in the case of the early establishment of white feminism, the strategy of counteridentification with men neglected the "multiple antagonisms" that queers of color have to negotiate around white normativity as well as heteronormativity.[39] To Qiao Collective, diasporic subjects who identify with any sense of American liberal values would only be subsumed under the "multicultural empire" and be "deeply circumscribed by Cold War anticommunism and its racist undertone." In this sense, the racial loss of Chinese Americans can only be amended through a process of counteridentification, a complete rejection of Americanism. The irony is that by arguing that Yang's subjectivity has been unconsciously "corrupted" by the "multicultural empire," it reduces the agency of a figure like Yang—a diasporic Chinese subject—to have any real capacity to criticize China as well.

The theme of formulating a diasporic counteridentification subjectivity as a pathway toward rediscovering the Chinese socialist tradition is quite visible across Qiao Collective's publications. In "Assimilation and Empire," the Chinese Canadian author Xin writes in the context of escalating anti-Asian violence and their denunciation of an assimilating path that their immigrant parents have wanted for them: "How can so-called 'North America' be the 'land of opportunity' of my parents' dreams for me when anti-Asian racism and white supremacy continue to run rampant? I spent most of my time in grade school and high school desperately trying to fit in with my white peers, shrugging off my Chinese heritage and distancing myself from those living in the 'authoritarian state' of China, all in the hopes that my friends would see me as 'Canadian,' as one of them."[40] The impossibility to fully assimilate and the continuation of racial microaggression that Xin faces pushes them to seek an identification otherwise. They criticize that "Asian assimilation into the US imperialist class is contingent upon becoming a native informant and confirming imperialist US talking points about China." Instead, only developing a politics of rejecting US militarization and imperialism in the Asia Pacific and a reidentification with Asian socialism can lead to liberation within the self and the diasporic communities.

Counteridentification as a strategy of forming diasporic belonging itself and the critique of the United States are not problems. The controversy of the rise of nostalgic projection of a socialist China that comes out of an anti-American politics gets particularly heightened when Qiao Collective and its affiliated leftist networks blatantly deny any wrongdoing by the Chinese state. Specifically, Qiao Collective took an uncritical pro–Chinese state stance on the issues of Hong Kong's 2019 pro-democracy movement and Xinjiang's reeducation camp. Take, for instance, their "Hong Kong Reading List" published in 2019, which according to them, "provides a critical lens on the driving forces of the Hong Kong protests: fervent anti-communism and a fetishization of abstract liberalism, British colonial nostalgia, anti-Chinese racism, and appeals to Western intervention."[41] Although these elements arguably may have existed in the Anti-ELAB protests, by strictly painting the movement as a "color revolution" and a "US-sponsored regime-change," their rhetoric completely aligned with Beijing's official stance, which criticized the grassroots mobilization as merely foreign interventions or incomplete colonization from the former British regime. Qiao Collective's aim is not only to provide an "alternative" perspective to Hong Kong's movement coverage in the West, which was mainly sympathetic to the protesters and condemned the unjustified police force used on civilians, but to articulate the event as yet another event of Western bashing of China: "The Hong Kong 'democracy movement' co-opts the language of 'self-determination' and 'autonomy' as a cover to bring Hong Kong more under Western colonial rule and to maintain Hong Kong as a capitalist imperialist base through which *the West can attack China*" (italics mine).[42] Their diasporic attachment views their projected inner self as the racialized Other bullied by Western power, and any attempt to examine the object of this identification (China) critically will be understood via the geopolitical scale of the West versus China, with no alternative.

Qiao Collective's anti-American counteridentification has reach into US leftist circles beyond diasporic Asian American communities. In September 2021, Qiao Collective cohosted a one-day conference with *Monthly Review* and People's Forum, which are both longtime US-based socialist organizations, in New York City. The conference, "China and the Left," drew at least 150 people in physical attendance, with thousands more who participated virtually. The conference overall stressed the robust Chinese state policies that have led to the successes of COVID-19 containment, the elimination of poverty since the Chinese Communist Party (CCP) takeover, and building a sovereign Global South nation that can defy US hegemony. What is interesting about Qiao Collective's politics is the parallel projection of antagonism between the United States and China as well as whiteness and Asianness vis-à-vis anti-Asian racism. Madison Tang, from the anti-war organization Code Pink, argues that US hybrid war against China is an Orientalist measure—framing it as "uncivilized, primitive, deceptive, despotic, and dishonest"—that aims to tame its influences in Asia, which echoes the "dehumanization and disposability of East and Southeast Asians" living in the "imperial core" of the United States.[43] Tang raises critiques against the constructing of a "good Asian" that must be founded on discrediting and rejecting communism and China itself, which has resulted in the largely depoliticized Chinese diaspora in the United States: "The 'good Chinese Americans' are the ones who actively oppose their country of origin, the Chinese government, and actively anti-communist."[44]

The racial loss and the political alienation due to the US-China rivalry is vast and real, yet the counteridentification affect that relies on a reattachment to China has prevented Qiao Collective's milieus to build constructive critiques of the Chinese government. This problem is shown through their analysis of various Chinese affairs, which border on disinformation. For instance, Sheila Xiao, a member of Pivot to Peace and a speaker on the same panel, argues that "there are six major myths . . . that have become the pillars of the US propaganda campaigns against China": (1) Hong Kong has had its freedom stripped from it, (2) the Uyghurs in western China are victims of state-sanctioned genocide and forced assimilation, (3) Tibetans have been denied their right to freedom, religion, and culture, (4) Taiwan is an independent country, (5) China is a totalitarian and police state, and (6) China is an imperial power bullying its neighbors, seizing disputed territories.[45] All of the above "myths," to them, are considered "anti-China" and "Sinophobic" propaganda, rather than genuine struggles of autonomy and freedom that have been sown by grassroots movements from Hong Kong, the Uyghurs, the Tibetans, Taiwan, and people from other Asian countries. The Critical China Scholars (CCS), a collective of left-leaning researchers who work on China-related issues, including Rebecca Karl, Tani Barlow, and Darren Byler, among others, issued a statement that intervenes in Qiao Collective's report on Xinjiang published by the *Monthly Review*, which outright identifies the internment camps as a myth fabricated by the National Endowment for Democracy and the Central Intelligence Agency. The CCS states, "We fully acknowledge the need for a critique of America's cynical and self-interested attacks on China's domestic policies. We are committed to that task. But the left must draw a line at apologia for the campaign of harsh Islamophobic repression now taking place in Xinjiang."[46] The statement reveals the hypocrisy of appropriating anti-imperialist discourses for Chinese apologism. Here, Qiao Collective's anti-American counteridentification ceases to be a critical stance of anti-imperialism and instead becomes a new form of identity politics in which the minoritarian subjects are caught in another binaristic framing of good versus bad and absorbing everything about China as a better counterexample of the evil American empire. To Qiao Collective, criticizing the Chinese state's Islamophobia is only a disingenuous and double-standard Sinopobic campaign because the West has the same problem, not because Islamophobic violence itself is wrong. Unfortunately, white supremacy precisely relies on such strategies of imitation and reproduction to expand its effects, as China has directly adapted elements of US-led counterterrorism security apparatuses since September 11 to discipline the Uyghurs in Xinjiang.[47] The fixation on one's racial loss, indeed, creates an uncritical bond with a new love object (China) in the name of racial belonging but ultimately misjudges the full-scale effects of white racial violence.

DISIDENTIFICATION

In seeking the political and creative possibilities of loss, David Eng and David Kazanjian propose a depathologized understanding of the melancholic attachments to loss that might generate a more productive conceptualization of temporality, where "melancholia's persistent struggle with its lost objects is not simply a 'grasping' and 'holding' on to a fixed notion of the past but rather a continuous engagement with loss and its remains."[48] By holding on to the object, the melancholic subject may have more capacity and flexibility to represent history and the various forms of loss—of a beloved person or "an abstraction which has taken the place of the person, such as fatherland, freedom, an ideal, and so on."[49] As dwelling in the past may offer the mourner a different sense of time and space, melancholia—the attachment to the object of loss—can provide a more nuanced and productive conceptualization of Asian American subjectivity beyond the binary of assimilation and oppression and the bicultural blues of inadequate becoming. For subjects who desire to uncover erased histories, the state of melancholia should not be considered as uniformly psychologically damaging.

Certainly, the risks of being stuck in the past or dwelling on losses are certainly not equal for all subjects, who as a consequence might be seen as permanent outcasts or utterly irrelevant. As I noted earlier, heightened racial surveillance and Sinophobia have intensified the feelings of paranoia, fear, and alienation of diasporic Chinese subjects. When we uncritically absorb such an affect, it risks becoming another form of identity politics rather than an effective critique of racism and imperialism. An alternative strategy of attachment, as proposed by Muñoz from thinking through queer Latinx's strategies of identity and culture making, is *disidentification*. He writes, "To disidentify is to read oneself and one's own life narrative in a moment, object, or subject that is not culturally coded to 'connect' with the disidentifying subject."[50] Unlike counteridentification, the process of disidentification does not simply turn against the mainstream but finds ways to create subversions from within. In the time of heightened racial tensions and geopolitical rivalries, I turned to diasporic queer Asian American activists, who navigate multiple spaces of conflicts and resistance in the wake of the anti-Asian violence as well as to the rise of pro-democracy movements in Asia. Standing steadfastly in an anti-imperialist position, these activists practice a form of disidentification with their US-based commitments and attachment to their home of origin in Asia and do not see them as contradictory. Instead, they collectively narrate a strategy of ambivalent belonging as a way to hold on to both places and the lost time. They have developed radical politics beyond assimilation and resistance to be sorted along the binarisms of backward versus progressive and the damaged versus the agentive in both queer and Asian American politics. Queers of color are often excluded from homonormative citizenship and become the *racialized remains* of white queer futurity. Specifically, queer Asian Americans' multiplicity of identities is often constructed as a site of irrecoverable and unresolved losses, where queerness is viewed as a Western construct and not fitting for Asian ethnic cultures.[51] However, queerness as a source of disidentification allows these activists to regard their negative affects of melancholia and grief not as quantifiable damages or inconsolable wounds but as motivation to find belonging in the liminal space of racialized geopolitics. The "unhappy queers" and "melancholic migrants" hold on to the negative affects that interrupt the presumed route of assimilation, allowing the body to encounter another kind of desire that "may even queer our aspirations."[52] That is, rather than simply turning against the assimilating love object of "America" and reattaching to the nostalgic object of "Asia" due to experiences of racialization and sexualization—as in counteridentification—these activists have sought transnational solidarity that rejects choosing sides in the US-China interimperial rivalries.

This loose network of diasporic queer Asian American activists—both first-generation and second-generation immigrants of Chinese, Japanese, Korean, Hong Kong, and Taiwanese descents who have spent time in both the United States and different parts of Asia—has been termed transnationally Asian.[53] The political milieu of which I have been a part originated from the New York City–based mobilization against the Trans-Pacific Partnership trade agreement among diasporic Asian American organizers, APIPS, in 2013, followed by the #Asians4BlackLives and #Justice4AkaiGurley movements between approximately 2015 and 2017, and the rapidly expanded transnational mobilization in terms of geographical scale and topics of concerns in the COVID-19 era since 2020. As the anti-imperialist campism grows into a new form of uncritical Chinese nationalism, these transnationally Asian activists have insisted on linking the racial struggles from the United States to a critique of the rise of authoritarian regimes in Asia. Whereas the campist discourses propagated the "effectiveness" of Chinese government in dealing with poverty, the social safety net, and the pandemic in contrast to the US neoliberal approach, Tammy Kim observes in her report on this political milieu: "By taking a transnationally Asian point of view, they were able to critique the American response without reflexively defending China or naively recycling praise of COVID-19 success stories."[54] They are affiliated with left-leaning diasporic media activist organizations including but not limited to Lausan (Hong Kong), Nodutdol (Korea), New Bloom (Taiwan), and Sloths against Nukes (Japan). I encountered these activists—roughly thirty members—during my fieldwork in New York City between 2013 and 2020, and about half of them, including myself, have moved out of New York City or the United States since the pandemic hit in 2020. However, I have been able to be in touch through virtual means.[55] Connected to the nature of their diasporic life, frequently moving across borders, the "transnationally Asian" milieu's disidentification approach is about finding ways to be continually attached to Asia, the object infused with trauma and pain, yet at the same time generate new capacity to actively resist dominant narratives of assimilation and Orientalization. Different from counteridentification where the subjects reinvent the creation of a new love object "China" in opposition to the idea of "America," these activists divert and transform their sense of racial loss into a broader geographical scale of psychic investment in communities beyond a singular national, racial, or ethnic affiliation. To understand how the politics of disidentification emerges requires that we think beyond the analytical unit of race and pay attention to the multiple uprisings that occur at the same time transnationally, from Justice for George Floyd and Stop Asian Hate that center on racial violence, to the multisited anti-authoritarian movements in Asia between 2019 and 2021.

The summer of 2020 changed the landscape of racial justice movements globally. The death of George Floyd in Minneapolis, an African American man who was brutally murdered by a white American police officer, Derek Chauvin, who held Floyd to the ground with his knee and choked Floyd to death after nine and a half minutes, sparked one of the largest social movements in the United States since the 1960s.[56] Jin,[57] a second-generation adoptee Korean American activist whom I met through the anti-Trans-Pacific Partnership organizing with APIPS and has been involved in multiracial activist work for more than fifteen years in New York City, told me that the scale of what she calls the "June Uprising" was unprecedented. Different from the more regional solidarity movement during the #Justice4AkaiGurley campaign regarding another incident of racialized police violence, the George Floyd incident was much more visible in its reach and more intense in terms of the level of mobilization: "The protests were happening every single day, every time of the day, the 'JusticeForGeorgeNYC' account [on Instagram] had to break it down by boroughs to announce the actions that were occurring." Jin articulated that part of the reason why the Asian American participants in the June Uprising had significantly increased, at least in comparison to the #Justice4AkaiGurley campaign around five years earlier, was because the rise in anti-Asian violence reporting made racial violence feel much more personal and urgent than ever before.

On the bright side, the social infrastructure of multiracial solidarity coalitions since the Liang-Gurley incident has built in more trust between Asian and Black communities. Many Black organizers protested anti-Asian hate alongside Asian Americans. While the pro-BLM side seemed to dominate Asian American narratives for the first time in June 2020, Jin also observed how the conservative pro-police voices grew louder among Asian Americans due to the visible attacks against Asian people. Multiracial politicians including Queens Borough president Donovan Richards, Representative Grace Meng, Senator Chuck Schumer, and Mayor Bill de Blasio led a rally and a march from Flushing Town Hall on May 2, 2021, chanting "Stop Asian Hate" to push for more federal and state budgets in law enforcement and the implementation of the COVID-19 Hate Crimes Act[58] to consolidate the mobilization efforts throughout the year.

Another Japanese activist, Akiko, whom I have met since through APIPS, raises another issue about the Stop Asian Hate rhetoric from a class perspective. As an undocumented restaurant worker, Akiko, whom I interviewed within the first few months of the COVID-19 pandemic, felt immensely insecure because of pay cuts, lack of health care, and the need to continue to take public transportation to work. She articulates the disingenuous interests that fixated on "race" in the campaigns around anti-Asian violence when Asian businesses were enduring difficult financial times due to both the pandemic and racial biases: "The liberal Asian Americans are calling to 'protect our neighborhoods' and 'protect our restaurants,' and lots of fundraising money are coming in. But they are going to the owners' pockets, not the workers." The racial and nationalist feelings mobilized around Asian American racial injury were indeed often class blind, as working-class Asian Americans needed to continually endure the risk of harassment and violence in the streets. "The point is to support restaurant workers' union organizing, not buying more takeout from the restaurants," said Akiko.

The organizing experiences of seeing how Asian Americanness can be pulled to either side of the political spectrum have led Jin to believe that there is nothing inherently "radical" about being Asian American but that this term must always be applied to the conditions we are situated in. She says, "It was a very radical idea at one point to be Asian American. Now it is no longer this way. I feel, at least in New York City, this movement was really strong in the '60s and '70s and built into something. But it's been forty-five years, you know? You get comfortable. The question is how do we shift the radical idea then to the conditions now?"

Both her adoptee and her queer identity pushed her to challenge any taken-for-granted assumptions about right or wrong because she hardly fits into the dominant immigrant and Asian American narrative. Her organizing with the Korean diasporic communities through Nodutdol is an attempt to break the monolithic narrative about Asian American assimilation by engaging with progressive activist organizations in both North and South Korea. Yet the more she is involved in transnational activism, the more she starts to question the diasporic romanticization of the "home country." For instance, Nodutdol advocates for the idea of *tongli*, peaceful unification of North and South Korea. For Jin, believing in this vision does not mean to resort to campist apologism on issues related to North Korea. "Going to North Korea and having the interpersonal relations is really important for me to understand the North Korea that is not seen in Western media," she said, "but we can still be critical of the government. In fact, we need to be critical of the government if we want to actually move toward unification." What Jin expresses here is a politics of disidentification—it refuses a wholesale attachment to either form of nationalism and makes commitments to engage with the multiple antagonisms and contradictions in both places.

This work of solidarity is certainly not easy. The emergence of young Asian Americans becoming politicized in the era of COVID-19 has not necessarily equated to a more cohesive ideology around Asian American radicalism. For diasporic Hong Konger activists, this may have been a particularly difficult and traumatic time, not only because of the Anti-ELAB movement but also the position of being caught in the middle of the US-China geopolitical conflicts. The Anti-ELAB movement started in the summer of 2019 in Hong Kong, where millions of Hong Kongers went into the streets to protest a bill introduced by the Hong Kong government that would allow the Beijing authorities to intervene in the judiciary autonomy of the Hong Kong court, altering the "One Country, Two Systems" promise of the Basic Laws since its handover from the British colonial regime to the PRC. In the meantime, the Stop Asian Hate mobilization in the United States had attracted large contingencies of Chinese nationals, where some participants were waving CCP flags to show national pride in various cities. This phenomenon alienated members of other Asian communities who face political persecution from the Chinese government, particularly Hong Kongers, Tibetans, Taiwanese, and Uyghurs in the US diasporas, where any critique against the Chinese state can risk being framed as Sinophobic and racist. In Washington, DC, a Stop Asian Hate rally on March

22, 2021 was confronted by pro-Uyghur protesters who held signs that stated, "Stop Uyghur Genocide," "Hold China Accountable," "CCP Killed 80 Million Chinese People," and "Stand Up for Freedom for All." In response, participants from the Stop Asian Hate rally called the pro-Uyghurs "racist."[59] The incident went viral on Twitter and marked the previously unspoken internal fracture within the Asian American mobilization, where the discourse of racial injury has been appropriated by Chinese nationalists to deny violence inflicted on other Asian communities. When "anti-China" is uncritically equated to "racism," it indeed becomes another discursive tool of shutting down dissent of the Chinese government.

This dynamic has been replicated by some of the leftist organizations in the United States besides Qiao Collective, such as an anti-war organization called ANSWER Coalition, which frames anti-Asian violence as an issue of "China-bashing," attempting to weaponize the moment of racial crisis to neutralize critique against the CCP. Promise Li points out that "conflating violence against Asian people and state-level conflicts impedes the struggle against Sinophobia and racism by furthering the artificial geopolitical conflict between U.S. and Chinese elites, and pitting regular Asians and Asian diaspora against one another."[60] After the DC incident, a Los Angeles–based pro-democracy organization, Hong Kong Forum, issued a statement to condemn both racism against Asian Americans and advocated for solidarity building with their "Taiwanese, Vietnamese, Filipinos, Uygur, Tibetan fellows," calling on Asian Americans to "empower ourselves and learn the Asian American's history adequately."[61] In reality, the splits along geopolitical lines have made it almost impossible for those who are stuck in the middle of the conflict to find safety and belonging. Shae, a New York City–based first-generation Hong Konger activist active in various Asian American campaigns as well as Lausan, the diasporic Hong Kong collective, was eager to facilitate dialogues and actions about Hong Kong's movement but was facing criticisms and attacks from the Asian American and the Hong Kong diasporic circles because of her affiliations in both spaces. On the one hand, she disagreed with the conflation of Sinophobia as a consequence of "China bashing" on issues relating to human rights abuses and political repression. On the other hand, her electoral campaign work for a city-level politician of mainland Chinese descent and her ongoing organizing work with the Manhattan Chinatown communities made her be seen somewhat as a "traitor" or a "left plastic"[62] by some of the Hong Kong diasporic groups. Shae points out,

> The tensions among Asian diasporic communities in the US were heightened since 2019 during the solidarity action for Hong Kong's Anti-ELAB

> movement. I could count in one hand of friends from my Asian American organizing communities that showed up for the Hong Kong rallies, for my identity, and for what's going on in Hong Kong. . . . While I was marshaling for the rallies, there were always Chinese people who yelled at us or sang the Chinese anthem really loudly to disturb the actions. . . . At the same time, I was working in Chinatown for tenant organizing. I got worried whether the Chinese tenants would have an issue with me because I was visible in the Hong Kong solidarity protests. But thankfully because of the pandemic, we were all wearing masks so no one would recognize me.

Despite the alienation from both spaces, Shae emphasized the importance of translation across communities. When the Atlanta shootings happened, she immediately jumped into the work for Red Canary Song, a grassroots collective of Asian and migrant sex workers, to highlight the frequently erased class and anti–sex work issues in how the massacre was framed by the mainstream press and Asian American communities. "The dominating Stop Asian Hate rhetoric about Sinophobia has reduced a lot of the nuanced politics. However, I continue to do translation and coordination work because I want to distinguish what the Chinese government has done and who the Chinese people are," says Shae about her ongoing commitment to disidentify with the polarizing discourses in the present. There are also some unexpected moments of recognition during her work that kept her going. She mentioned one day she was wearing black to be in solidarity with the Anti-ELAB movement in Hong Kong around the fall of 2019, and a Taiwanese uncle in her tenant organizing space asked if she "wore black to protest in silence," and it was the first time that she felt seen, even if it was just a brief encounter of recognition.

Certainly, not all Chinese diasporas support the Chinese state's violence against ethnic minorities or are apologetic for the state's human rights abuse and territorial expansionism. During the June Uprising, a group of diasporic Chinese feminists began to mobilize support for the BLM activities under #ChineseForBlackLives across US cities.[63] Consisted of mostly first-generation, young international students from China, the loose feminist collective began their political inspiration via Black feminist writing and was inspired by the #MeToo movement in China. As the George Floyd incident happened, the feminist collective translated slogans and posters to reach out to Chinese restaurants and other vendors in the Chinatowns of various US cities to advocate for solidarity with the Black communities. The feminists I have encountered are not shy about challenging the wrongdoings of the Chinese state, especially calling out its ill treatments of African immigrants in Guangzhou during the

COVID-19 outbreak, where many were evicted from their home and put into forced quarantine simply based on their race.[64] According to Kun Huang, a Chinese diasporic activist scholar, this new rise of feminist network is sharply different from the pro-police Chinese Americans in 2016. She writes, "Unlike their peers who prioritize Chinese national identity and privilege a binary framework of Sino-US comparison, progressive diaspora activists tend to pursue more nuanced, context-based, comparative analysis, engage in localized and transnational action, and display more complex patterns of group identification and community belonging."[65] The insurgency of Chinese feminist collective shows how the diasporic Asian communities can build coalition with Asian American social movements through their immigrant community infrastructure. Rather than preoccupied with the assimilationist demands, the immigrant activists are "unapologetically foreign"[66]—that is, their politics is driven not by the psychic racial loss but a different hope for cross-racial solidarity. While the pandemic has created new geopolitical fault lines within Asian American communities, we also witness the growing of transnational resistance beyond national, racial, and ethnic borders.

Amid the multiple struggles in the two summers of uprisings, the "transnationally Asian" activists dealt with the affect of racial injury not through rejecting the centrality of race in their analysis of US state violence but through seeking transnational points of connection without falling into a fixated nostalgic attachment with the nation-state. On October 19 and 22, 2020, a virtual conference titled "Transnationally Asian" hosted by Lausan, New Bloom, and New Naratif, a pro-democracy media collective in Southeast Asia, took place.[67] The presenters were mostly bilingual or trilingual diasporic Asian organizers with educational experiences in the West but who had been intimately involved in the local politics of Hong Kong, Taiwan, Singapore, and Malaysia. Their media strategies attempted to distinguish from the often conservative-leaning Anglophone local news outlets in Asia, run by white expats, experts in creating safe and secure online communication methods against state surveillance. Their politics addressed their shared tenuous relationships with "multiple empires" from the perspectives of diasporic Asians.[68] As a presenter and participant who strongly identified with the politics of the group, I was, like Shae, where I felt seen for the first time in a space that organized specifically around the interconnectedness of the transpacific. I realized that perhaps the capacity of this type of movement to bridge different locally based movements has allowed the sense of stuckness as a racialized subject to find alternative paths of belonging that are constantly shifting rather than firmly located in a state, a flag, or a people. By holding on to the sense of loss and frustration as a motivating affect of seeking belonging otherwise, disidentification subverts both the racial politics of assimilating through racial injury and the nationalist sentiments of neutralizing critiques against non-Western authoritarian regimes. It diversifies the politics of a given group—in this case Asian Americans—and strengthens different kinds of affiliation between groups.

Unruly Subjects

Despite the nationalist pressure to assimilate and to "move on" as highlighted in the #thisis2016 campaign, both the counteridentification and disidentification forms of diasporic attachments reject simply moving on and are, rather, engaging in a process of dwelling in the history and presence of colonial relations. As Anne Anlin Cheng argues, "Like melancholia, racism is hardly ever a clear rejection of the other."[69] The racial other in the white society is usually melancholily possessed and maintained, rather than an outright relinquishment or exclusion. Even under the colonial structure of segregation where the racial other is captured in a geographically separate site, the colonizers would invest an immense amount of psychic energy of fear and desire in the colonized subject.[70] When it comes to facing discrimination and injury by the racial other, reducing their experience to an inevitable self-hatred or self-ostracism is thus too simplistic and prescriptive. Anne Anlin Cheng points out that the subjective agency of the racialized subject should be considered as "a convoluted, ongoing, generative, and at times self-contradicting negotiation with pain."[71] The insistence on anti-American counteridentification, however, has led some Asian American subjects to quickly seek a new love object for belonging. The activists I spoke to were wary of the emergent popularity of Qiao Collective–like organizations that may reduce the nuances of anti-imperialist politics to a form of "revolutionary aesthetics" that is ideologically messy and troubling. For instance, a self-identified mixed-raced Asian artist who created under the name Vienna Rye has become an Asian American community influencer with 123,000 followers on Instagram. Rye's images are beautifully crafted with essences that mirror third worldist aesthetics, citing revolutionary lines from famous people such as W. E. B. Du Bois, Malcolm X, and Arundhati Roy, with images of Xi Jinping, Kim Jong-un, and Fidel Castro in the same frame with the text: "The cruel spectacle of Amerikkkan 'democracy' is burning itself down from the inside out."[72] The histories of third world anti-colonial struggles are certainly valuable, but the decontextualized reattachments of these ideas to present-day authoritarian leaders are dangerous for building any relevant and nuanced politics of anti-imperialism. However, more and more Asian Americans have become politicized through visual routes, and the imagination of radical politics is dominated by the fast track of visual cues. The results are a fractured Asian American community along geopolitical fault lines. As Promise Li writes about the homogenizing discourse of anti-Asian violence being synonymous to China-bashing, "This is not the time for unity."[73]

Disidentification thus becomes a critical and necessary method to reimagine the possibility of Asian Americanness; because of its ambivalent attachments to nations and a permanent state in the diaspora, activists must conceptualize their loss not as something immediately resolvable through identifying with a new love object but rather as a process of mourning against assimilation and the empire. These activists illustrate alternative forms of subjective agency to live and resist in the colonized society beyond the binary of identification and negation. Therefore, rather than prescribing how the public in general should "get over" the fact that colonial and imperial histories are part of what constitutes Asian Americanness—to simply celebrate the multicultural ideal of #thisis2016—the attachment to losses and the unresolved tensions of their multiple commitments can indeed be sites of regeneration. Seeking something beyond another nostalgic love object for comfort and belonging, disidentification insists on being with the unruly attachments to communities beyond the imagery of any singular nation-state.

The unresolved questions of immigrant identity, as social psychologist Kay Deaux[74] has pointed out, come from an ontological anxiety over the issues of patriotism and nationalism. The hyphenated identities are challenged over and over again in social sciences, policy, and public representations precisely because the racial and ethnic identity and the American identity are thought of as fundamentally incompatible. That is, even when the two sides of these identities are acknowledged, there is still pressure for the immigrant subject to declare allegiance and loyalty to one national identity only. This sense of nationalism is pervasive and deeply rooted in US immigration discourse, despite the effort of multicultural rhetoric that proposes the framework of being on the hyphen. What the diasporic Asian American activists have highlighted, from both sides, is a perpetual sense of instability of the hyphen in which it is not something one should simply resolve or "choose a side" of. Rather, the narratives indicate "a dialectic labor of psychological reconciliation" that pieces together what Selcuk Sirin and Michelle Fine term the uncompromising "hyphenated selves"[75] on the fault lines of geopolitical conflicts, colonial histories, and transnational struggles. In a sense, the activists' melancholic attachment to the tension between mourning one's national and racial loss and concern extended toward a collective history of anti-imperialism and anti-colonialism *is* the hyphenated site that regenerates radical possibility of affiliation beyond being subsumed to a singular national identity. As I write in the era of rising nationalisms and geopolitical contests, the willfulness to hold on to the hyphenated tensions between assimilation and opposition, as well as belonging and marginalization, becomes ever more pressing. To trouble the hegemonic narrative of becoming Asian American in the theorization of immigrant subjectivity, we must create alternative frameworks that not only pay attention to the process of citizen formation but also take into account the stubborn resistance against being subjugated to either side of the border, and the multiple commitments across national and racial boundaries.

EPILOGUE

Sideways to Asian America

On June 13, 2020, hundreds of multiracial participants holding protest signs in both English and Mandarin gathered in the 228 Peace Memorial Park in Taipei, Taiwan to show solidarity with the global Black Lives Matter (BLM) movement after George Floyd's death. Taiwan, where race has seldom been a political topic in the mainstream, was suddenly put in the front of the news coverage. The crowd consisted of local Taiwanese and foreigners of divergent racial and national backgrounds. The same signs I had just seen in the protests in New York City prior to my departure, such as "#SayOurNames" and "I Can't Breathe," showed up in the protest-scape of Taipei. At the moment, I had just relocated from New York to Taipei, after twenty years of living in the United States, yet suddenly the two worlds did not feel as far apart as I had originally imagined. During the height of the COVID-19 pandemic, where infection and death rates soared globally, Taiwan's local infection rates were relatively under control and life went on as usual, making it almost a parallel universe. In Taipei, around the New Bloom activist circle, I began to see many young Taiwanese Americans make the same move as I did, coming to Taiwan not only to seek refuge from the pandemic but also to build different kinds of transnational networks. These millennial "returnees" mostly had very weak connection to the social and political life in Taiwan, but as the United States was failing to create a coherent strategy of combating the pandemic and the racial animosity intensified by the growing white ethnonationalism, many Asian Americans began to see moving to Asia as a viable option, if not permanently, at least temporarily.

In Taiwan, the diasporic milieu I am part of is largely invested in building multiethnic and multiracial coalition with the migrant worker and Indigenous communities locally to change the "transnational scene" that was previously dominated by white male expats. Workshops, lectures, and discussions among Southeast Asian, Black, Indigenous, Han Taiwanese, Hong Kongers, and diasporic Asian Americans were held monthly in New Bloom's space in Wanhua, Taipei, which was reminiscent of the activist spaces I frequented in Brooklyn. It seems that the pandemic has drastically pushed forward a new era of external deterritorialization in Asian American politics and identity formation in which young Asian Americans are looking at Asia not just as a nostalgic object or problematic identity but as a place of resolution—that is, a site that contains new cultural and political possibilities, rather than a dead end to their Asian American belonging. More specifically, Taiwan, in the transnational Asian American imagination, breaks away from the oscillation of Asian American identity on the poles of being oppressed or being assimilated. It propels the diasporic subjects to think and feel alongside the multiple struggles occurring in the transnational landscape beyond the analytical unit of US-centric racial formation. While identity politics within the United States stagnated domestically, Asian Americans seem to be increasingly looking for a sideways position of politicization, rather than one that goes directly through a US-centric racial discourse of historical injury.

Throughout this book, I have stressed that the study of Asian American subjectivity necessitates a geopolitical analysis at the transnational scale. Although economically heavily codependent, the US and Chinese global superpowers have been involved in competitive relations almost on all fronts since the trade war that was initiated by the Trump administration via increasing tariffs on China in 2018. In the meantime, China has exerted growing economic and political influence in the Asian region and beyond through projects such as the Belt and Road Initiative and military pressures against surrounding communities and states including Taiwan, Hong Kong, Tibet, and Xinjian. The Biden administration has continued this new Asia policy of an open "Indo-Pacific" and is seeking new strategic partnership with India. The vision for China being the "responsible stakeholder"[1] thesis under President Barack Obama and Secretary of State Hillary Clinton is no longer effective, as Chinese state capitalism insists on functioning with a semi-liberalized economy and increasingly closed-off political system. The COVID-19 pandemic, since early 2020, has shown how quickly the geopolitical alignments shift, fragment, and merge into different shapes. "Asia" cannot be simply understood as a cohesive and autonomous regional entity "beyond" the imperial centers of Euro-America, but rather, it has always been integrated in a Western-led imperialist and capitalist apparatus in contested forms.

As Jini Kim Watson notes, "The Pacific, indeed, has long been a place full of solutions."[2] The current spatial rearrangement does not change the projected and imagined futurity of Asia Pacific. More than ever, Asia Pacific is now the global site of militaristic, financial, ecological, technological, and nuclear contestations. Aimee Bahng points out that the speculation of the early twenty-first century as the "Asian century" has depended on its capacity for global capitalist financialization and its lurking potential of ecological disaster.[3] The coexistence of hope and devastation, solution and crisis, accumulation and destruction continue to produce the codependent notions of Asia Pacific and futurity as well as the Western imagination of racialized Asian subjects. Therefore, rather than taking the position of the "beyond Black and white" that often leads us to a one-directional future uncritically and easily appropriated by neoliberal capitalism, I have turned the queer vision of "sideways"[4] to Asian America to examine the curved and unconventional routes of power that grow *beside* the very production of Asian American space-time. Instead of simply taking racial trauma and racial identity collectivity as the formulating point of Asian Americanist analysis, sideways asks us to look at the temporospatial assemblage as a whole—its geopolitical struggle, neoliberal aspirations, racial nostalgia, and affective diasporas. A sideways perspective resists using the United States as the primary object of inquiry in Asian American studies, rejects race as a natural and cohesive identity in Asian American psychology, and highlights the need for Asian studies to look at the effects of white supremacy and racialization globally. A sideways analysis pays attention to both the expansion of empire and imperialism acting through and against Asian America, and the possibility of alternative affiliations besides the cohesiveness of an Asian American race.

As I argued in chapter 1, Asian Americanness emerged in the field of American psychology precisely as a concept of geographical significance originating in World War II and was later neutralized as an alternative racial position beyond the Black-white paradigm. However, the unyielding forces of US imperialism at large and in American psychology in particular provided the "perpetual foreigner" a path toward recognition and inclusion through an allegiance to the US nation-state. The anti-war and anti-imperialist origin of the Asian American civil rights movement is partly appropriated into a new bureaucratic structure of Asian American professionalization under the paradigm of US neoliberal multiculturalism, mitigating the crisis of racial relations domestically and globally.

The diasporic visions of anti-imperialist politics that have emerged lately are attempts to break away from the previous decades of internal territorialization, yet not without producing new kinds of contradictions. As a result, the tension of Asian American representation and contestation of its political goals is ever more intensified under the rise of China. It not only troubles the inter-Asia relations but also creates diasporic ramifications among Asian American communities. The strong desire to reinvest in a 1960s anti-imperialist and anti-colonial vision of Asian-Black solidarity thus must confront the new geopolitical alignments and the authoritarian governments that have appropriated the racial sentiments to justify repression in non-Western sites. These challenges and contradictions thus demand new paradigms to examine Asian Americanness as always already a geopolitical formation and theorize racial relations away from the depoliticized multiculturalism of "beyond Black and white." Despite the poststructuralist skepticism regarding identity, the intersectional power hierarchy that is based on "old" forms of domination—colonialism, imperialism, white supremacy, and heteropatriarchy—continues to regulate and manage relations of domination and submission.[5]

Alexander Wehelliye stresses the need to *ontologize race*—that is, to place race "front and center in considerations of political violence . . . as a set of sociopolitical processes of differentiation and hierarchization, which are projected onto the putatively biological human body."[6] Similarly, in this book, I have attempted to conceptualize Asian Americanness ontologically but not representationally—that is, existing and functioning through its own spatial and temporal logic, not as a subcategory of race or a "happenstance" of the effects of white supremacy that largely relies on a theory of race based in a Black-white racial paradigm. As a mechanism of arranging events and matter, my insistence on theorizing Asian Americanness as an assemblage is to highlight its discursive power through modes of scientific categorization, geopolitical positing, and temporal projection that are mapped onto the accumulative knowledge about a type of body. In other words, what we recognize as an "Asian American population" is inseparable from its technological, geopolitical, and temporal arrangements. The "Asian American body" does not exist prior to the assemblage.

My utilization of assemblage illustrates Asian Americanness not as a solidified object that moves in the field of racial construction but rather, as the field itself that drives the knowledge, representation, scale, duration, and intensity of Asian American "raceness." Amit Rai terms racial assemblage "the ecology of sensation,"[7] where a multiplicity of subjectivities is captured and integrated with various moving elements in the field and start to feel "real" across populations. For instance, Asian American foreignness is rarely felt as an expression of direct physical or social distance but a cultural Otherness that remains ideologically and economically congruent with Western imperial and capitalist interests. This foreignness is not a complete outsider status but the position of "model-minority nations" in the postcolonial nation-state development, which is granted that status as a sovereign entity while residing within the global hegemonic regime and acting as a bargaining chip for the imperial power center. It cannot simply be explained by a single axis of racial hierarchy but is driven simultaneously by a spatial distancing and a cultural desire away and toward its field, a threat to and an aspiration toward the American future. The power of racial assemblage is also its capacity to affect events and create new patterns of habituation.[8] The racial crisis that BLM has highlighted and the interracial conflicts that the movement has made explicit between Asian and African Americans were indeed not new but are intensified through the process of rearranging racial relations. They are the recycled racial contradictions lurking in US society ever since the founding of this country that is based in the racial stratification of labor, rights, and citizenship as well as the patterns of socialization habituated across communities. By engaging in both a historical and geopolitical analysis, we can see how the flexibility of Asian Americanness precisely resides in its capacity of regenerating from the position of the foreign Other to the foreign within ever since World War II, which continues to rescale the affective spacing between Asianness and Americanness and mediates US relations with Asian Pacific nations through military occupation and economic cooperation. In other words, the Black and Asian conflict is as much about the shifting positions of racial status between the two racial categories as is about US interests in producing new norms of neoliberal multiculturalism from the previous agendas of racial liberalism.

Throughout this book, I have troubled the "radical outsiderness" of Asian Americanness to the US racial order that is often portrayed in Asian Americanist studies, as Viet Thanh Nguyen argues, where minor acts of agency by Asian American subjects are highlighted to justify Asian Americans as a central moral subject of the field via their own injured history.[9] Rather, Asian Americanness *travels*. It is not a predetermined positionality but circulates with the evolving global politics and movements of capital and war, producing its "raceness" through science, protests, and affect. Hence, Asian American subjectivity cannot be solely defined by one's race, biology, culture, national origin, or even the "shared experience" of discrimination, because such conceptualization of agency often inevitably naturalizes a liberal politics of representation that further solidifies the centrality of American nationalism and the underlying narratives of a masculinist racial victimhood, patriarchal family, and heteronormativity. Instead of thinking about power as functioning vertically between the oppressor and the subordinator and agency as "acting up" against the top, the sideways strategy of queer growth allows the "back-and-forth connections and extensions that are not reproductive"[10] and spreads "sideways and backwards—more than a simple thrust toward height and forward time."[11] Sideways points to an array of possibilities and positions beyond the linear immigrant narrative of "becoming integrated'" with time, the vertical ascent on the racial hierarchy ladder toward whiteness, and instead a constant movement of leaving and reentering that builds on the sticky, resistive forces beside the others. In other words, whereas the Asian Americanist approach to agency emphasizes the group's racial injury discrimination and trauma that necessitates a solidifying collective identity as the source of political agency, the sideways approach rejects a singular point of identification and builds movements from multiple points of entry with others who may or may not be politicized through a unifying identity.

The sideways movement toward agency can also be understood through Eve Sedgwick's metaphor of the "analogue" relations of values instead of the on-off switch of the "digital" relations to affect.[12] The "many values" model of theorizing drawn from psychologist Silvan Tomkins's theory of affect opposes the binary logic of positivity versus negativity and instead proposes an array of possibilities toward feeling, identifying, and experiencing affects. Whereas the poststructuralist position of critical scholarship often relies on a *paranoid attachment* to the "strong theory" that structures around "one affect, or maybe two, of whatever kind—whether ecstasy, sublimity, self-shattering, *jouissance*, suspicion, abjection, knowingness, horror, grim satisfaction, or righteous indignation,"[13] Sedgwick proposes the analogue style of relating to negative events that rejects the definite positions of the oppressor and the oppressed. This sideways approach to agency is expressed by diasporic Asian American activists' *backward feelings*[14] to seeking anti-nationalist forms of attachments by reconnecting with colonial histories and trauma, where embracing their diasporic foreign background opens up regenerative affects that allow them to move away from the singular narrative of assimilating to the hegemonic identity of Asian American. Rachel Lee elaborates this sideways approach as a method of the Asian Americanist critique that is "reparative in its distributed, complex settings of many distributed agencies and contingencies."[15] Countering the "singular blame-agent" position, the sideways movement extends and expands with others, detouring the trajectory of racial becoming toward the neoliberal future or the avenging path of racial injury. It demands a temporality elsewhere, an alternative way of belonging and growth beyond the constraints of biological and ethnic ties. To borrow from Kandice Chuh's Asian Americanist critique, "Asian Americanist discourse must look to itself to ensure that the partial and variegated freedoms enjoyed by both Asian American studies and various Asian-raced peoples are not merely celebrated but are leading to an elsewhere."[16] The agentive potentials of Asian Americanness are generated sideways to the borders, in between the spaces of home, and they rescue a geopolitical and anti-imperialist lens of understanding history, community, identity, and futurity.

The anti-imperialist and geopolitically minded vision of Asian American politics is certainly not new, especially in the era before Hart-Celler immigration reform. The BLM movements have regalvanized an Asian American engagement with the intersectional politics of race *and* class that builds on an internationalist vision of Asian American identity—as migrants, refugees, and workers—as both the product of and force of resistance against empires. Similarly, the sideways approach builds on a similar desire toward transnational solidarity. However, what is different among the recent transnational milieus of Asian American activists is that the geopolitical elements of their politics are not only the source from which to re-create radical political imagination about the United States but invested in local struggles rooted in Asia and thus putting forward an internationalist outlook from the standpoint of non-US actors. In this sense, the injured affect of Asian Americans can be suspended, at least temporarily, in the side-by-side relations with the various mass struggles in Asia.

Writing in the global conservative turn, we are witnessing a new era of total attacks on racial justice, gender equality, sexual autonomy, immigration, and Indigenous rights, and a full frontal warfare between Russia and Ukraine that is almost reminiscent of elements of World War II that we thought were already history. From the left, Eastern European activists have pointed out the limits of the US-centric position of anti-war and anti-imperialism on the Russian invasion of Ukraine, termed "US-plaining," in which the myopic view not only left Russia unaccountable to its imperialist ambition but also denies Ukrainian agency in fighting for their sovereignty. The overemphasis on American agency and responsibility from this stance can often lead to another form of arrogant isolationism from the Western left. Volodymyr Artiukh, an anthropologist on Eastern Europe, writes, "The Western left is doing what it has been doing the best: analysing the American neo-imperialism, the expansion of NATO," and yet, "the world is not exhaustively described as shaped by or reacting upon the actions of the US. It has gained dynamics of its own, and the US and Europe is in reactive mode in many areas."[17] In some aspects, the possibility of a progressive Asian American politics must confront its US-centric analysis of empire and imperialism and take into account the new geopolitical dynamics that are shaping Asian Americanness from the diaspora. Regarding the insistence on an internationalist stance against all forms of empire, we can especially learn from the progressive Hong Kong activists who have been caught between the US-China interimperial rivalries. In the midst of the war, Hong Kong activists' support for Ukraine was framed by the pro-Beijing camp as more evidence of their "anti-government" and "anti-China" sentiments and was largely repressed. Nonetheless, a statement from Hong Kong University students addresses not only their unwavering stance against all forms of imperialism but the globally connected histories of war and violence:

> Since the beginning of the war, different actors have taken varying approaches to the Russian invasion. Pro-Russia chauvinists have watched the escalation of the situation with glee, whereas Western and East Asian countries have refrained from taking substantial action. Ironically, the Taliban—which brutally and violently suppressed the Afghan people—has weighed in and called for negotiation on both sides. Provoking aggression, civil war, and subsequent chaos are the tools of imperialism. In the midst of this chaos, people who have been tormented by war and oppressed by different regimes need to unite once again and rebuild the anti-war fronts that we previously saw in response to the wars in Vietnam and Iraq. We oppose not only the military aggression commanded by Putin, but also NATO provocation, which altogether has led to the crisis in Ukraine. We stand in solidarity with thousands of anti-war demonstrators in Russia to insist on an internationalist anti-war stance.[18]

The recognition of historically situated violence from both the West and East, the hypocrisy of regimes who refuse to take sides in the conflicts, and the call for anti-war fronts from the legacies of mobilization against the wars in Vietnam and Iraq demonstrate the necessary and critical vision for a progressive Asian American politics, despite that the statement is not drafted by those who see themselves as Asian Americans. As I have argued in this book, the claim over a singular Asian American identity is no longer unproblematic. New intersectional analysis is needed to tease apart those who are hijacking the category for neoliberal advancement and those who are seeking coalitional possibilities of revaluing collective life beyond the boundaries of identities. While mainstream Asian American politics continues to center on issues of representation and the debates over assimilation and oppression, I see the returning of its roots on building transnational and cross-identity solidarity the key to making Asian Americanness stay relevant in today's world.

Our contemporary troubling conditions necessitate a conceptualization of intersectionality not as a politic of recognition of similarity but as a willfulness of putting one's body behind others and orienting the body toward a definite trajectory.[19] In a sense, one does not have to own the same body or experience the same event to be in solidarity. Rather, it is the stretchiness of the body that extends itself in the same direction that creates an energetic relation and commitment. A politics of willfulness does not center one's own injured feelings but traces the sentiments as affective attunements to multifaced struggles. From BLM to mass protests for democracy in Hong Kong, from the decolonizing struggles in Hawaiʻi and other Asian Pacific states to fights for sovereignty in Taiwan, the notion of Asian Americanness must be reshaped and expanded way beyond the current debates about model minority or Asian-Black racial antagonism and incorporate the "foreign-within" questions regarding mass deportation, mass incarceration, militarism and wars, land ownership, sexual and gender-based violence, forced displacement, surveillance, economic deprivation, and racial and religious profiling. To will for a sideways movement to a progressive vision of Asian America is to situate oneself in between the spatial confinements of nation-states and the temporal boundaries of the past and future in order to have an open and clear angle to the wide landscape that has constituted Asian Americanness. To will is to refuse the erasure of colonial and racial histories and create a horizon to extend one's arms to the subjects at the margins, against the hegemonic current of becoming a singular identity. As Sara Ahmed articulates, with willfulness, "you feel the momentum when you are going the wrong way."[20] We must become the bodies of persistence, growing sideways through our very effort of reaching out toward something that is not yet present.

Notes

Introduction. Feeling Asian American

1. Li Zhou, "Andrew Yang Told Asian Americans to Prove Their Americanness. Here's Why That's Wrong," Vox, April 3, 2020, https://www.vox.com/2020/4/3/21206760/andrew-yang-washington-post-asian-americans-opinion.

2. Jay Caspian Kang, "We Need to Put a Name to This Violence," *New York Times*, March 3, 2021, http://nytimes.com/2021/03/06/opinion/asian-american-violence-race.html.

3. Karen E. Fields and Barbara J. Fields, *Racecraft: The Soul of Inequality in American Life* (New York: Verso, 2014).

4. Fields and Fields, *Racecraft*, 19.

5. Brian Massumi, "The Autonomy of Affect," *Cultural Critique*, no. 31 (Autumn 1995): 83–109.

6. Massumi, "Autonomy of Affect," 96.

7. Kandice Chuh, *Imagine Otherwise: On Asian Americanist Critique* (Durham, NC: Duke University Press, 2003), 8.

8. Patricia Clough, "The New Empiricism: Affect and Sociological Method," *European Journal of Social Theory* 12, no. 1 (February 2009): 43–61.

9. Ali Lara, "Mapping Affect Studies," *Athenea Digital* 20, no. 2 (July 2020).

10. Jasbir K. Puar, *Terrorist Assemblage: Homonationalism in Queer Times* (Durham, NC: Duke University Press, 2007), 206.

11. José Esteban Muñoz, *The Sense of Brown* (Durham, NC: Duke University Press, 2020).

12. José Esteban Muñoz, "Feeling Brown, Feeling Down: Latina Affect, the Performativity of Race, and the Depressive Position," *Signs: Journal of Women in Culture and Society* 31, no. 3 (Spring 2006): 680.

13. Claire Jean Kim, "The Racial Triangulation of Asian Americans," *Politics & Society* 27, no. 1 (March 1999).

14. Christopher B. Patterson, "Brown Theory: A Storied Manifest of Our World," *positions: asia critique* 31, no. 1 (February 2023).

15. Cathy Park Hong, *Minor Feelings: An Asian American Reckoning* (New York: One World, 2020).

16. Hong, *Minor Feelings*, 55–56.

17. Lauren Berlant, *Cruel Optimism* (Durham, NC: Duke University Press, 2011).

18. Jodi Melamed, "The Spirit of Neoliberalism: From Racial Liberalism to Neoliberal Multiculturalism," *Social Text* 24, no. 4 (Winter 2006).

19. Hong, *Minor Feelings*, 54.

20. Frantz Fanon, *Black Skin, White Masks*, trans. Richard Philcox (New York: Grove, 2008), 42.

21. Derek Hook, "Fanon and the Psychoanalysis of Racism," in *Critical Psychology*, ed. Derek Hook (Lansdowne, South Africa: Juta Academic Publishing, 2004).

22. Hook, "Fanon and the Psychoanalysis of Racism," 118.

23. Fanon, *Black Skin, White Masks*, 124.

24. Fanon, *Black Skin, White Masks*, 124.

25. Derek Hook, "A Critical Psychology of the Postcolonial," *Theory & Psychology* 15, no. 4 (August 2005).

26. David K. Yoo and Eiichiro Azuma, eds., *The Oxford Handbook of Asian American History* (New York: Oxford University Press, 2016).

27. Daryl J. Maeda, "Black Panthers, Red Guards, and Chinamen: Constructing Asian American Identity through Performing Blackness, 1969–1972," *American Quarterly* 57, no. 4 (December 2005).

28. William Wei, *The Asian American Movement* (Philadelphia: Temple University Press, 2010).

29. Wendy Brown, "Wounded Attachments," *Political Theory* 21, no. 3 (August 1993): 390–91.

30. Brown, "Wounded Attachments."

31. Protect Oakland Chinatown (@protectoaklandchinatown), "Chinese Exclusion Act 1882, Japanese Internment 1942, Trump Calls Us Kung Flu," Instagram photo, March 1, 2021, https://www.instagram.com/p/CL2YnqaBgO1/?igshid=1p1ggpnao6kis.

32. Michael Liu, Kim Geron, and Tracy A. M. Lai, *The Snake Dance of Asian American Activism: Community, Vision, and Power* (Washington, DC: Lexington Books, 2008).

33. "Stop Asian Hate" is a slogan that has been widely adopted by activists who fight against anti-Asian violence across the United States during the COVID-19 pandemic since 2021. It is not necessarily linked to the organization Stop AAPI Hate, which is a grassroots organization that conducts research, actions, and policy recommendations around the

same issue. The slogan has also been used by government agencies to raise awareness on anti-Asian violence, such as the government of New York City. "Stop Asian Hate," City of New York, https://www.nyc.gov/site/cchr/community/stop-asian-hate.page.

34. Shu-mei Shih, "The Concept of the Sinophone," *PMLA* 126, no. 3 (May 2011).

35. Charlie Yi Zhang, Wen Liu, and Casey Lee, "Ethno-racial Paranoia and Affective Cold Warism: Remapping Rival US-PRC Imperial Formations," *American Quarterly* 74, no. 3 (September 2022).

36. Zhang, Liu, and Lee, "Ethno-racial Paranoia," 710.

37. Paolo Virno, "The Ambivalence of Disenchantment," in *Radical Thought in Italy: A Potential Politics*, ed. Paolo Virno and Michael Hardt (Minneapolis: University of Minnesota Press, 2006), 17.

38. Wen Liu, "Against the Politics of Injury: On the Dangers of Asian American Liberal Antiracism," *positions politics: episteme* no. 6 (June 2021), https://positionspolitics.org/against-the-politics-of-injury-on-the-dangers-of-asian-american-liberal-antiracism/.

39. Silvan Tomkins, *Affect Imagery Consciousness: Volume I: The Positive Affects* (New York: Springer, 1962), 190.

40. Manuel DeLanda, *Assemblage Theory* (Edinburgh: Edinburgh University Press, 2016).

41. DeLanda, *Assemblage Theory*, 10.

42. Laura Hyun Yi Kang, *Compositional Subjects: Enfiguring Asian/American Women* (Durham, NC: Duke University Press, 2002).

43. Eric Liu, *The Accidental Asian: Notes of a Native Speaker* (New York: Vintage Books, 1998), 34.

44. Chuh, *Imagine Otherwise*, 12.

45. Anne Anlin Cheng, *The Melancholy of Race: Psychoanalysis, Assimilation, and Hidden Grief* (New York: Oxford University Press, 2000).

46. David L. Eng and David Kazanjian, eds., *Loss: The Politics of Mourning* (Berkeley: University of California Press, 2003).

47. David L. Eng and Shinhee Han, *Racial Melancholia, Racial Dissociation: On the Social and Psychic Lives of Asian Americans* (Durham, NC: Duke University Press, 2019).

48. Kurt Danziger, *Constructing the Subject: Historical Origins of Psychological Research* (Cambridge: Cambridge University Press, 1994).

49. Nikolas Rose, "Power and Subjectivity: Critical History and Psychology," in *Historical Dimensions of Psychological Discourse*, ed. Carl F. Graumann and Kenneth J. Gergen (Cambridge: Cambridge University Press, 1996).

50. Karen K. Ho, "Crazy Rich Asians Is Going to Change Hollywood. It's about Time," *Time*, August 15, 2018, https://time.com/longform/crazy-rich-asians/.

51. Claire N. Park, "'Crazy Rich Asians' Stars on How the Film 'Transcends Race,'" *Harvard Crimson*, August 12, 2018, https://www.thecrimson.com/article/2018/8/12/crazy-rich-asians-feature/.

52. Melamed, "The Spirit of Neoliberalism."

53. Melamed, "The Spirit of Neoliberalism."

54. Matt Hamilton, "'No More Chinese' Graffiti in San Francisco Prompts Hate Crime Investigation," *Los Angeles Times*, September 7, 2015, https://www.latimes.com/local/lanow/la-me-ln-chinese-graffiti-san-francisco-hate-crime-investigation-20150907-story.html.

55. Nicholas Kristof, "The Asian Advantage," *New York Times*, October 10, 2015, https://www.nytimes.com/2015/10/11/opinion/sunday/the-asian-advantage.html.

56. Richard E. Nisbett, *Intelligence and How to Get It: Why Schools and Cultures Count* (New York: Norton, 2009).

57. Abby Budiman and Neil G. Ruiz, "Key Facts about Asian Origin Groups in the U.S.," Pew Research Center, April 29, 2021, https://www.pewresearch.org/fact-tank/2021/04/29/key-facts-about-asian-origin-groups-in-the-u-s/.

58. Virno, "The Ambivalence of Disenchantment," 15.

59. Claire Jean Kim, "Are Asians the New Blacks? Affirmative Action, Anti-Blackness, and the 'Sociometry'of Race," *Du Bois Review: Social Science Research on Race* 15, no. 2 (Fall 2018).

60. Khin Mai Aung and Russell Chun, "Nicholas Kristof Thinks All Asian Americans Are Alike: *The New York Times* Gets the 'Asian Advantage' All Wrong," *Salon*, October 13, 2015, https://www.salon.com/2015/10/12/nicholas_kristof_thinks_all_asian_americans_are_alike_what_the_new_york_times_gets_wrong_about_the_so_called_asian_advantage/.

61. William Petersen, "Success Story, Japanese-American Style," *New York Times*, January 9, 1966, http://inside.sfuhs.org/dept/history/US_History_reader/Chapter14/modelminority.pdf.

62. Keith Osajima, "Asian Americans as the Model Minority: An Analysis of the Popular Press Image in the 1960s and 1980s," in *A Companion to Asian American Studies*, ed. Kent A. Ono (Oxford: Blackwell, 2005): 216–19.

63. For instance, see Nellie Tran and Dina Birman, "Questioning the Model Minority: Studies of Asian American Academic Performance," *Asian American Journal of Psychology* 1, no. 2 (June 2010).

64. Julie J. Park and Amy Liu, "Interest Convergence or Divergence? A Critical Race Analysis of Asian Americans, Meritocracy, and Critical Mass in the Affirmative Action Debate," *Journal of Higher Education* 85, no. 1 (January/February 2014).

65. Paul Ong, "The Affirmative Action Divide," in *Asian American Politics: Law, Participation, and Policy*, ed. Don T. Nakanishi and James S. Lai (Washington, DC: Rowman & Littlefield, 2003).

66. Amy Chua, *Battle Hymn of the Tiger Mother* (New York: Bloomsbury, 2011).

67. Ruth Wilson Gilmore, *Golden Gulag: Prisons, Surplus, Crisis, and Opposition in Globalizing California* (Berkeley: University of California Press, 2007), 28.

68. Jodi Melamed, "Racial Capitalism," *Critical Ethnic Studies* 1, no. 1 (Spring 2015): 79.

69. Anna Tsing, "Supply Chains and the Human Condition," *Rethinking Marxism: A Journal of Economics, Culture & Society* 21, no. 2 (April 2009).

70. Jane L. Collins, *Threads: Gender, Labor, and Power in the Global Apparel Industry* (Chicago: University of Chicago Press, 2009), 162.

71. Kim, "Racial Triangulation."

72. Iyko Day, *Alien Capital: Asian Racialization and the Logic of Settler Colonial Capitalism* (Durham, NC: Duke University Press, 2016).

73. Iyko Day, "The Yellow Plague and Romantic Anticapitalism," *Monthly Review* 72, no. 3 (July 2020): 64–73.

74. Chuh, *Imagine Otherwise.*

75. Michel Foucault, *The Archaeology of Knowledge and the Discourse on Language*, trans. A. M. Sheridan Smith (New York: Pantheon, 1972), 33.

76. Sumie Okazaki, "Beyond Questionnaires: Conceptual and Methodological Innovations in Asian American Psychology," in *Asian American Psychology: The Science of Lives in Context* eds. Gordon C. Nagayama Hall and Sumie Okazaki (Washington, DC: American Psychological Association, 2002).

77. E. J. R. David and Sumie Okazaki, "Colonial Mentality: A Review and Recommendation for Filipino American Psychology," *Cultural Diversity and Ethnic Minority Psychology* 12, no. 1 (January 2006). See also Kevin L. Nadal, *Filipino American Psychology: A Handbook of Theory, Research, and Clinical Practice* (Hoboken: Wiley, 2020); and Sunil Bhatia, "Orientalism in Euro-American and Indian Psychology: Historical Representations of Natives in Colonial and Postcolonial Contexts," *History of Psychology* 5, no. 4 (November 2002).

78. Abby Budiman and Neil G. Ruiz, "Key Facts about Asian Americans, a Diverse and Growing Population," Pew Research Center, April 29, 2021, https://www.pewresearch.org/fact-tank/2021/04/29/key-facts-about-asian-americans/.

79. Anna L. Tsing, *Friction: An Ethnography of Global Connection* (Princeton: Princeton University Press, 2005), 6.

80. Promise Li, "Fighting Anti-Asian Violence Cannot Include Apologism for the Chinese State," Lausan, April 4, 2021, https://lausancollective.com/2021/fighting-anti-asian-violence/.

81. Wilson Walker, "Hundreds Rally in Oakland against Hate Directed at Asian American, Pacific Islander Community," CBS Bay Area, April 3, 2021, https://sanfrancisco.cbslocal.com/2021/04/03/rally-oakland-against-hate-directed-asian-american-pacific-islander/.

82. José Esteban Muñoz, *Disidentifications: Queers of Color and the Performance of Politics* (Minneapolis: University of Minnesota Press, 1999).

83. E. Tammy Kim, "Transnationally Asian: A New Media Neighborhood for an Emerging World," *Columbia Journalism Review*, July 21, 2020, https://www.cjr.org/special_report/transnationally_asian.php.

84. Kathryn Bond Stockton, *The Queer Child, or Growing Sideways in the Twentieth Century* (Durham, NC: Duke University Press, 2009).

85. Rachel C. Lee, *The Exquisite Corpse of Asian America: Biopolitics, Biosociality, and Posthuman Ecologies* (New York: New York University Press, 2014).

86. Lois Weis and Michelle Fine, *Working Method: Research and Social Justice* (New York: Routledge, 2004).

87. Eve Kosofsky Sedgwick, *Touching Feeling: Affect, Pedagogy, Performativity* (Durham, NC: Duke University Press, 2003), 21.

Chapter 1. Psychology and Racial Flexibility

1. Michel Foucault, *The History of Sexuality: Volume 1: An Introduction*, trans. Robert Hurley (New York: Pantheon, 1978).

2. Kurt Danziger, *Constructing the Subject: Historical Origins of Psychological Research* (Cambridge: Cambridge University Press, 1994).

3. Nikolas Rose, *The Psychological Complex: Psychology, Politics and Society in England, 1869–1939* (London: Routledge Kegan & Paul, 1985).

4. Michel Foucault, *Power/Knowledge: Selected Interviews and Other Writings 1972–1977*, ed. Colin Gordon, trans. Colin Gordon, Leo Marshall, John Mepham, and Kat Soper (New York: Pantheon, 1980), 133.

5. Stanley Sue and Derald W. Sue, "Chinese-American Personality and Mental Health," *Amerasia Journal* 1, no. 2 (1971).

6. Foucault, *The History of Sexuality*, 43.

7. Manuel DeLanda, *Assemblage Theory* (Edinburgh: Edinburgh University Press, 2016).

8. Foucault, *The History of Sexuality*.

9. Sunil Bhatia, "Orientalism in Euro-American and Indian Psychology: Historical Representations of Natives in Colonial and Postcolonial Contexts," *History of Psychology* 5, no. 4 (November 2002): 376.

10. Graham Richards, *Race, Racism and Psychology: Towards a Reflexive History* (New York: Routledge, 1997).

11. Robert Williams, "A History of the Association of Black Psychologists: Early Formation and Development," *Journal of Black Psychology* 1, no. 1 (August 1974).

12. Alexandra Rutherford, Kelli Vaughn-Blount, and Laura C. Ball, "Responsible Opposition, Disruptive Voices: Science, Social Change, and the History of Feminist Psychology," *Psychology of Women Quarterly* 34, no. 4 (December 2010).

13. Thomas Teo, "Critical Psychology: A Geography of Intellectual Engagement and Resistance," *American Psychologist* 70, no. 3 (April 2015): 243.

14. Foucault, *The Archaeology of Knowledge*.

15. Wade Pickren, "Tension and Opportunity in Post–World War II American Psychology," *History of Psychology* 10, no. 3 (August 2007): 279.

16. Ellen Herman, *The Romance of American Psychology: Political Culture in the Age of Experts* (Berkeley: University of California Press, 1995), 2.

17. Frank Summers, "Making Sense of the APA: A History of the Relationship between Psychology and the Military," *Psychoanalytic Dialogues* 18, no. 5 (September 2008).

18. In a conference hosted by the American University, Dr. E. K. Karcher Jr. advocated for the closer engagement between behavioral sciences and US warfare, particularly to

investigate the "human factors" and "psychological screening" to better predict the army officers' field performance. See E. K. Karcher Jr., "Army Social Science Programs and Plans," in *Symposium Proceedings: The U.S. Army's Limited War Mission and Social Science Research*, ed. William A. Lybrand (Washington, DC: Special Operations Research Office, American University, 1962).

19. Stephen Soldz, "Healers or Interrogators: Psychology and the United States Torture Regime," *Psychoanalytic Dialogues* 18, no. 5 (September 2008).

20. Robert V. Guthrie, *Even the Rat Was White: A Historical View of Psychology* (New York: Pearson Education, 2004).

21. James M. Jones and Thomas F. Pettigrew, "Kenneth B. Clark (1914–2005)," *American Psychologist* 60, no. 6 (September 2005).

22. William H. Grier and Price M. Cobbs, *Black Rage* (New York: Basic Books, 1968).

23. Sidney Lens, *Permanent War: The Militarization of America* (New York: Schocken, 1987).

24. Catherine Lutz, "Epistemology of the Bunker: The Brainwashed and Other New Subjects of Permanent War," in *Inventing the Psychological: Toward a Cultural History of Emotional Life in America*, ed. Joel Pfister and Nancy Schnog (New Haven: Yale University Press, 1997), 246.

25. Iyko Day, *Alien Capital: Asian Racialization and the Logic of Settler Colonial Capitalism* (Durham, NC: Duke University Press, 2016).

26. Day, *Alien Capital*, 31–34.

27. Day, *Alien Capital*, 33.

28. Colleen Lye, "The Afro-Asian Analogy," *PMLA* 123, no. 5 (October 2008).

29. Edward Said, *Orientalism* (New York: Vintage, 1979).

30. David Forgacs, ed., *The Gramsci Reader: Selected Writings 1916–1935* (New York: New York University Press, 2000).

31. Said, *Orientalism*, 7.

32. Day, *Alien Capital*.

33. Frank H. Wu, *Yellow: Race in America Beyond Black and White* (New York City: Basic Books, 2002).

34. Richards, *Race, Racism and Psychology*, xii.

35. Beth Lew-Williams, *The Chinese Must Go: Violence, Exclusion, and the Making of the Alien in America* (Boston: Harvard University Press, 2018), 5.

36. Andrew Gyory, *Closing the Gate: Race, Politics, and the Chinese Exclusion Act* (Chapel Hill: University of North Carolina Press, 1998).

37. Manu Karuka, *Empire's Tracks: Indigenous Nations, Chinese Workers, and the Transcontinental Railroad* (Berkeley: University of California Press, 2019).

38. Karuka, *Empire's Tracks*, 161.

39. Lew-Williams, *The Chinese Must Go*, 6.

40. Robert Seager, "Some Denominational Reactions to Chinese Immigration to California, 1856–1892," *Pacific Historical Review* 28, no. 1 (February 1959).

41. Seager, "Some Denominational Reactions," 53.

42. Robert F. Berkhofer Jr., *Salvation and the Savage: An Analysis of Protestant Missions and American Indian Response, 1787–1862* (Lexington: University Press of Kentucky, 2014), 13.

43. Alexander H. Leighton, *The Governing of Men: General Principles and Recommendations Based on Experience at a Japanese Relocation Camp* (Princeton: Princeton University Press, 2016).

44. David Harvey, "The Golden Age of Post-War Capital," *David Harvey's Anti-Capitalist Chronicles* (Podcast), April 8, 2021, https://anticapitalistchronicles.libsyn.com/the-golden-age-of-post-war-capital-0.

45. Raymond B. Cattell, "The Dimensions of Culture Patterns by Factorization of National Characters," *Journal of Abnormal and Social Psychology* 44, no. 4 (October 1949): 462–63.

46. Cattell, "The Dimensions of Culture Patterns," 443.

47. Michael Keevak, *Becoming Yellow: A Short History of Racial Thinking* (Princeton: Princeton University Press, 2011).

48. Geert Hofstede, *Culture's Consequences: International Differences in Work-Related Values* (Newbury Park, CA: Sage, 1980).

49. The Chinese Culture Connection, "Chinese Values and the Search for Culture-Free Dimensions of Culture," *Journal of Cross-Cultural Psychology* 18, no. 2 (June 1987).

50. Geert Hofstede and Michael Harris Bond, "The Confucius Connection: From Cultural Roots to Economic Growth," *Organizational Dynamics* 16, no. 4 (Spring 1988).

51. Hofstede, *Culture's Consequences*, 14–15.

52. Else Frenkel-Brunswik and Joan Havel, "Prejudice in the Interviews of Children: I. Attitudes toward Minority Groups," *Pedagogical Seminary and Journal of Genetic Psychology* 82, no. 1 (March 1953): 121.

53. Frenkel-Brunswik and Havel, "Prejudice in the Interviews of Children," 134.

54. John H. Rohrer, "The Test Intelligence of Osage Indians," *Journal of Social Psychology* 16, no. 1 (1942) showed that the level of white ancestry had no effects on Osage Indian people's IQ; Herman G. Canady, "The Problem of Equating the Environment of Negro-White Groups for Intelligence Testing in Comparative Studies," *Journal of Social Psychology* 17, no. 1 (1943) also stressed the importance of environmental factors and thus argued that it was impossible to measure Blacks and whites in unequal contexts.

55. Ruth Benedict and Gene Weltfish, *The Races of Mankind* (New York: Public Affairs Committee, 1943), 2.

56. Richards, *Race, Racism and Psychology*, 224.

57. Herman, *The Romance of American Psychology*, 26.

58. Leighton, *The Governing of Men*.

59. Leighton, *The Governing of Men*, 49–50.

60. Leighton, *The Governing of Men*, 359–60.

61. Leighton, *The Governing of Men*, 366.

62. Ivan P. Pavlov, *Lectures on Conditioned Reflexes: Vol. 2: Conditioned Reflexed and Psychiatry* (New York: International Publishers, 1941).

63. William Sargant, *Battle for the Mind: A Physiology of Conversion and Brain-Washing*, (Baltimore: Penguin, 1961).

64. Charlie Williams, "Public Psychology and the Cold War Brainwashing Scare," *History & Philosophy of Psychology* 21, no. 1 (January 2020).

65. Susan L. Carruthers, *Cold War Captives* (Berkeley: University of California Press, 2009).

66. Lawrence E. Hinkle and Harold G. Wolff. "The Methods of Interrogation and Indoctrination Used by the Communist State Police," *Bulletin of the New York Academy of Medicine* 33, no. 9 (1957): 600–615.

67. Robert Lifton, *Thought Reform and the Psychology of Totalism: A Study of "Brainwashing" in China* (New York: Norton, 1961), 388–89.

68. Lifton, *Thought Reform*, 396–97.

69. Lifton, *Thought Reform*, 288–90.

70. Lifton, *Thought Reform*, 266.

71. Ellen D. Wu, *The Color of Success: Asian Americans and the Origins of the Model Minority* (Princeton: Princeton University Press, 2014), 11.

72. Wu, *The Color of Success*, 19.

73. Richards, *Race, Racism and Psychology*, 225.

74. The earlier deployment of psychological testing methods aimed to examine whether the Chinese or Japanese subjects' response was "normal enough" compared to white subjects. Kuo-Shu Yang, Huan-Yuan Tzuo, and Ching-Yi Wu, "Rorschach Responses of Normal Chinese Adults: II. The Popular Responses," *Journal of Social Psychology* 60, no. 2 (1963).

75. Robert W. Scofield and Chin-Wan Sun, "A Comparative Study of the Differential Effect upon Personality of Chinese and American Child Training Practices," *Journal of Social Psychology* 52, no. 2 (1960).

76. Frenkel-Brunswik and Havel, "Prejudice in the Interviews of Children." See also E. Terry Prothro and Otha King Miles, "Social Distance in the Deep South as Measured by a Revised Bogardus Scale," *Journal of Social Psychology* 37, no. 2 (1953): 171; and Rose Zeligs, "Children's Concepts and Stereotypes of Turk, Portuguese, Roumanian, Arab, Chinese, French-Canadian, Mulatto, South American, Hawaiian, and Australian," *Pedagogical Seminary and Journal of Genetic Psychology* 83, no. 1 (September 1953).

77. Frenkel-Brunswik and Joan Havel, "Prejudice in the Interviews of Children."

78. Frenkel-Brunswik and Joan Havel, "Prejudice in the Interviews of Children," 121.

79. Frenkel-Brunswik and Joan Havel, "Prejudice in the Interviews of Children," 120.

80. Erika Lee, *The Making of Asian America: A History* (New York: Simon & Schuster, 2015).

81. Richards, *Race, Racism and Psychology*, 245.

82. Everett S. Lee and Xue-lan Rong, "The Educational and Economic Achievement of Asian-Americans," *Elementary School Journal* 88, no. 5 (May 1988): 545.

83. Richards, *Race, Racism and Psychology*, 237–38.

84. Richards, *Race, Racism and Psychology*, 252.

85. Frederick T. L. Leong and Sumie Okazaki, "History of Asian American Psychology," *Cultural Diversity and Ethnic Minority Psychology* 15, no. 4 (October 2009): 352.

86. Rhacel S. Parreñas and Lok C. D. Siu, eds., *Asian Diasporas: New Formations, New Conceptions* (Stanford: Stanford University Press, 2007).

87. Viet Thanh Nguyen and Janet Hoskins, "Introduction: Transpacific Studies: Critical Perspectives on an Emerging Field," in *Transpacific Studies: Framing an Emerging Field*, ed. Janet Hoskins and Viet Thanh Nguyen (Honolulu: University of Hawai'i Press, 2014), 6.

88. Geert Hofstede, *Cultures and Organizations: Software of the Mind* (London: McGraw-Hill, 1991), 165–66.

89. Stanley Sue, Derald W. Sue, and David W. Sue, "Asian Americans as a Minority Group," *American Psychologist* 30, no. 9 (September 1975).

90. Sue, Sue, and Sue, "Asian Americans," 906.

91. Sue, Sue, and Sue, "Asian Americans," 908.

92. Wu, *Color of Success*, 2.

93. See Lee and Rong, "The Educational and Economic Achievement of Asian-Americans"; and Sue, Sue, and Sue, "Asian Americans."

94. Sue and Sue, "Chinese-American Personality and Mental Health."

95. The authors used the male pronouns to describe the "Asian-American," which indicates that they had a specific male figure of the new personality-ethnic category. I followed their usage to signify how the original theory may indeed carry gender biases.

96. Sue and Sue, "Chinese-American Personality," 42.

97. Sue and Sue, "Chinese-American Personality," 42–43.

98. Foucault, *The History of Sexuality*.

99. Jack Drescher, "Out of DSM: Depathologizing Homosexuality," *Behavioral Sciences* 5, no. 4 (December 2015).

100. Sue and Sue, "Chinese-American Personality," 43.

101. David Eng, *Racial Castration: Managing Masculinity in Asian America* (Durham, NC: Duke University Press, 2001).

102. Sue and Sue, "Chinese-American Personality," 41.

103. Sue and Sue, "Chinese-American Personality," 45.

104. Stanley Sue and Sumie Okazaki, "Asian-American Educational Achievements: A Phenomenon in Search of an Explanation," *American Psychologist* 45, no. 8 (August 1990).

105. Cited in Sue and Sue, "Chinese-American Personality," 43. Originally from Gordon W. Allport, *The Nature of Prejudice* (New York: Doubleday, 1958), 141.

106. Shigehiro Oishi, Selin Kesebir, and Benjamin H. Snyder, "Sociology: A Lost Connection in Social Psychology," *Personality and Social Psychology Review* 13, no. 4 (November 2009).

107. Edna Bonacich, "A Theory of Middleman Minorities," *American Sociological Review* 38, no. 5 (October 1973).

108. Lee and Rong, "Educational and Economic Achievement," 559.

109. Sue, Sue, and Sue, "Asian Americans as a Minority Group."

110. David Crystal, "Asian Americans and the Myth of the Model Minority," *Social Casework* 70, no. 7 (September 1989).

111. Crystal, "Asian Americans," 406.

112. Michael Omi and Howard Winant, *Racial Formation in the United States*, 3rd ed. (New York: Routledge, 2014).

113. Viet Thanh Nguyen, *Race and Resistance: Literature and Politics in Asian America* (Oxford: Oxford University Press, 2002), 15.

114. Justin C. Perry, Kristen S. Vance, and Janet E. Helms, "Using the People of Color Racial Identity Attitude Scale among Asian American College Students: An Exploratory Factor Analysis," *American Journal of Orthopsychiatry* 79, no. 2 (April 2009): 258.

115. Omi and Winant, *Racial Formation*.

116. Omi and Winant, *Racial Formation*, 219.

117. Nguyen, *Race and Resistance*, 20.

118. Teresa W. Julian, Patrick C. McKenry, and Mary W. McKelvey, "Cultural Variations in Parenting: Perceptions of Caucasian, African-American, Hispanic, and Asian-American Parents," *Family Relations* 43, no. 1 (January 1994).

119. Perry, Vance, and Helms, "Using the People of Color Racial Identity Attitude Scale," 252.

120. Perry, Vance, and Helms, "Using the People of Color Racial Identity Attitude Scale," 253.

121. Perry, Vance, and Helms, "Using the People of Color Racial Identity Attitude Scale," 258.

122. Perry, Vance, and Helms, "Using the People of Color Racial Identity Attitude Scale," 259.

123. Derald W. Sue, Christina M. Capodilupo, Gina C. Torino, Jennifer M. Bucceri, Aisha Holder, Kevin L. Nadal, and Marta Esquilin, "Racial Microaggressions in Everyday Life: Implications for Clinical Practice," *American Psychologist* 62, no. 4 (May–June 2007): 271.

124. Derald W. Sue, Jennifer Bucceri, Annie I. Lin, Kevin L. Nadal, and Gina C. Torino, "Racial Microaggressions and the Asian American Experience," *Cultural Diversity and Ethnic Minority Psychology* 13, no. 1 (January 2007).

125. John B. McConahay, "Modern Racism, Ambivalence, and the Modern Racism Scale," in *Prejudice, Discrimination, and Racism*, ed. John. F. Dovidio and Samuel. L. Gaertner. (Cambridge, MA: Academic Press, 1986).

126. Donald R. Kinder and David O. Sears, "Prejudice and Politics: Symbolic Racism versus Racial Threats to the Good Life," *Journal of Personality and Social Psychology* 40, no. 3 (March 1981).

127. John F. Dovidio and Samuel L. Gaertner, "Aversive Racism and Selection Decisions: 1989 and 1999," *Psychological Science* 11, no. 4 (July 2000).

128. Sue et al., "Racial Microaggressions and the Asian American Experience," 89.

129. Pauline Agbayani-Siewert, "Assumptions of Asian American Similarity: The Case of Filipino and Chinese American Students," *Social Work* 49, no. 1 (January 2004): 39–51. See also Jeanne L. Tsai, Heather Mortensen, Ying Wong, and Dan Hess, "What Does 'Being American' Mean? A Comparison of Asian American and European American Young Adults," *Cultural Diversity and Ethnic Minority Psychology* 8, no. 3 (August 2002).

130. Angela Reyes, *Language, Identity, and Stereotype among Southeast Asian American Youth: The Other Asian* (New York: Routledge, 2006).

131. Alberta M. Gloria and Tamara A. Ho, "Environmental, Social, and Psychological Experiences of Asian American Undergraduates: Examining Issues of Academic Persistence," *Journal of Counseling & Development* 81, no. 1 (Winter 2003).

132. Nguyen, *Race and Resistance.*

133. Su Yeong Kim, Yishan Shen, Yang Hou, Kelsey E. Tilton, Linda Juang, and Yijie Wang, "Annual Review of Asian American Psychology, 2014," *Asian American Journal of Psychology* 6, no. 4 (December 2015).

134. Uichol Kim and Maria B. J. Chun, "Educational 'Success' of Asian Americans: An Indigenous Perspective," *Journal of Applied Developmental Psychology* 15, no. 3 (July–September1994); Samuel S. Peng and DeeAnn Wright, "Explanation of Academic Achievement of Asian American Students," *Journal of Educational Research* 87, no. 6 (July–August 1994).

135. Tiffany Yip, Charissa S. L. Cheah, Lisa Kiang, and Gordon C. Nagayama Hall, "Rendered Invisible: Are Asian Americans a Model or a Marginalized Minority?" *American Psychologist* 76, no. 4 (May–June 2021): 576.

136. Yip et al., "Rendered Invisible," 576.

137. Jodi Melamed, "The Spirit of Neoliberalism: From Racial Liberalism to Neoliberal Multiculturalism," *Social Text* 24, no. 4 (Winter 2006).

Chapter 2. Black Lives Matter and Asian American Political Fracture

The chapter is revised from the author's article in the *Journal of Asian American Studies*, Volume 21, Number 3, October 2018. Published with permission by Johns Hopkins University Press. Copyright © 2018 The Johns Hopkins University Press.

1. Michael G. Flaherty, "Time Work: Customizing Temporal Experience," *Social Psychology Quarterly* (March 2003). See also the application of "time work" in racialization: Crystal Marie Fleming, *Resurrecting Slavery: Racial Legacies and White Supremacy in France* (Philadelphia: Temple University Press, 2017).

2. "The Rise of Asian Americans," Pew Research Center, June 19, 2012, https://www.pewresearch.org/social-trends/2012/06/19/the-rise-of-asian-americans/.

3. "Black Lives Matter" is a hashtag, a phrase of political expression, an organization with multiple chapters, and also a broad political movement that first gained widespread attention through the labor of Black youth activists in Ferguson who began organizing

after the killing of Michael Brown. The movement is built on the backs of not just the founders but the countless families and communities whose loved ones have had their lives stolen by police and state violence. Their work has continued through organizations such as Black Youth Project 100 and many more throughout the country since the Ferguson mobilization. In this paper, I use the term as a politics that centers Black resistance against state violence that has been expressed through numerous protests across the United States, rather than as a specific organization.

4. Christian Edlagan and Kavya Vaghul, "How Data Disaggregation Matters for Asian Americans and Pacific Islanders," Washington Center for Equitable Growth, December 14, 2016, https://equitablegrowth.org/how-data-disaggregation-matters-for-asian-americans-and-pacific-islanders/.

5. See Viet Thanh Nguyen, *Race and Resistance: Literature and Politics in Asian America* (Oxford: Oxford University Press, 2002), 21, for analysis of intra-racial Asian American politics; Claire Jean Kim, *Bitter Fruits: The Politic of Black-Korean Conflict in New York City* (New Haven: Yale University Press, 2003) for Asian-Black class-oriented racial conflicts; and Aihwa Ong, *Neoliberalism as Exception: Mutations in Citizenship and Sovereignty* (Durham, NC: Duke University Press, 2006) for transnational Asian politics in neoliberal time.

6. Kim, *Bitter Fruits.*

7. Rowena Robles, *Asian Americans and the Shifting Politics of Race: The Dismantling of Affirmative Action at an Elite Public High School* (New York: Routledge, 2013).

8. Rowena Robles, "The Asian American as Victim and Success Story: A Discursive Analysis of the *Brian Ho v. SFUSD* Lawsuit," *Asian American Policy Review* 13 (January 2004): 73–88.

9. Elizabeth Freeman, *Beside You in Time: Sense Methods and Queer Sociabilities in the American Nineteenth Century* (Durham, NC: Duke University Press, 2019), 6.

10. Jon Stratton and Ien Ang, "Multicultural Imagined Communities: Cultural Difference and National Identity in Australia and the USA," *Continuum* 8, no. 2 (1994).

11. Rey Chow, *The Protestant Ethnic and the Spirit of Capitalism* (New York: Columbia University Press, 2002), 30.

12. Nguyen, *Race and Resistance.*

13. Wendy Cheng, "Strategic Orientalism: Racial Capitalism and the Problem of 'Asianness,'" *African Identities* 11, no. 2 (2013).

14. APIPS was a grassroots coalition specifically formed to oppose the Trans-Pacific Partnership Act, a neoliberal trade pact called the "Pivot to Asia" by the Obama administration, which became defunct under the Trump administration. It aimed to counter the growing economic and political influences of China in the Asia Pacific region by forming a trade bloc in the region and reinserting military intervention and presence.

15. Peter Kwong, *The New Chinatown* (New York: Hill & Wang, 1996). Kwong has discussed the splits between "Uptown Chinese" and "Downtown Chinese" in NYC as being a result of the increase in professional-class immigrants due to immigrant reform in 1965 and the influx of foreign capital from diasporic Chinese investors in Asia to the city. These investors not only took advantage of working-class Chinese labor but also drove

up real estate prices in Chinatown, Manhattan, exacerbating the class and ideological splits between the working-class Downtown Chinese and the post-1965 upwardly mobile Uptown Chinese.

16. Christa Craven and Dána-Ain Davis, "Feminist Activist Ethnography," in *Feminist Activist Ethnography: Counterpoints to Neoliberalism in North America,* ed. Christa Craven and Dána-Ain Davis (Lanham, MD: Lexington Books, 2013).

17. Zheng Wang, "The Chinese Dream: Concept and Context," *Journal of Chinese Political Science* 19, no. 1 (March 2014).

18. Jodi Melamed, "The Spirit of Neoliberalism: From Racial Liberalism to Neoliberal Multiculturalism," *Social Text* 24, no. 4 (Winter 2006).

19. Jeffrey S. Juris and Alex Khasnabish, eds., *Insurgent Encounters: Transnational Activism, Ethnography, and the Political* (Durham, NC: Duke University Press, 2013).

20. The key events around the Liang-Gurley conflict I included in this article are the following: (1) a vigil for Akai Gurley and his family hosted by a coalition of pro-BLM Asian American organizations on March 15, 2015, (2) a Support Your Local Police rally hosted by CAACR on March 8, 2015, (3) a Justice for Peter Liang march hosted by CAACR on April 26, 2015, and (4) a protest in front of the Chinese press company *Sing Tao Daily,* led by a faction of the Asians for Black Lives group in NYC on May 20, 2016.

21. Margaret Wetherell and Jonathan Potter, *Mapping the Language of Racism: Discourse and the Legitimation of Exploitation* (New York: Columbia University Press, 1992).

22. Eduardo Bonilla-Silva, *Racism without Racists: Colorblind Racism and the Persistence of Racial Inequality in the United States,* 6th ed. (Lanham, MD: Rowman & Littlefield, 2022); Michael Omi and Howard Winant, *Racial Formation in the United States,* 3rd ed. (New York: Routledge, 2014).

23. The political expression has various iterations such as "Black and Muslim Lives Matter" and "Black Trans Lives Matter."

24. Jasbir Puar, "'The Turban Is Not a Hat': Queer Diaspora and Practices of Profiling," in *Beyond Biopolitics: Essays on the Governance of Life and Death,* ed. Patricia T. Clough and Craig Willse (Durham, NC: Duke University Press, 2011), 73.

25. Vittorio Hernandez, "White House Petition to Withdraw Indictment of Peter Liang Gets over 120,000 Signatures," *Yibada,* February 22, 2016, http://en.yibada.com/articles/105622/20160222/white-house-petition-to-withdraw-indictment-of-peter-liang-gets-over-120-000-signatures.htm.

26. "梁彼得案發酵 紐約華人捐款請願反應熱烈" [Peter Liang's case facilitated donations from many Chinese in New York], *Epoch Times,* February 14, 2016, http://www.epochtimes.com/b5/16/2/14/n4639405.htm.

27. "梁彼得案折射不公，美国司法还有很长的路要走" [Peter Liang's unjust legal case. The US legal system still has a long way to go)], *People's Daily,* February 23, 2016, http://www.thepaper.cn/newsDetail_forward_1434685.

28. Matt Schiavenz, "The Banality of Televised Anti-Chinese Racism," *The Atlantic,* November 22, 2013, https://www.theatlantic.com/china/archive/2013/11/the-banality-of-televised-anti-chinese-racism/281776/.

29. The original "We the People" petition that demanded the cancellation of Jimmy Kimmel's show on the ABC network is no longer available online. For details about the petition, see Ted Johnson, "White House Responds to Jimmy Kimmel's China Controversy," *Variety*, January 10, 2014, https://variety.com/2014/tv/news/white-house-responds-to-jimmy-kimmels-china-controversy-1201045362/.

30. Although there are no public records showing that the two mobilizations (ABC and Pro-Liang) are led and funded by the same group or individuals, the discussions and calls for action of the two events occurred in the same WeChat groups I observed during the time, which suggests overlapping participation.

31. Chris Fuchs, "Complaint Filed against Yale, Dartmouth, and Brown Alleging Discrimination," NBC News, May 23, 2016, http://www.nbcnews.com/news/asian-america/groups-file-complaint-against-yale-dartmouth-brown-alleging-discrimination-n578666; see also Emil Guillermo, "More than 160 Asian-American Groups File Briefs in Support of Affirmative Action," NBC News, November 4, 2015, https://www.nbcnews.com/news/asian-america/more-160-asian-american-groups-file-briefs-support-affirmative-action-n456666.

32. "美國華社發起聲援華裔警察梁彼得大遊行" [Chinese American communities initiated marches for Officer Peter Liang], BBC, February 20, 2016, https://www.bbc.com/zhongwen/trad/world/2016/02/160220_us_peterliang_chinese/. All translations of the Chinese-language news and texts are mine unless otherwise noted.

33. Esther Wang, "Republican behind Sunday's Pro-Cop Rally Sees 'Racial Arsonists' Everywhere," *The Gothamist*, March 9, 2015, https://gothamist.com/news/republican-behind-sundays-pro-cop-rally-sees-racial-arsonists-everywhere.

34. "A Mature and Rational March."

35. Ong, *Neoliberalism as Exception*.

36. "曠新年:中國新左派的銷沉" [Kuang Xin Nian: The doom and gloom of the Chinese New Left], *Groundbreaking*, July 15, 2015, http://www.inmediahk.net/node/1035923.

37. Wang, "Chinese Dream," 2.

38. Viola Rothschild, "Online Reaction Revealed Much about Chinese Tension with an Influx of African Immigrants," *Foreign Policy*, May 5, 2015, http://foreignpolicy.com/2015/05/05/what-china-saw-when-baltimore-shook-with-anger/.

39. "人民日报钟声：巴尔的摩之乱并不偶然" [The voice of *People's Daily*: The chaos in Baltimore is not a coincidence], *People's Daily*, April 30, 2015, http://opinion.people.com.cn/n/2015/0430/c1003-26928411.html. Translations of all quotations from this article are my own.

40. See the translated full text of Xi Jinping's speech by Taylor Soper, "Full Text: China President Xi Gives Policy Speech in Seattle, Wants to Fight Cybercrime with the U.S.," Geek Wire, September 22, 2015, http://www.geekwire.com/2015/full-text-china-president-xi-gives-policy-speech-in-seattle-pledges-to-fight-cybercrime-with-u-s/.

41. Wang, "Chinese Dream," 9.

42. Allen R. Carlson, Anna Costa, Prasenjit Duara, James Leibold, Kevin Carrico, Peter H. Gries, Naoko Eto, Suisheng Zhao, and Jessica C. Weis, "Race, Knowledge

Production, and Chinese Nationalism: Nations and Nationalism Roundtable Discussion on Chinese Nationalism and National Identity," *Nations and Nationalism* 22, no. 3 (July 2016): 431.

43. Noted by David Greenwald, "Sunday Commentary II: Moving Past Blaming the Protesters," *The Davis Vanguard*, December 28, 2014, https://www.davisvanguard.org/2014/12/sunday-commentary-ii-moving-past-blaming-the-protesters/.

44. "Silent Asians" (啞裔): the pronunciation of the words "Asian" and "silence" is the same in Chinese, and thus the phrase has been popularized around the pro-Liang actions by the Chinese press.

45. For a comprehensive description of how #Asians4BlackLives activists mobilized across the United States, see May Fu, Simmy Makhijani, Anh-Thu Pham, Meejin Richart, Joanne Tien, and Diane Wong, "#Asians4BlackLives: Notes from the Ground," *Amerasia Journal* 45, no. 2 (2019).

46. Fu et al., "#Asians4BlackLives."

47. "Third World Resistance for Black Power Reclaiming MLK's Legacy of Militant Internationalism: Linking Third World Struggle with Black Resistance," #Asians4BlackLives, Tumblr, January 16, 2016, http://a4bl.tumblr.com/post/108277670394/official-statement-third-world-resistance-for.

48. Sahra Vang Nguyen, "Activating Asian America," 18 Million Rising, Tumblr, 2015, http://18mr.tumblr.com/post/107384818264/last-week-i-spoke-on-a-panel-at-the-museum-of.

49. Vijay Prashad, *Everybody Was Kung Fu Fighting: Afro-Asian Connections and the Myth of Cultural Purity* (Boston: Beacon, 2002). See also Yuichiro Onishi, *Transpacific Antiracism: Afro-Asian Solidarity in 20th-Century Black America, Japan, and Okinawa* (New York: New York University Press, 2013).

50. Chih-Ming Wang and Yu-Fang Cho, "Introduction: The Chinese Factor and American Studies, Here and Now," *American Quarterly* 69, no. 3 (September 2017).

51. Brian Hioe, "The Qiao Collective and Left Diasporic Chinese Nationalism," *New Bloom Magazine*, June 22, 2020, https://newbloommag.net/2020/06/22/qiao-collective-nationalism/.

52. Fabio Lanza, "Of Rose-Coloured Glasses, Old and New," *Made in China Journal*, October 20, 2021, https://madeinchinajournal.com/2021/10/20/of-rose-coloured-glasses-old-and-new/.

53. As previously mentioned, I use "BLM" (Black Lives Matter) here not as a particular organization but as a set of politics inspired by the Ferguson protests against police and state violence. In the context of my ethnographic work, it includes the activists in the Justice for Akai Gurley campaign as well as those who mobilized through the Asians4BlackLives hashtag.

54. Chris Fuchs, "Debate over Police Accountability, after Peter Liang Conviction, Spans Generations," NBC News, February 29, 2016, http://www.nbcnews.com/news/asian-america/debate-over-police-accountability-after-pet er-liang-conviction-spans-generations-n527926.

55. Letters for Black Lives, "Dear Mom, Dad, Uncle, Auntie: Black Lives Matter to Us, Too," *Medium*, July 12, 2016, https://lettersforblacklives.com/dear-mom-dad-uncle-auntie-black-lives-matter-to-us-too-7ca577d59f4c.

56. For an analysis of how age influences Asian American political participation, see Janelle S. Wong, "The Effects of Age and Political Exposure on the Development of Party Identification among Asian American and Latino Immigrants in the United States," *Political Behavior* 22, no. 4 (December 2000).

57. Adam Liptak, "Supreme Court Rejects Affirmative Action Programs at Harvard and U.N.C.," *New York Times*, June 29, 2023, https://www.nytimes.com/2023/06/29/us/politics/supreme-court-admissions-affirmative-action-harvard-unc.html.

58. Promise Li, "Asian American Conservatives Have Become Key Allies of White Supremacy," *The National*, July 6, 2023, https://www.thenation.com/article/society/asian-american-conservatives-white-supremacy/.

59. Asian Americans Advancing Justice, "Inclusion, Not Exclusion: Spring 2016 Asian American Voter Survey," A25, https://www.advancingjustice-aajc.org/sites/default/files/2016-09/Inclusion%20Not%20Exclusion%20voter%20survey.pdf.

60. Claire Jean Kim, "The Trial of Peter Liang and the Confronting Reality of Asian American Privilege," *Los Angeles Times*, April 21, 2016, https://www.latimes.com/opinion/opinion-la/la-ol-peter-liang-asian-american-privilege-20160421-snap-story.html.

Chapter 3. Racial Loss, Diasporic Attachments, and Anti-Imperialism

1. Michael Luo, "An Open Letter to the Woman Who Told My Family to Go Back to China," *New York Times*, October 9, 2016, https://www.nytimes.com/2016/10/10/nyregion/to-the-woman-who-told-my-family-to-go-back-to-china.html?_r=0.

2. Michael Luo, Chris M. Kwok, Anthony C. Ocampo, Grace Meng, Simran J. Singh, Erika Lee, Anand Giridharadas, and Arun Venugopal, "Confronting Racism against Asian-Americans," *New York Times*, October 18, 2016, https://www.nytimes.com/interactive/2016/10/17/us/asian-american-confronting-racism.html.

3. Luo et al., "Confronting Racism."

4. Timothy Bella, "Asian American Official Condemns Anti-Asian Violence by Removing Shirt, Showing His Military Scars: 'Is This Patriot Enough?'" *Washington Post*, March 27, 2021, https://www.washingtonpost.com/politics/2021/03/27/lee-wong-military-patriot-video/.

5. Wendy Brown, "Wounded Attachments," *Political Theory* 21, no. 3 (August 1993): 391.

6. Anne Anlin Cheng, *The Melancholy of Race: Psychoanalysis, Assimilation, and Hidden Grief* (New York: Oxford University Press, 2000), 23.

7. Lisa Lowe, *Immigrant Acts: On Asian American Cultural Politics* (Durham, NC: Duke University Press, 1996), 5.

8. On theory and the bicultural framework, see Teresa LaFromboise, Hardin L. K. Coleman, and Jennifer Gerton, "Psychological Impact of Biculturalism: Evidence and Theory," *Psychological Bulletin* 114, no. 3 (November 1993); on the Asian American case,

see Andrea J. Romero, Scott C. Carvajal, Fabian Valle, and Michele Orduña, "Adolescent Bicultural Stress and Its Impact on Mental Well-Being among Latinos, Asian Americans, and European Americans," *Journal of Community Psychology* 35, no. 4 (May 2007).

9. Verónica Benet-Martínez, Janxin Leu, Fiona Lee, and Michael W. Morris, "Negotiating Biculturalism: Cultural Frame Switching in Biculturals with Oppositional versus Compatible Cultural Identities," *Journal of Cross-Cultural Psychology* 33, no. 5 (September 2002).

10. Ien Ang, *On Not Speaking Chinese: Living between Asia and the West* (New York: Routledge, 2001).

11. "Double consciousness" originally written by W. E. B. Du Bois, *The Souls of Black Folk* (Oxford: Oxford University Press, 2009) and cited in Benet-Martínez, Leu, and Lee, "Negotiating Biculturalism," 490.

12. Cheng, *Melancholy of Race*, 3

13. APIPS came together as a coalition in 2013 in response to the Trans-Pacific Partnership Agreement. See also chapter 2, endnote 12.

14. Brian Hioe, "The Qiao Collective and Left Diasporic Chinese Nationalism," *New Bloom Magazine*, June 22, 2020, https://newbloommag.net/2020/06/22/qiao-collective-nationalism/.

15. David Klion, "What Should the Left Do about China?" *The Nation*, January 11, 2022, https://www.thenation.com/article/world/china-left-foreign-policy/.

16. Christopher Connery, "On the Continuing Necessity of Anti-Americanism," *Inter-Asia Cultural Studies* 2, no. 3 (2001).

17. Klion, "What Should the Left Do about China?"

18. Sara Braun, "Stop AAPI Hate: Statement on House Passage of the COVID-19 Hate Crimes Act," Stop AAPI Hate, May 18, 2021, https://stopaapihate.org/statement-on-house-passage-of-the-covid-19-hate-crimes-act/.

19. Sara Braun, "National Council of Asian Pacific Americans (NCAPA), Stop AAPI Hate, and 21 Organizations Urge President Biden to Protect AAPI Communities ahead of Administration's Release of Findings on the Origins of COVID-19," Stop AAPI Hate, August 19, 2021, https://stopaapihate.org/statement-biden-administration-letter/.

20. Qiao Collective (@qiaocollective), "We are excited to announce our formation as Qiao," Twitter, January 18, 2020, https://twitter.com/qiaocollective/status/1218318830998474753.

21. Kandice Chuh, *Imagine Otherwise: On Asian Americanist Critique* (Durham, NC: Duke University Press, 2003).

22. Leo T. S. Ching, *Anti-Japan: The Politics of Sentiment in Postcolonial East Asia* (Durham, NC: Duke University Press, 2019), ii.

23. José Esteban Muñoz, *Disidentifications: Queers of Color and the Performance of Politics* (Minneapolis: University of Minnesota Press, 1999).

24. Due to the fact that the nature of Qiao Collective's and China Is Not Our Enemy's mobilizing style is around creating public-facing discourses rather than locally based cam-

paigns, I was unable to get acquainted with the organizers and my sources were limited to the texts they have made public.

25. Lili Shi and Yadira Perez Hazel, "Introduction: Locating Feminism in Asian Diasporas," *WSQ: Women's Studies Quarterly* 47, no. 1 (Spring/Summer 2019).

26. Daniele Conversi, "Irresponsible Radicalisation: Diasporas, Globalisation and Long-Distance Nationalism in the Digital Age," *Journal of Ethnic and Migration Studies* 38, no. 9 (2012).

27. Denise Aghanian, *The Armenian Diaspora: Cohesion and Fracture* (Lanham, MD: University Press of America, 2007); Yossi Shain, *Kinship and Diasporas in International Affairs* (Ann Arbor: University of Michigan Press, 2007).

28. Nancy Bernkopf Tucker, *Strait Talk: United States—Taiwan Relations and the Crisis with China* (Cambridge, MA: Harvard University Press, 2011).

29. Xu Wu, *Chinese Cyber Nationalism: Evolution, Characteristics, and Implications* (Lanham, MD: Lexington Books, 2007).

30. Hailong Liu, ed., *From Cyber-Nationalism to Fandom Nationalism: The Case of Diba Expedition in China* (Abingdon, UK: Routledge, 2020).

31. Chenchen Zhang, "Right-Wing Populism with Chinese Characteristics? Identity, Otherness and Global Imaginaries in Debating World Politics Online," *European Journal of International Relations* 26, no. 1 (March 2020).

32. Conversi, "Irresponsible Radicalization," 1363.

33. Svetlana Boym, *The Future of Nostalgia* (New York: Basic Books, 2001), xiii–xvi.

34. Boym, *The Future of Nostalgia*, xviii.

35. Boym, *The Future of Nostalgia*, 49.

36. Tom Phillips, "Chinese Student Abused for Praising 'Fresh Air of Free Speech' in US," *The Guardian*, May 23, 2022, https://www.theguardian.com/world/2017/may/23/china-yang-shuping-free-speech-university-of-maryland-us-student.

37. Phillips, "Chinese Student Abused for Praising."

38. Qiao Collective, "Can the Chinese Diaspora Speak?" *Monthly Review*, July 1, 2021, https://monthlyreview.org/2021/07/01/can-the-chinese-diaspora-speak/.

39. Muñoz, *Disidentifications*, 22.

40. Xin, "Assimilation and Empire," Qiao Collective, April 1, 2021, https://www.qiaocollective.com/articles/assimilation-empire/.

41. "Hong Kong Reading List," Qiao Collective, March 11, 2019, https://www.qiaocollective.com/education/hong-kong.

42. "Hong Kong Reading List."

43. Qiao Collective, Robert G. Lee, Madison Tang, Sheila Xiao, and Roxanne Dunbar-Ortiz, "Yellow Peril, Red Scare: Orientalism, Anti-Asian Racism, New Cold War on China," The People's Forum NYC, YouTube video, September 19, 2021, https://youtu.be/6bJGDAT1HBE.

44. Qiao Collective et al., "Yellow Peril, Red Scare," circa 44:00.

45. Qiao Collective et al., "Yellow Peril, Red Scare," circa 55:00.

46. "Open Letter to *Monthly Review* on Xinjiang and the Qiao Collective," Critical China Scholars, October 19, 2020, https://criticalchinascholars.org/interventions/.

47. Darren Byler, *Terror Capitalism: Uyghur Dispossession and Masculinity in a Chinese City* (Durham, NC: Duke University Press, 2021).

48. David L. Eng and David Kazanjian, eds., *Loss: The Politics of Mourning* (Berkeley: University of California Press, 2003).

49. Sigmund Freud, *On Murder, Mourning and Melancholia* (London: Penguin, 2005), 203.

50. Muñoz, *Disidentifications*, 12.

51. Y. Barry Chung and Motoni Katayama, "Ethnic and Sexual Identity Development of Asian-American Lesbian and Gay Adolescents," *Professional School Counseling* 1, no. 3 (February 1998); Dawn M. Szymanski and, Mi Ra Sung, "Minority Stress and Psychological Distress among Asian American Sexual Minority Persons," *Counseling Psychologist* 38, no. 6 (August 2010).

52. Sara Ahmed, *The Promise of Happiness* (Durham, NC: Duke University Press, 2010), 120.

53. E. Tammy Kim, "Transnationally Asian: A New Media Neighborhood for an Emerging World," *Columbia Journalism Review*, July 21, 2020, https://www.cjr.org/special_report/transnationally_asian.php.

54. Kim, "Transnationally Asian."

55. Specifically, with New Bloom, most members have moved to Taiwan where I am currently residing; hence, I am able to stay connected on a regular basis.

56. Larry Buchanan, Quoctrung Bui, and Jugal K. Patel, "Black Lives Matter May Be the Largest Movement in U.S. History," *New York Times*, July 3, 2020, https://www.nytimes.com/interactive/2020/07/03/us/george-floyd-protests-crowd-size.html.

57. All interviewees' names that appear in this chapter have been changed to pseudonyms for confidentiality.

58. Adam Harding, "'Rise against Hate: Rally Condemns Spike in Violence against Asians in NYC," NBC New York, May 2, 2020, https://www.nbcnewyork.com/news/local/rise-against-hate-rally-condemns-spike-in-violence-against-asians-in-nyc/3032065/.

59. Carl Samson, "Pro-Uyghur Protesters Called Racists at Stop Asian Hate Rally in Washington D.C.," Yahoo! News, March 25, 2021, https://news.yahoo.com/pro-uyghur-protesters-called-racists-205307961.html.

60. Promise Li, "Fighting Anti-Asian Violence Cannot Include Apologism for the Chinese State," International Viewpoint, April 11, 2021, http://internationalviewpoint.org/spip.php?article7101.

61. Hong Kong Forum, Los Angeles (@HKFLA), "#StopAsianHate!" Facebook photo, March 19, 2021, https://www.facebook.com/HKFLA/posts/2938220903102629.

62. "Left plastic" (左膠) is a term that has been adopted by Hong Kong activists in the Anti-ELAB movement to criticize progressive elites who are seen as too idealistic and thus out of touch with the grounded reality and sufferings of the Hong Kong people under Chinese repression.

63. See #ChineseForBlackLives's Instagram account: https://www.instagram.com/chineseforblacklives/?hl=en.

64. Personal communication with activist scholar Kun Huang, March 11, 2021.

65. Kun Huang, "Chinese Diaspora Activism in the Age of Sinophobia and Anti-Asian Racism," *positions politics* 6 (2021), https://positionspolitics.org/chinese-diaspora-activism-in-the-age-of-sinophobia-and-anti-asian-racism/

66. Huang, "Chinese Diaspora Activism."

67. Lausan Collective, "Transnationally Asian Digital Conference," YouTube video, October 27, 2020, https://youtu.be/hlbSPEiWWoo.

68. Lausan Collective, "Our Relationship with Empire," YouTube video, October 24, 2020, https://youtu.be/grylE__goqY.

69. A. Cheng, *The Melancholy of Race.*

70. Derek Hook, *A Critical Psychology of the Postcolonial: The Mind of Apartheid* (New York: Routledge, 2012).

71. A. Cheng, *Melancholy of Race,* 15.

72. vienna rye (@vrye), "The Cruel Spectacle of Amerikkkan 'Democracy,'" Instagram photo, January 7, 2021, https://www.instagram.com/vrye/. The author has since deleted the post.

73. Promise Li, "Fighting Anti-Asian Violence."

74. Kay Deaux, "To Be an American: Immigration, Hyphenation, and Incorporation," *Journal of Social Issues* 64, no. 4 (December 2008).

75. Selcuk R. Sirin and Michelle Fine, "Hyphenated Selves: Muslim American Youth Negotiating Identities on the Fault Lines of Global Conflict," *Applied Development Science* 11, no. 3 (2007): 151.

Epilogue. Sideways to Asian America

1. Robert B. Zoellick, Deputy Secretary of State, "Whither China: From Membership to Responsbility?" Remarks to National Committee on U.S.-China Relations, September 21, 2005, https://2001–2009.state.gov/s/d/former/zoellick/rem/53682.htm.

2. Jini Kim Watson, "Postscript: On Transpacific Futurities," *Journal of Asian American Studies* 20, no. 1 (February 2017): 119.

3. Christine Mok and Aimee Bahng, "Transpacific Overtures: An Introduction," *Journal of Asian American Studies* 20, no. 1 (2017).

4. Kathryn Bond Stockton, *The Queer Child, or Growing Sideways in the Twentieth Century* (Durham, NC: Duke University Press, 2009).

5. Chandra Talpade Mohanty, "Transnational Feminist Crossings: On Neoliberalism and Radical Critique," *Signs: Journal of Women in Culture and Society* 38, no. 4 (Summer 2013).

6. Alexander G. Weheliye, *Habeas Viscus: Racializing Assemblages, Biopolitics, and Black Feminist Theories of the Human* (Durham, NC: Duke University Press, 2014), 5.

7. Amit S. Rai, "Race Racing: Four Theses on Race and Intensity," *Women's Studies Quarterly* 40, no. 1/2 (Spring/Summer2012): 67.

8. Rai, "Race Racing," 73.

9. Viet Thanh Nguyen, *Race and Resistance: Literature and Politics in Asian America* (Oxford: Oxford University Press, 2002).

10. Stockton, *The Queer Child*, 13.

11. Stockton, *The Queer Child*, 4.

12. Eve Kosofsky Sedgwick, *Touching Feeling: Affect, Pedagogy, Performativity* (Durham, NC: Duke University Press, 2003):149.

13. Sedgwick, *Touching Feeling*, 149.

14. Heather Love, *Feeling Backward: Loss and the Politics of Queer History* (Cambridge, MA: Harvard University Press, 2009).

15. Rachel C. Lee, *The Exquisite Corpse of Asian America: Biopolitics, Biosociality, and Posthuman Ecologies* (New York: New York University Press, 2014).

16. Kandice Chuh, *Imagine Otherwise: On Asian Americanist Critique* (Durham, NC: Duke University Press, 2003), 145.

17. Volodymyr Artiukh, "US-plaining Is Not Enough. To the Western Left, on Your and Our Mistakes," *Commons*, March 1, 2022, https://commons.com.ua/en/authors/artyuh-volodimir/.

18. A group of Hong Kong University students and socialism defenders, "Internationalism amidst Repression: Hong Kong Students against the War in Ukraine," Lausan Collective, March 28, 2022, https://lausancollective.com/2022/internationalism-amidst-repression/.

19. Sara Ahmed, *Willful Subjects* (Durham, NC: Duke University Press, 2014).

20. Ahmed, *Willful Subjects*, 144.

Select Bibliography

Agbayani-Siewert, Pauline. "Assumptions of Asian American Similarity: The Case of Filipino and Chinese American Students." *Social Work* 49, no. 1 (January 2004): 39–51.

Aghanian, Denise. *The Armenian Diaspora: Cohesion and Fracture*. Lanham, MD: University Press of America, 2007.

Ahmed, Sara. *The Promise of Happiness*. Durham, NC: Duke University Press, 2010.

Ahmed, Sara. *Willful Subjects*. Durham, NC: Duke University Press, 2014.

Allport, Gordon W. *The Nature of Prejudice*. New York: Doubleday, 1958.

Ang, Ien. *On Not Speaking Chinese: Living between Asia and the West*. New York: Routledge, 2001.

Benedict, Ruth, and Gene Weltfish. *The Races of Mankind*. New York: Public Affairs Committee, 1943.

Benet-Martínez, Verónica, Janxin Leu, Fiona Lee, and Michael W. Morris. "Negotiating Biculturalism: Cultural Frame Switching in Biculturals with Oppositional versus Compatible Cultural Identities." *Journal of Cross-Cultural Psychology* 33, no. 5 (September 2002): 492–516.

Berkhofer, Robert F., Jr. *Salvation and the Savage: An Analysis of Protestant Missions and American Indian Response, 1787–1862*. Lexington: University Press of Kentucky, 2014.

Berlant, Lauren. *Cruel Optimism*. Durham, NC: Duke University Press, 2011.

Bhatia, Sunil. "Orientalism in Euro-American and Indian Psychology: Historical Representations of Natives in Colonial and Postcolonial Contexts." *History of Psychology* 5, no. 4 (November 2002): 376–98.

Bonacich, Edna. "A Theory of Middleman Minorities." *American Sociological Review* 38, no. 5 (October 1973): 583–94.

Bonilla-Silva, Eduardo. *Racism without Racists: Colorblind Racism and the Persistence of Racial Inequality in the United States*. 6th ed. Lanham, MD: Rowman & Littlefield, 2022.

Boym, Svetlana. *The Future of Nostalgia*. New York: Basic Books, 2001.

Brown, Wendy. "Wounded Attachments." *Political Theory* 21, no. 3 (August 1993): 390–410.

Byler, Darren. *Terror Capitalism: Uyghur Dispossession and Masculinity in a Chinese City*. Durham, NC: Duke University Press, 2021.

Canady, Herman G. "The Problem of Equating the Environment of Negro-White Groups for Intelligence Testing in Comparative Studies." *Journal of Social Psychology* 17, no. 1 (July 1943): 3–15.

Carlson, Allen R., Anna Costa, Prasenjit Duara, James Leibold, Kevin Carrico, Peter H. Gries, Naoko Eto, Suisheng Zhao, and Jessica C. Weiss. "Nations and Nationalism Roundtable Discussion on Chinese Nationalism and National Identity." *Nations and Nationalism* 22, no. 3 (July 2016): 415–46.

Carruthers, Susan L. *Cold War Captives*. Berkeley: University of California Press, 2009.

Cattell, Raymond B. "The Dimensions of Culture Patterns by Factorization of National Characters." *Journal of Abnormal and Social Psychology* 44, no. 4 (October 1949): 443–69.

Cheng, Anne Anlin. *The Melancholy of Race: Psychoanalysis, Assimilation, and Hidden Grief*. New York: Oxford University Press, 2000.

Cheng, Wendy. "Strategic Orientalism: Racial Capitalism and the Problem of 'Asianness.'" *African Identities* 11, no. 2 (2013): 148–58.

The Chinese Culture Connection. "Chinese Values and the Search for Culture-Free Dimensions of Culture." *Journal of Cross-Cultural Psychology* 18, no. 2 (June 1987): 143–64.

Ching, Leo T. S. *Anti-Japan: The Politics of Sentiment in Postcolonial East Asia*. Durham, NC: Duke University Press, 2019.

Chow, Rey. *The Protestant Ethnic and the Spirit of Capitalism*. New York: Columbia University Press, 2002.

Chua, Amy. *Battle Hymn of the Tiger Mother*. New York: Bloomsbury, 2011.

Chuh, Kandice. *Imagine Otherwise: On Asian Americanist Critique*. Durham, NC: Duke University Press, 2003.

Chung, Y. Barry, and Motoni Katayama. "Ethnic and Sexual Identity Development of Asian-American Lesbian and Gay Adolescents." *Professional School Counseling* 1, no. 3 (February 1998): 21–25.

Clough, Patricia. "The New Empiricism: Affect and Sociological Method." *European Journal of Social Theory* 12, no. 1 (February 2009): 43–61.

Collins, Jane L. *Threads: Gender, Labor, and Power in the Global Apparel Industry*. Chicago: University of Chicago Press, 2009.

Connery, Christopher. "On the Continuing Necessity of Anti-Americanism." *Inter-Asia Cultural Studies* 2, no. 3 (2001): 399–405.

Conversi, Daniele. "Irresponsible Radicalisation: Diasporas, Globalisation and Long-Distance Nationalism in the Digital Age." *Journal of Ethnic and Migration Studies* 38, no. 9 (2012): 1357–79.

Craven, Christa, and Dána-Ain Davis. "Feminist Activist Ethnography," In *Feminist Activist Ethnography: Counterpoints to Neoliberalism in North America*, edited by Christa Craven and Dána-Ain Davis, 1–20. Lanham, MD: Lexington Books, 2013.

Crystal, David. "Asian Americans and the Myth of the Model Minority." *Social Casework* 70, no. 7 (September 1989): 405–13.

Danziger, Kurt. *Constructing the Subject: Historical Origins of Psychological Research*. Cambridge: Cambridge University Press, 1994.

David, E. J. R., and Sumie Okazaki. "Colonial Mentality: A Review and Recommendation for Filipino American Psychology." *Cultural Diversity and Ethnic Minority Psychology* 12, no. 1 (January 2006): 1–16.

Day, Iyko. *Alien Capital: Asian Racialization and the Logic of Settler Colonial Capitalism*. Durham, NC: Duke University Press, 2016.

Day, Iyko. "The Yellow Plague and Romantic Anticapitalism." *Monthly Review* 72, no. 3 (July 2020): 64–73.

Deaux, Kay. "To Be an American: Immigration, Hyphenation, and Incorporation." *Journal of Social Issues* 64, no. 4 (December 2008): 925–43.

DeLanda, Manuel. *Assemblage Theory*. Edinburgh: Edinburgh University Press, 2016.

Dovidio, John F., and Samuel L. Gaertner. "Aversive Racism and Selection Decisions: 1989 and 1999." *Psychological Science* 11, no. 4 (July 2000): 315–19.

Drescher, Jack. "Out of DSM: Depathologizing Homosexuality." *Behavioral Sciences* 5, no. 4 (December 2015): 565–75.

Du Bois, W. E. B. *The Souls of Black Folk*. Oxford: Oxford University Press, 2009.

Eng, David. *Racial Castration: Managing Masculinity in Asian America*. Durham, NC: Duke University Press, 2001.

Eng, David L., and Shinhee Han. *Racial Melancholia, Racial Dissociation: On the Social and Psychic Lives of Asian Americans*. Durham, NC: Duke University Press, 2019.

Eng, David L., and David Kazanjian, eds. *Loss: The Politics of Mourning*. Berkeley: University of California Press, 2003.

Fanon, Frantz. *Black Skin, White Masks*. Translated by Richard Philcox. New York: Grove, 2008.

Fields, Karen E., and Barbara J. Fields. *Racecraft: The Soul of Inequality in American Life*. New York: Verso, 2014.

Flaherty, Michael G. "Time Work: Customizing Temporal Experience." *Social Psychology Quarterly* 66, no. 1 (2003): 17–33.

Fleming, Crystal Marie. *Resurrecting Slavery: Racial Legacies and White Supremacy in France*. Philadelphia: Temple University Press, 2017.

Forgacs, David, ed. *The Gramsci Reader: Selected Writings 1916–1935*. New York: New York University Press, 2000.

Foucault, Michel. *The Archaeology of Knowledge and the Discourse on Language*. Translated by A. M. Sheridan Smith. New York: Pantheon, 1972.

Foucault, Michel. *The History of Sexuality: Volume 1: An Introduction*. Translated by Robert Hurley. New York: Pantheon, 1978.

Foucault, Michel. *Power/Knowledge: Selected Interviews and Other Writings 1972–1977*. Edited by Colin Gordon. Translated by Colin Gordon, Leo Marshall, John Mepham, and Kat Soper. New York: Pantheon, 1980.

Freeman, Elizabeth. *Beside You in Time: Sense Methods and Queer Sociabilities in the American Nineteenth Century*. Durham, NC: Duke University Press, 2019.

Frenkel-Brunswik, Else, and Joan Havel. "Prejudice in the Interviews of Children: I. Attitudes toward Minority Groups." *Pedagogical Seminary and Journal of Genetic Psychology* 82, no. 1 (March 1953): 91–136.

Freud, Sigmund. *On Murder, Mourning and Melancholia*. London: Penguin, 2005.

Fu, May, Simmy Makhijani, Anh-Thu Pham, Meejin Richart, Joanne Tien, and Diane Wong. "#Asians4BlackLives: Notes from the Ground." *Amerasia Journal* 45, no. 2 (2019): 253–70.

Gilmore, Ruth Wilson. *Golden Gulag: Prisons, Surplus, Crisis, and Opposition in Globalizing California*. Berkeley: University of California Press, 2007.

Gloria, Alberta M., and Tamara A. Ho. "Environmental, Social, and Psychological Experiences of Asian American Undergraduates: Examining Issues of Academic Persistence." *Journal of Counseling & Development* 81, no. 1 (Winter 2003): 93–105.

Grier, William H., and Price M. Cobbs. *Black Rage*. New York: Basic Books, 1968.

Guthrie, Robert V. *Even the Rat Was White: A Historical View of Psychology*. 2nd ed. New York: Pearson Education, 2004.

Gyory, Andrew. *Closing the Gate: Race, Politics, and the Chinese Exclusion Act*. Chapel Hill: University of North Carolina Press, 1998.

Herman, Ellen. *The Romance of American Psychology: Political Culture in the Age of Experts*. Berkeley: University of California Press, 1995.

Hinkle, Lawrence E., and Harold G. Wolff. "The Methods of Interrogation and Indoctrination Used by the Communist State Police." *Bulletin of the New York Academy of Medicine* 33, no. 9 (1957): 600–615.

Hofstede, Geert. *Culture's Consequences: International Differences in Work-Related Values*. Newbury Park, CA: Sage, 1980.

Hofstede, Geert. *Cultures and Organizations: Software of the Mind*. London: McGraw-Hill, 1991.

Hofstede, Geert, and Michael Harris Bond. "The Confucius Connection: From Cultural Roots to Economic Growth." *Organizational Dynamics* 16, no. 4 (Spring 1988): 5–21.

Hong, Cathy Park. *Minor Feelings: An Asian American Reckoning*. New York: One World, 2020.

Hook, Derek. "A Critical Psychology of the Postcolonial." *Theory & Psychology* 15, no. 4 (August 2005): 475–503.

Hook, Derek. *A Critical Psychology of the Postcolonial: The Mind of Apartheid*. New York: Routledge, 2012.

Hook, Derek. "Fanon and the Psychoanalysis of Racism." In *Critical Psychology*, edited by Derek Hook, 114–37. Lansdowne, South Africa: Juta Academic Publishing, 2004.

Jones, James M., and Thomas F. Pettigrew. "Kenneth B. Clark (1914–2005)." *American Psychologist* 60, no. 6 (September 2005): 649–51.

Julian, Teresa W., Patrick C. McKenry, and Mary W. McKelvey. "Cultural Variations in Parenting: Perceptions of Caucasian, African-American, Hispanic, and Asian-American Parents." *Family Relations* 43, no. 1 (January 1994): 30–37.

Juris, Jeffrey S., and Alex Khasnabish, eds. *Insurgent Encounters: Transnational Activism, Ethnography, and the Political*. Durham, NC: Duke University Press, 2013.

Kang, Laura Hyun Yi. *Compositional Subjects: Enfiguring Asian/American Women*. Durham, NC: Duke University Press, 2002.

Karcher, E. K., Jr. "Army Social Science Programs and Plans." In *Symposium Proceedings: The U.S. Army's Limited War Mission and Social Science Research*, edited by William A. Lybrand, 348–62. Washington, DC: Special Operations Research Office, American University, 1962. https://apps.dtic.mil/dtic/tr/fulltext/u2/613594.pdf.

Karuka, Manu. *Empire's Tracks: Indigenous Nations, Chinese Workers, and the Transcontinental Railroad*. Berkeley: University of California Press, 2019.

Keevak, Michael. *Becoming Yellow: A Short History of Racial Thinking*. Princeton: Princeton University Press, 2011.

Kim, Claire Jean. "Are Asians the New Blacks? Affirmative Action, Anti-Blackness, and the 'Sociometry' of Race." *Du Bois Review: Social Science Research on Race* 15, no. 2 (Fall 2018): 217–44.

Kim, Claire Jean. *Bitter Fruits: The Politic of Black-Korean Conflict in New York City*. New Haven: Yale University Press, 2003.

Kim, Claire Jean. "The Racial Triangulation of Asian Americans." *Politics & Society* 27, no. 1 (March 1999): 105–38.

Kim, Su Yeong, Yishan Shen, Yang Hou, Kelsey E. Tilton, Linda Juang, and Yijie Wang. "Annual Review of Asian American Psychology, 2014." *Asian American Journal of Psychology* 6, no. 4 (December 2015): 291–332.

Kim, Uichol, and Maria B. J. Chun. "Educational 'Success' of Asian Americans: An Indigenous Perspective." *Journal of Applied Developmental Psychology* 15, no. 3 (July–September 1994): 329–39.

Kinder, Donald R., and David O. Sears. "Prejudice and Politics: Symbolic Racism versus Racial Threats to the Good Life." *Journal of Personality and Social Psychology* 40, no. 3 (March 1981): 414–31.

Kwong, Peter. *The New Chinatown*. New York: Hill & Wang, 1996.

LaFromboise, Teresa, Hardin L. K. Coleman, and Jennifer Gerton. "Psychological Impact of Biculturalism: Evidence and Theory." *Psychological Bulletin* 114, no. 3 (November 1993): 395–412.

Lara, Ari. "Mapping Affect Studies." *Athenea Digital* 20, no. 2 (July 2020): 1–18.

Lee, Erika. *The Making of Asian America: A History*. New York: Simon & Schuster, 2015.

Lee, Everett S., and Xue-lan Rong. "The Educational and Economic Achievement of Asian-Americans." *Elementary School Journal* 88, no. 5 (May 1988): 545–60.

Lee, Rachel C. *The Exquisite Corpse of Asian America: Biopolitics, Biosociality, and Posthuman Ecologies*. New York: New York University Press, 2014.

Leighton, Alexander H. *The Governing of Men: General Principles and Recommendations Based on Experience at a Japanese Relocation Camp*. Princeton: Princeton University Press, 2016.

Lens, Sidney. *Permanent War: The Militarization of America*. New York: Schocken, 1987.

Leong, Frederick T. L., and Sumie Okazaki. "History of Asian American Psychology." *Cultural Diversity and Ethnic Minority Psychology* 15, no. 4 (October 2009): 352–62.

Lew-Williams, Beth. *The Chinese Must Go: Violence, Exclusion, and the Making of the Alien in America*. Boston: Harvard University Press, 2018.

Lifton, Robert. *Thought Reform and the Psychology of Totalism: A Study of "Brainwashing" in China*. New York: Norton, 1961.

Liu, Eric. *The Accidental Asian: Notes of a Native Speaker*. New York: Vintage, 1998.

Liu, Hailong, ed. *From Cyber-Nationalism to Fandom Nationalism: The Case of Diba Expedition in China*. Abingdon, UK: Routledge, 2020.

Liu, Michael, Kim Geron, and Tracy A. M. Lai. *The Snake Dance of Asian American Activism: Community, Vision, and Power*. Lanham, MD: Lexington Books, 2008.

Liu, Wen. "Against the Politics of Injury: On the Dangers of Asian American Liberal Antiracism." *positions politics: episteme* no. 6 (June 2021). https://positionspolitics.org/against-the-politics-of-injury-on-the-dangers-of-asian-american-liberal-antiracism/.

Love, Heather. *Feeling Backward: Loss and the Politics of Queer History*. Cambridge, MA: Harvard University Press, 2009.

Lowe, Lisa. *Immigrant Acts: On Asian American Cultural Politics*. Durham, NC: Duke University Press, 1996.

Lutz, Catherine. "Epistemology of the Bunker: The Brainwashed and Other New Subjects of Permanent War." In *Inventing the Psychological: Toward a Cultural History of Emotional Life in America*, edited by Joel Pfister and Nancy Schnog, 245–67. New Haven: Yale University Press, 1997.

Lye, Colleen. "The Afro-Asian Analogy." *PMLA* 123, no. 5 (October 2008): 1732–36.

Maeda, Daryl J. "Black Panthers, Red Guards, and Chinamen: Constructing Asian American Identity through Performing Blackness, 1969–1972." *American Quarterly* 57, no. 4 (December 2005): 1079–103.

Massumi, Brian. "The Autonomy of Affect." *Cultural Critique*, no. 31 (Autumn 1995): 83–109.

McConahay, John B. "Modern Racism, Ambivalence, and the Modern Racism Scale." In *Prejudice, Discrimination, and Racism*, edited by John F. Dovidio and Samuel L. Gaertner, 91–125. Cambridge, MA: Academic Press, 1986.

Melamed, Jodi. "Racial Capitalism." *Critical Ethnic Studies* 1, no. 1 (Spring 2015): 76–85.

Melamed, Jodi. "The Spirit of Neoliberalism: From Racial Liberalism to Neoliberal Multiculturalism." *Social Text* 24, no. 4 (Winter 2006): 1–24.

Mohanty, Chandra Talpade. "Transnational Feminist Crossings: On Neoliberalism and Radical Critique." *Signs: Journal of Women in Culture and Society* 38, no. 4 (Summer 2013): 967–91.

Mok, Christine, and Aimee Bahng. "Transpacific Overtures: An Introduction." *Journal of Asian American Studies* 20, no. 1 (February 2017): 1–9.

Muñoz, José Esteban. *Disidentifications: Queers of Color and the Performance of Politics.* Minneapolis: University of Minnesota Press, 1999.

Muñoz, José Esteban. "Feeling Brown, Feeling Down: Latina Affect, the Performativity of Race, and the Depressive Position." *Signs: Journal of Women in Culture and Society* 31, no. 3 (Spring 2006): 675–88.

Muñoz, José Esteban. *The Sense of Brown.* Durham, NC: Duke University Press, 2020.

Nadal, Kevin L. *Filipino American Psychology: A Handbook of Theory, Research, and Clinical Practice.* 2nd ed. (Hoboken: Wiley, 2020).

Nguyen, Viet Thanh. *Race and Resistance: Literature and Politics in Asian America.* Oxford: Oxford University Press, 2002.

Nguyen, Viet Thanh, and Janet Hoskins. "Introduction: Transpacific Studies: Critical Perspectives on an Emerging Field." In *Transpacific Studies: Framing an Emerging Field,* edited by Janet Hoskins and Viet Thanh Nguyen, 1–38. Honolulu: University of Hawaiʻi Press, 2014.

Nisbett, Richard E. *Intelligence and How to Get It: Why Schools and Cultures Count.* New York: Norton, 2009.

Oishi, Shigehiro, Selin Kesebir, and Benjamin H. Snyder. "Sociology: A Lost Connection in Social Psychology." *Personality and Social Psychology Review* 13, no. 4 (November 2009): 334–53.

Okazaki, Sumie. "Beyond Questionnaires: Conceptual and Methodological Innovations in Asian American Psychology," In *Asian American Psychology: The Science of Lives in Context,* edited by Gordon C. Nagayama Hall and Sumie Okazaki, 13–39. Washington, DC: American Psychological Association, 2002.

Omi, Michael, and Howard Winant. *Racial Formation in the United States.* 3rd ed. New York: Routledge, 2014.

Ong, Aihwa. *Neoliberalism as Exception: Mutations in Citizenship and Sovereignty.* Durham, NC: Duke University Press, 2006.

Ong, Paul. "The Affirmative Action Divide." In *Asian American Politics: Law, Participation, and Policy,* edited by Don T. Nakanishi and James S. Lai, 377–406. Washington, DC: Rowman & Littlefield, 2003.

Onishi, Yuichiro. *Transpacific Antiracism: Afro-Asian Solidarity in 20th-Century Black America, Japan, and Okinawa.* New York: New York University Press, 2013.

Osajima, Keith. "Asian Americans as the Model Minority: An Analysis of the Popular Press Image in the 1960s and 1980s." In *A Companion to Asian American Studies,* edited by Kent A. Ono, 215–25. Oxford: Blackwell, 2005.

Park, Julie J., and Amy Liu. "Interest Convergence or Divergence? A Critical Race Analysis of Asian Americans, Meritocracy, and Critical Mass in the Affirmative Action Debate." *Journal of Higher Education* 85, no. 1 (January/February 2014): 36–64.

Parreñas, Rhacel S., and Lok C. D. Siu, eds. *Asian Diasporas: New Formations, New Conceptions.* Stanford: Stanford University Press, 2007.

Patterson, Christopher B. "Brown Theory: A Storied Manifest of Our World." *positions: asia critique* 31, no. 1 (February 2023): 91–116.

Pavlov, Ivan P. *Lectures on Conditioned Reflexes: Vol. 2: Conditioned Reflexed and Psychiatry*. New York: International Publishers, 1941.

Peng, Samuel S., and DeeAnn Wright. "Explanation of Academic Achievement of Asian American Students." *Journal of Educational Research* 87, no. 6 (July-August 1994): 346–52.

Perry, Justin C., Kristen S. Vance, and Janet E. Helms. "Using the People of Color Racial Identity Attitude Scale among Asian American College Students: An Exploratory Factor Analysis." *American Journal of Orthopsychiatry* 79, no. 2 (April 2009): 252–60.

Pickren, Wade. "Tension and Opportunity in Post–World War II American Psychology." *History of Psychology* 10, no. 3 (August 2007): 279–99.

Prashad, Vijay. *Everybody Was Kung Fu Fighting: Afro-Asian Connections and the Myth of Cultural Purity*. Boston: Beacon, 2002.

Prothro, E. Terry, and Otha King Miles. "Social Distance in the Deep South as Measured by a Revised Bogardus Scale." *Journal of Social Psychology* 37, no. 2 (1953): 171–74.

Puar, Jasbir K. *Terrorist Assemblage: Homonationalism in Queer Times*. Durham, NC: Duke University Press, 2007.

Puar, Jasbir K. "'The Turban Is Not a Hat': Queer Diaspora and Practices of Profiling." In *Beyond Biopolitics: Essays on the Governance of Life and Death*, edited by Patricia T. Clough and Craig Willse, 65–105. Durham, NC: Duke University Press, 2011.

Rai, Amit S. "Race Racing: Four Theses on Race and Intensity." *Women's Studies Quarterly* 40, no. 1/2 (Spring/Summer 2012): 64–75.

Reyes, Angela. *Language, Identity, and Stereotype among Southeast Asian American Youth: The Other Asian*. New York: Routledge, 2006.

Richards, Graham. *Race, Racism and Psychology: Towards a Reflexive History*. New York: Routledge, 1997.

Robles, Rowena. "The Asian American as Victim and Success Story: A Discursive Analysis of the *Brian Ho v. SFUSD* Lawsuit." *Asian American Policy Review* 13 (January 2004): 73–88.

Robles, Rowena. *Asian Americans and the Shifting Politics of Race: The Dismantling of Affirmative Action at an Elite Public High School*. New York: Routledge, 2013.

Rohrer, John H. "The Test Intelligence of Osage Indians." *Journal of Social Psychology* 16, no. 1 (June 1942): 99–105.

Romero, Andrea J., Scott C. Carvajal, Fabian Valle, and Michele Orduña. "Adolescent Bicultural Stress and Its Impact on Mental Well-Being among Latinos, Asian Americans, and European Americans." *Journal of Community Psychology* 35, no. 4 (May 2007): 519–34.

Rose, Nikolas. "Power and Subjectivity: Critical History and Psychology." In *Historical Dimensions of Psychological Discourse*, edited by Carl F. Graumann and Kenneth J. Gergen, 103–24. Cambridge: Cambridge University Press, 1996.

Rose, Nikolas. *The Psychological Complex: Psychology, Politics and Society in England, 1869–1939*. London: Routledge Kegan & Paul, 1985.

Rutherford, Alexandra, Kelli Vaughn-Blount, and Laura C. Ball. "Responsible Opposition, Disruptive Voices: Science, Social Change, and the History of Feminist Psychology." *Psychology of Women Quarterly* 34, no. 4 (December 2010): 460–73.

Said, Edward. *Orientalism*. New York: Vintage, 1979.

Sargant, William. *Battle for the Mind: A Physiology of Conversion and Brain-Washing*. Baltimore: Penguin, 1961.

Scofield, Robert W., and Chin-Wan Sun. "A Comparative Study of the Differential Effect upon Personality of Chinese and American Child Training Practices." *Journal of Social Psychology* 52, no. 2 (1960): 221–24.

Seager, Robert. "Some Denominational Reactions to Chinese Immigration to California, 1856–1892." *Pacific Historical Review* 28, no. 1 (February 1959): 49–66.

Sedgwick, Eve Kosofsky. *Touching Feeling: Affect, Pedagogy, Performativity*. Durham, NC: Duke University Press, 2003.

Shain, Yossi. *Kinship and Diasporas in International Affairs*. Ann Arbor: University of Michigan Press, 2007.

Shi, Lili, and Yadira Perez Hazel. "Introduction: Locating Feminism in Asian Diasporas." *WSQ: Women's Studies Quarterly* 47, no. 1 (Spring/Summer 2019): 13–28.

Shih, Shu-mei. "The Concept of the Sinophone." *PMLA* 126, no. 3 (May 2011): 709–18.

Sirin, Selcuk R., and Michelle Fine. "Hyphenated Selves: Muslim American Youth Negotiating Identities on the Fault Lines of Global Conflict." *Applied Development Science* 11, no. 3 (2007): 151–63.

Soldz, Stephen. "Healers or Interrogators: Psychology and the United States Torture Regime." *Psychoanalytic Dialogues* 18, no. 5 (September 2008): 592–613.

Stockton, Kathryn Bond. *The Queer Child, or Growing Sideways in the Twentieth Century*. Durham, NC: Duke University Press, 2009.

Stratton, Jon, and Ien Ang. "Multicultural Imagined Communities: Cultural Difference and National Identity in Australia and the USA." *Continuum* 8, no. 2 (1994): 124–58.

Sue, Derald W., Jennifer Bucceri, Annie I. Lin, Kevin L. Nadal, and Gina C. Torino. "Racial Microaggressions and the Asian American Experience." *Cultural Diversity and Ethnic Minority Psychology* 13, no. 1 (January 2007): 72–81.

Sue, Derald W., Christina M. Capodilupo, Gina C. Torino, Jennifer M. Bucceri, Aisha Holder, Kevin L. Nadal, and Marta Esquilin. "Racial Microaggressions in Everyday Life: Implications for Clinical Practice." *American Psychologist* 62, no. 4 (May–June 2007): 271–86.

Sue, Stanley, and Sumie Okazaki. "Asian-American Educational Achievements: A Phenomenon in Search of an Explanation." *American Psychologist* 45, no. 8 (August 1990): 913–20.

Sue, Stanley, and Derald W. Sue. "Chinese-American Personality and Mental Health." *Amerasia Journal* 1, no. 2 (1971): 36–49.

Sue, Stanley, Derald W. Sue, and David W. Sue. "Asian Americans as a Minority Group." *American Psychologist* 30, no. 9 (September 1975): 906–10.

Summers, Frank. "Making Sense of the APA: A History of the Relationship between Psychology and the Military." *Psychoanalytic Dialogues* 18, no. 5 (September 2008): 614–37.

Szymanski, Dawn M., and Mi Ra Sung. "Minority Stress and Psychological Distress among Asian American Sexual Minority Persons." *Counseling Psychologist* 38, no. 6 (August 2010): 848–82.

Teo, Thomas. "Critical Psychology: A Geography of Intellectual Engagement and Resistance." *American Psychologist* 70, no. 3 (April 2015): 243–54.

Tomkins, Silvan. *Affect Imagery Consciousness: Volume I: The Positive Affects*. New York: Springer, 1962.

Tran, Nellie, and Dina Birman. "Questioning the Model Minority: Studies of Asian American Academic Performance." *Asian American Journal of Psychology* 1, no. 2 (June 2010): 106–18.

Tsai, Jeanne L., Heather Mortensen, Ying Wong, and Dan Hess. "What Does 'Being American' Mean? A Comparison of Asian American and European American Young Adults." *Cultural Diversity and Ethnic Minority Psychology* 8, no. 3 (August 2002): 257–73.

Tsing, Anna L. *Friction: An Ethnography of Global Connection*. Princeton: Princeton University Press, 2005.

Tsing, Anna L. "Supply Chains and the Human Condition." *Rethinking Marxism: A Journal of Economics, Culture & Society* 21, no. 2 (April 2009): 148–76.

Tucker, Nancy Bernkopf. *Strait Talk: United States–Taiwan Relations and the Crisis with China*. Cambridge, MA: Harvard University Press, 2011.

Virno, Paolo. "The Ambivalence of Disenchantment." In *Radical Thought in Italy: A Potential Politics*, edited by Paolo Virno and Michael Hardt, 13–36. Minneapolis: University of Minnesota Press, 2006.

Wang, Chih-Ming, and Yu-Fang Cho. "Introduction: The Chinese Factor and American Studies, Here and Now." *American Quarterly* 69, no. 3 (September 2017): 443–63.

Wang, Zheng. "The Chinese Dream: Concept and Context." *Journal of Chinese Political Science* 19, no. 1 (March 2014): 1–13.

Watson, Jini Kim. "Postscript: On Transpacific Futurities." *Journal of Asian American Studies* 20, no. 1 (February 2017): 119–24.

Weheliye, Alexander G. *Habeas Viscus: Racializing Assemblages, Biopolitics, and Black Feminist Theories of the Human*. Durham, NC: Duke University Press, 2014.

Wei, William. *The Asian American Movement*. Philadelphia: Temple University Press, 2010.

Weis Lois, and Michelle Fine. *Working Method: Research and Social Justice*. New York: Routledge, 2004.

Wetherell, Margaret, and Jonathan Potter. *Mapping the Language of Racism: Discourse and the Legitimation of Exploitation*. New York: Columbia University Press, 1992.

Williams, Charlie. "Public Psychology and the Cold War Brainwashing Scare." *History & Philosophy of Psychology* 21, no. 1 (January 2020): 21–30.

Williams, Robert. "A History of the Association of Black Psychologists: Early Formation and Development." *Journal of Black Psychology* 1, no. 1 (August 1974): 9–24.

Wong, Janelle S. "The Effects of Age and Political Exposure on the Development of Party Identification among Asian American and Latino Immigrants in the United States." *Political Behavior* 22, no. 4 (December 2000): 341–71.

Wu, Ellen D. *The Color of Success: Asian Americans and the Origins of the Model Minority*. Princeton: Princeton University Press, 2014.

Wu, Frank H. *Yellow: Race in America Beyond Black and White*. New York: Basic Books, 2002.

Wu, Xu. *Chinese Cyber Nationalism: Evolution, Characteristics, and Implications*. Lanham, MD: Lexington Books, 2007.

Yang, Kuo-Shu, Huan-Yuan Tzuo, and Ching-Yi Wu. "Rorschach Responses of Normal Chinese Adults: II. The Popular Responses." *Journal of Social Psychology* 60, no. 2 (1963): 175–86.

Yip, Tiffany, Charissa S. L. Cheah, Lisa Kiang, and Gordon C. Nagayama Hall. "Rendered Invisible: Are Asian Americans a Model or a Marginalized Minority?" *American Psychologist* 76, no. 4 (May–June 2021): 575–81.

Yoo, David K., and Eiichiro Azuma, eds. *The Oxford Handbook of Asian American History*. New York: Oxford University Press, 2016.

Zeligs, Rose. "Children's Concepts and Stereotypes of Turk, Portuguese, Roumanian, Arab, Chinese, French-Canadian, Mulatto, South American, Hawaiian, and Australian." *Pedagogical Seminary and Journal of Genetic Psychology* 83, no. 1 (September 1953): 171–78.

Zhang, Charlie Yi, Wen Liu, and Casey Lee. "Ethno-racial Paranoia and Affective Cold Warism: Remapping Rival US-PRC Imperial Formations." *American Quarterly* 74, no. 3 (September 2022): 499–521.

Zhang, Chenchen. "Right-Wing Populism with Chinese Characteristics? Identity, Otherness and Global Imaginaries in Debating World Politics Online." *European Journal of International Relations* 26, no. 1 (March 2020): 88–115.

Index

WEN LIU is an assistant research fellow at the Institute of Ethnology, Academia Sinica, Taiwan.

The University of Illinois Press
is a founding member of the
Association of University Presses.

University of Illinois Press
1325 South Oak Street
Champaign, IL 61820-6903
www.press.uillinois.edu